T0244751

A Midsummer Night's Dream

Other Books of Interest from St. Augustine's Press

William Shakespeare (Jan H. Blits, Editor), *Hamlet*

Nalin Ranasinghe, *Shakespeare's Reformation:
Christian Humanism and the Death of God*

Ralph McInerny, *Shakespearean Variations*

Jeremy Black, *The Importance of Being Poirot*

Jeremy Black, *In Fielding's Wake*

Jeremy Black, *Defoe's Britain*

Jeremy Black, *Smollett's Britain*

Anne Drury Hall, *Where the Muses Still Haunt: The Second Reading*

David K. O'Connor, *Plato's Bedroom: Ancient Wisdom and Modern Love*

Marvin R. O'Connell, *Telling Stories that Matter: Memoirs and Essays*

Francisco Insa, *The Formation Affectivity: A Christian Approach*

Pete Fraser, *Twelve Films about Love and Heaven*

Anne Drury Hall, *Where the Muses Still Haunt: The Second Reading*

Alexandre Kojève, *The Concept, Time, and Discourse*

David Lowenthal, *Slave State: Rereading Orwell's 1984*

Gene Fendt, *Camus' Plague: Myth for Our World*

Nathan Lefler, *Tale of a Criminal Mind Gone Good*

Nalin Ranasinghe, *The Confessions of Odysseus*

John Poch, *God's Poems: The Beauty of Poetry and the Christian Imagination*

Roger Scruton, *The Politics of Culture and Other Essays*

Rainer Maria Rilke, *The Sonnets of Maria Rilke*

Marion Montgomery, *With Walker Percy at the Tupperware Party*

Stanley Rosen, *The Language of Love:
An Interpretation of Plato's Phaedrus*

Will Morrisey, *Shakespeare's Politic Comedy*

Will Morrissey, *Herman Melville's Ship of State*

A Midsummer Night's Dream

WILLIAM SHAKESPEARE
EDITED, WITH INTRODUCTION AND NOTES
BY JAN H. BLITS

ST. AUGUSTINE'S PRESS
South Bend, Indiana

Copyright © 2024 by Jan H. Blits

All rights reserved. No part of this book may be reproduced, stored in a retrieval system, or transmitted, in any form or by any means, electronic, mechanical, photocopying, recording, or otherwise, without the prior permission of St. Augustine's Press.

Manufactured in the United States of America.

1 2 3 4 5 6   29 28 27 26 25 24

Library of Congress Control Number: 2024934647

Paperback ISBN: 978-1-58731-532-9
Ebook ISBN: 978-1-58731-533-6

∞ The paper used in this publication meets the minimum requirements of the American National Standard for Information Sciences — Permanence of Paper for Printed Materials, ANSI Z39.48-1984.

St. Augustine's Press
www.staugustine.net

TABLE OF CONTENTS

PREFACE

The seriousness of tragedies seems self-evident. The seriousness of comedies is not so apparent. Not surprisingly, while the early development of tragedy is known, "comedy," Aristotle writes, "because it was of no stature from the beginning passed unnoticed" (Aristotle, *Poetics*, 1449a38–b1). Indeed, according to Plutarch, "the Athenians considered the writing of comedy so undignified and vulgar a business that there was a law forbidding a member of the Areopagus to write comedies."[1] A serious edition of a comedy thus runs at least two risks. It may seem to take the comedy more seriously than the comedy warrants or its author intends, making the study's author no less laughable than his subject—and humorless to boot. And it may make unfunny the work whose humor it is discussing. Explained jokes are, after all, no longer funny jokes.

Despite these risks, this edition of *A Midsummer Night's Dream* takes the comedy seriously. Like my editions of other Shakespeare plays, it gives full weight to Shakespeare's dramatic setting, which other editors (and scholars) almost always ignore or at least fail adequately to consider. Ancient Athens is the core, not the mere background, of *MND*. As we shall see, Shakespeare focuses particularly on the love of the beautiful and the triumph of learning and art, along with the rise of democracy, which, as Pericles famously claims, are the hallmarks of classical Athens (Thucydides, *The Peloponnesian War*, 2.40.1).

MND is of course not a history play in any usual sense. It is rather a poetic-philosophic portrayal, with comic embellishments and droll distortions, of the nature of the ancient Athenian

---

1   Plutarch, *Whether the Athenians Were More Famous in War or in Wisdom*, 348b.

---

regime. In contrast to ordinary history plays, time in *MND* is often synchronic. Athens' Thesean founding and its Periclean peak, though centuries apart, are shown to concur. Indeed, Cadmus, who introduced the alphabet to Greece some seven or eight centuries before the Trojan War,[2] is said to have been Hippolyta's hunting companion in Crete. Prehistory and history—barbarism and civilization—are presented as contemporaneous. Time in the play is similarly askew. For example, while midsummer coincides with the first of May, the duration before Theseus' wedding is said to be four days but plays out over just two. Location is likewise often illusive. The woods, where most of the play's action occurs, are at once a poetic fairyland and a prosaic property protected by the Duke's own forester. They are, and are not, part of Athens. Most notably, the founding of Athens, though focal to the play, is left implicit or allusive. We do not see Theseus' legendary gathering of Attica's villages to form Athens. We see instead his overthrowing the patriarchal authority of fathers in determining their daughters' marriages. The equivalence of these two actions, Shakespeare shows, ties together the play's love and political themes.

Failure to consider classical Athens as central to MND will cause a reader to miss not only the play's remarkable substance, but much of its sparkling comedy as well. Far from impeding the play's humor, focusing on Athens helps to bring out multi-layers of comedy that Shakespeare put there.

The relation between comedy and tragedy is, in fact, a running theme of *MND*. I have therefore attached a Coda which briefly takes up a surprising aspect of this theme.

---

2   Herodotus, *Histories*, 5.58.1.

NOTE ON THE TEXT

The text for this edition is the First Quarto (1600), which is generally the authoritative text. The Second Quarto (1619, erroneously dated 1600), reprints the First, with minor differences. The text of the play included in the First Folio (1623) is based on the Second Quarto. It corrects some misprints, slightly modifies some language, and adds or expands some stage directions. While I modernize the spelling and punctuation, I avoid substantive emendations except when the reason seems compelling.

INTRODUCTION

A Midsummer Night's Dream portrays the foundation and the flourishing of ancient Athens. Despite the centuries' difference in time, the play melds Theseus' founding of the city and the Athenian love of the beautiful and the triumph of art. Yet, at first glance, Athens itself and its political world appear largely absent from the play. Notwithstanding Pericles' claim that the Athenians regard the man who takes no part in public affairs, not as one who meddles in nothing, but as one who is good for nothing,[1] no one in *MND* seems to show the slightest interest in public affairs. All the characters are absorbed, instead, in their private lives. Not only do Lysander and Demetrius flee Athens for love, giving not a moment's thought to their obligations to their city. Even Theseus, Athens' legendary founder and ruler, confesses that, "being over-full of self-affairs" (1.1.113), he has been diverted from his public duties by his private love.

While Shakespeare traces the founding of the Roman Republic to the establishment of the tribunate and the city's mixed regime,[2] he depicts the founding of Athens without mentioning any Athenian political office or institution, or, indeed, without directly mentioning Theseus' unification of the villages of Attica, traditionally considered his great founding act.[3] Shakespeare gives Theseus the title of Duke, which is neither Greek in origin

---

1   Thucydides, 2.40.2.
2   *Coriolanus*, 1.1.203–20.
3   "[A]fter the death of his father…, [Theseus] undertook a marvelous great enterprise. For he brought all the inhabitants of the whole province of Attica to be within the city of Athens and made them all one corporation, which were before dispersed into diverse villages" (Plutarch, *Theseus*, 24.1; North, 52). See also Thucydides, 2.15.

1

nor definite in meaning.[4] Apart from Theseus, the only Athenian who might be thought to have a public office or function is Philostrate. But although his Greek name means "lover of battle," his sole duty is to serve as Theseus' "manager of mirth" (5.1.35).

All the Athenian noblemen in the play—Theseus, Egeus, Lysander, Demetrius, and Philostrate—have the names of famous warriors or the name "lover of battle" itself. But all are either lovers, the angry father of a lover, or the provider of private pleasures.[5] Even Shakespeare's title points away from politics to a purely private realm. The difference between Shakespeare's presentations of the foundings of Athens and of Rome reflects the essential difference between the two cities themselves. Republican Rome is a thoroughly political world. To the Romans, no good stands higher than political honor and glory. The private realm is suppressed by or subordinated to the public realm, though the two realms remain in an irresolvable tension with each other. The city of citizen soldiers is also the city of godlike ambition on the one hand and filial piety on the other. Rome is thus the stuff of tragedy. As we see in *Coriolanus*, the hero who prides himself above all on his godlike self-sufficiency ultimately has no place in the city he saves or in the family he reveres.[6] In Athens, by contrast, despite the city's imperial greatness and glory, politics is not the highest, let alone the only, human activity. The Athenians are

---

4   "Duke," from the Latin *dux*, means "commander," "guide," or "leader," particularly of an army. In Plutarch, Theseus' title is king (Plutarch, *Theseus*, 24.2; *Comparison of Theseus and Romulus*, 2.1). Hence, Lysander's reference to Theseus' "royal walks" (5.1.31). However, when founding Athens, Theseus promised the nobles that it would "not [be] subject to the power of any sole prince" (Plutarch, *Theseus*, 25.2; North, 1:52). See, further, 1.1.20n.

5   The words "act" and "deed" never appear in *MND*. "Action" occurs twice, once meaning a full rehearsal of the artisans' play (3.1.5) and once referring to Cobweb's bringing Bottom a honeybag (4.1.14). "Actor(s)" appears five times, always in the theatrical sense.

6   *Coriolanus*, 3.3.120–35, 5.3.22ff.

lovers of the beautiful and of the mind. "We are lovers of the beautiful with thrift, and lovers of wisdom without softness," Pericles proudly proclaims (Thucydides, 2.40.1). Athena is the goddess of wisdom as well as of war. The highest and most distinctive Athenian activities are thus private, not public.[7] Where love and art enter Rome only late and only as forms of Greek corruption,[8] the love of the beautiful and the triumph of art are the essence of Athens at its glorious peak.[9]

Love and art, and their close connections, lie at the heart of *MND*. In addition to Theseus' associating lovers, lunatics, and poets (5.1.4–17), the young lovers think of their own love as literature and of their beloveds as works of art,[10] and Oberon and Puck look upon the lovesick entanglements in the woods as theater ("Shall we their fond pageant see?" [3.2.114; also 3.2.118–19, 353]). The artisans, though literal-minded and unerotic themselves, prepare and perform a tragedy about love (1.2.11–91; 3.1.8–98; 5.1.56–57, 108–338). And Oberon imitates a poetic imitation of a

---

7   Whereas the words "city" and "country" occur 40 times each in *Coriolanus* and always in a political sense, "city" is mentioned only twice in *MND* and only in a nonpolitical sense (1.2.96; 2.1.215) and "country" just once, also in a nonpolitical sense (3.2.458). While in *Coriolanus* "the people" (including its variants) is spoken 77 times, in *MND* the commoners are never explicitly identified as a political class, but always as practitioners of individual manual arts or trades (2.2.9–10; 4.1.9–10; 4.2.7–10; 5.1.72–73), and "civil" never means civic, but always calm or courteous (2.1.152; 3.2.147).

8   Horace, *Letters*, 2.1.156–57; Plutarch, *Marcellus*, 21; *Cato the Elder*, 22–23.

9   Where the Athenians associate the noble with the beautiful (*to kalon*), the Romans associate it with the decorous, the seemly, the suitable, or the fitting (Cicero, *On Duties*, 1.93). Thus, while the word "noble" appears more often in *Coriolanus* than in any other Shakespeare play, "beauty" and "beautiful" are never mentioned. Plutarch, accordingly, contrasts "beautiful and famous Athens" with "invincible and glorious Rome," as "two most illustrious cities of the world" (Plutarch, *Theseus*, 1.2–3, 2.1).

10 For example, 1.1.132–55, 235–39; 2.1.230–31; 2.2.121.

---

lover (Corin), who is himself a poetic imitator ("Playing on pipes of corn, and versing love"), pursuing a poetic imitation of a beloved (Phillida) (2.1.65–68). Throughout the play, love not only inspires poetry and poetry inspires love, but each imitates the other. As "imitation" means both emulation and simulation,[11] love imitates poetry by beautifying its object, while poetry imitates love by representing it. Love and poetry—the passion and its expression—imitate each other.

Love and poetry find common ground in the imagination. As Theseus observes, poetry and love involve seeing or imagining what is absent (5.1.4–22). Art, particularly dramatic poetry, impersonates its characters ("[T]ell them that I, Pyramus, am not Pyramus, but Bottom the weaver" [3.1.19–20]), while love idealizes its object ("[T]he lover... / Sees Helen's beauty in the brow of Egypt" [5.1.10–11]). Both involve seeing something as something else. The double vision of imagination stands out in dramatic art, where, contrary to what the artisans fear (1.2.70–78; 3.1.8–21, 26–44; 5.1.214–21), imitations announce their simultaneous reality and unreality. They are what they are not, and are not what they are: Bottom is, and is not, Pyramus. And we, as spectators, naturally distinguish between the image and the reality, the imitation and the imitated as well as between the actor and the character.

Such doubleness of vision is essential to human thinking. Humans naturally see double: "Methinks I see these things with parted eye / When everything seems double" (4.1.188–89). We see what is before us with our body's eye and see what it means with our mind's eye. Able to separate the significance of a sight from the sight itself, we are able to see or to imagine what is absent and therefore to generalize, utter aphorisms, speak in metaphors, play on words, name one thing by another, idealize or beautify, make promises and vows, pretend or suspect others of doing so, offer tokens, form lists, and compose poems and plays—all of which abound in *MND*.

---

11   Aristotle, *Poetics*, 1448b4–19.

Dreams and literalness are opposite our natural double vision. Instead of recognizing an image as an image, when we dream or are literal-minded, we take the likeness for the thing itself. Rather than distinguishing the image from the reality, we believe the reality of the image: "What a dream was here / ... / Methought a serpent ate my heart away" (2.2.148). The distinction between something and its likeness vanishes. The natural doubleness of thinking collapses into one.

Love, paradoxically, combines the doubleness of drama and the literalism of dreams. Like drama or art in general, love beautifies or idealizes its object. It naturally projects an imaginary form upon what it sees: "Things base and vile, holding no quantity, / Love can transpose to form and dignity" (1.1.232–33). But love also tends to deny that it embellishes. Owing precisely to the strength of its spell, it claims that it does not adorn or transform but sees its object faithfully:

So is mine eye enthralled to thy shape;
And thy fair virtue's force perforce doth move me
On the first view to say, to swear, I love thee.
(3.1.134–36)

A contradictory combination of idealization and literalness, love first beautifies its object, but then takes its own idealization literally. Notwithstanding that the one depends upon the imagination while the other shows no trace of imagination at all, in the end the lover's view of his beloved at least partly matches the players' view of their art.

Nearly everything in *MND* has a dual character or is double. Theseus, having won Hippolyta with his sword, promises to marry her in "another key" (1.1.18). Hermia's father insists that she "consent" to his "consent" to whom she marries (1.1.25, 40; 4.1.157, 158). Theseus tells Hermia that her eyes must look with her father's judgment (1.1.57). Hermia and Lysander meet in the woods where they met once before on another May Day morning and where Hermia and Helena used to meet when they were young (1.1.166–67, 214–17). Helena wishes to be Hermia "translated" (1.1.191). Bottom, who is "translated" or "transformed" (3.1.113–14; 4.1.63), becomes half man, half ass, while Hercules, who is himself half human, half divine, once fought a creature that was half man, half beast (5.1.44–47). Oberon and Titania quarrel over a "changeling" boy (2.1.120). Oberon's love juice duplicates Cupid's fiery arrow (2.1.155–720). Lysander and Demetrius are "two…rival enemies" (4.1.141). Puck mistakes one for the other, turning a true love false rather than a false love true (3.2.88–91). Both the fairies and the players are "shadows" (3.2.347; 5.1.208, 409). Hermia and Lysander are "two bosoms and a single troth" (2.2.49), while Hermia and Helena were once

> Like to a double cherry, seeming parted,
> But yet an union in partition,
> Two lovely berries molded on one stem.
>   (3.2.209–11)

Lysander makes vows to both women, "truth kill[ing] truth" (3.2.129). Puck, who initially finds the greatest amusement in "two at once woo[ing] one" (3.2.118), finally welcomes that "[t]wo of both kinds makes up four" (3.2.438). In addition, the moon, whose own light is a reflection, is both passionate and passionless,[12] at once full and new.[13] The season is both spring and summer. Theseus emphasizes that four days remain until his wedding (1.1.2–3), yet the play's action covers just two. And whereas the play begins with lovers either sundered or threatened with separation, it ends with the "couples…eternally…knit" (4.1.180).

Not surprisingly, doubles and quasi-doubles often take the form of imitation. Combining imitation's twin meanings,[14] the

---

12 For example, 1.1.3–6, 9–11, 30, 73, 89–90; 2.1.141, 156, 162; 4.1.72; 5.1.135–37.

13 For example, 1.1.2–11, 209–10; 1.2.95; 2.1.60; 2.2.85; 3.1.48–54; 3.2.177–82.

14 See Introduction, n11.

artisans, emulating Athenian actors, perform a stage drama—a drama, moreover, based on a traditional love story (Ovid, *Metamorphoses*, 4.55–166). The artisans' play, while an imitation of an imitation, also closely parallels the plight and plan of Hermia and Lysander. Shakespeare's play and the play within the play mirror each other, the one as comedy, the other as tragedy. Indeed, while "Pyramus and Thisbe" is played twice, once in rehearsal and once in performance, the actors' incompetence transforms the putative tragedy into an unintended comedy. The tragedy becomes "tragical mirth" (5.1.57). Besides Oberon's thoroughgoing imitative pursuit of a beloved (2.1.65–68), an Indian woman "imitate[s]" ships imitating her (2.1.128–34); Helena, reversing the myth, imitates Daphne chasing Apollo (2.1.230–31); Egeus accuses Lysander of "feigning love" (1.1.31); and Helena accuses the other young lovers of "counterfeit[ing] sad looks" to mock her (3.2.237). Moreover, the lovers are to think the events in the woods were a dream (3.2.370–71; 4.1.67–68). Bottom thinks they were and would have Quince write a ballad of the dream, which he would sing at the end of the artisans' play (4.1.203–17). Puck, who himself mimics the shape and sound of almost anything (2.1.44–57; 3.1.101–6), regards the lovers' imbroglio as a play, in which he is playwright and stage manager, actor and audience. And while also "an auditor" and "[a]n actor too" in the artisans' rehearsal (3.1.75–76), he is both character and actor in *MND*'s epilogue (5.1.409–24) and the onstage narrator of events which we had already seen for ourselves (3.2.6–34). In short, throughout the play, art imitates life imitating art. Image and reality are not so much opposed as brought curiously together.

Such ambiguity especially characterizes the fairies. "[F]airy land" (2.1.65; 122; 4.1.60) is a kingdom of unstinted imagination. In it, time, place, causality, and identity lose their natural character. Necessity seems suspended. While the fairies tend not just to speak but to recite elaborate narratives, their narrative accounts prove to be fictitious even within the fiction of Shakespeare's play. Titania describes at considerable length vast floods and disastrous unseasonable weather, brought on, she says, by her quarrel with

Oberon (2.1.82–117). Yet, nothing else in the play suggests or even permits the floods or disorder. Apart from the fog that Puck produces to keep the male rivals apart (3.2.355–59), there are no fogs, floods, famine, or signs of winter in summer. Nor does anyone appear concerned with such conditions when deciding to go into the woods. Quite the contrary, the lovers, artisans, and fairies alike describe the woods as undisturbed. The lovers and fairies even speak of Phoebe (the moon) or the fairies themselves placing dewdrops on the grass and flowers (1.1.211, 2.1.14–15). Titania's narrative—the longest speech in the play—is at odds with the rest of the play. It is an image without an original.

More glaringly, Philostrate contradicts not just words, but actions of the fairies that we see for ourselves. Bottom is the only human to see any of the fairies. Yet, he cannot recall what he saw and supposes that his amorous encounter with Titania was a dream. And when he decides to have Quince write a ballad of the dream, Bottom names the ballad for what he says the dream lacks: "[I]t shall be called 'Bottom's Dream,' because it hath no bottom" (4.2.214–15). Bottom may, for once, be correct. What he saw may indeed have no foundation, no bottom. It may truly have been a dream. In a play with many strange twists, none appears more curious—and more needless—than Philostrate's thrice-uttered insistence that he saw the entire "Pyramus and Thisbe" rehearsed (5.1.64–65, 67–68, 77), even though we see Puck interrupting it after just ten lines (3.1.73ff.). Philostrate's repeated claim, which seems wholly unnecessary to the plot in any ordinary sense, effectively denies that the amatory interlude with the ass-headed Bottom and the love-juiced Titania ever took place.

Now, because it is closely joined to the imagination, love for the young lovers is primarily looking at the beloved. It is connected more to sight than to touch. Oberon's love juice—a comic exaggeration of falling in love at first sight—underscores the intimate tie.[15] However, where the young lovers illustrate that

---

15 The word "eye[s]" appears in *MND* more often than in other Shakespeare plays (79 times).

love lies in the eyes, Theseus, by contrast, decries its dependence on sight. To him, lovers, like lunatics, claim to see what exists merely in their imagination. "Lovers and madmen have such seething brains," he says, with a telling pun, "Such shaping fantasies, that apprehend / More than cool reason ever comprehends" (5.1.4–6). And just as fear leads the lunatic to see more devils than hell could hold, and love leads the lover to see great beauty even in an ugly face, the poet, whose "imagination bodies forth / The forms of things unknown," gives bodily shape to "airy nothing" (5.1.14–16). For Theseus, the heroic warrior, what can be touched is real and what exists in the imagination has not only a reduced reality, but is entirely illusory. Accordingly, just as the young lovers tend to confuse letters and love, Theseus does so, but with the opposite import. For him, the resemblance among "[t]he lover, the lunatic, and the poet," who "[a]re of imagination all compact" (5.1.7–8), lowers the lover and the poet to the level of the lunatic. Ironically, the founder of the city renowned for the love of beauty and the highest accomplishments in art, disparages both love and art as mere madness. In a most important way, Athens' founder does not fit into the city which he founds. If heroic ambition places Coriolanus outside of Rome, heroic taste places Theseus outside of Athens. The hero who is himself an "antique fable" (5.1.3), and who has emulated another antique fable (5.1.44–47), has no taste for literary tales.

Shakespeare presents Theseus as a sexually impatient lover. Whether four days or three hours, waiting for his desire's satisfaction is "the anguish of a torturing hour" (1.1.1–6, 5.1.32–37). That Theseus waits at all, however, is surprising, for he is notorious for ravishing and abandoning women:

Didst not thou lead him through the glimmering night,
From Perigouna, whom he ravished;
And make him with fair Aegles break his faith,
With Ariadne and Antiopa?

                                                                        (2.1.77–80)

9

Yet, notwithstanding his unrestrained, even brutal, past,[16] Theseus is an eager bridegroom who, despite his tormenting desire and his having conquered his bride in war, awaits his wedding day. The play ends with the lawful fulfillment of his desire, as well as that of the other lovers. Shakespeare's portrayal shows the change in Theseus from heroic to moral virtue, from heroic unrestraint to civic self-control in sexual desire.[17] Erotic desire is civilized or tamed in Theseus and, by implication, in Athens as well.

Love is not only moderated in Theseus' Athens. It is also liberated. Despite the apparent absence of politics in the play, Theseus establishes the Athenian political regime. He overthrows the authority of fathers and hence of the household gods ("To you your father should be as a god" [1.1.47]) and does so in the name of freedom or "consent" in marriage (1.1.40, 82; cp. 1.1.25, 4.1.157–58). As already noted, ancient tradition places Athens' founding in Theseus' unification of the demes or villages of Attica. Shakespeare, however, locates it in Theseus' liberating love from patriarchal authority. Love is linked to marriage on the one hand and freed from patriarchal authority on the other. The claims of lawful erotic love defeat those of generation. The love of the beautiful replaces the absolute power of fathers over their offspring.

It is surely no accident that Shakespeare gives Hermia's father the name Egeus, which ancient sources attribute to Theseus' father. According to Plutarch, Theseus, who was at least indirectly responsible for his father's death, "cannot be cleared of parricide" (Plutarch, *Comparison of Theseus and Romulus*, 5.2; North, 1:115).[18] Whereas *MND* begins with a father invoking "the ancient privilege of Athens" (1.1.41) to marry his daughter to whatever man he wishes ("[W]hat is mine my love shall render him; / And she is mine" [1.1.96–97]), it ends with the father absent from his

---

16 See, further, Plutarch, *Theseus*, 8.2–3, 19.1–3, 20.1–2, 26.1–2, 29.1–2, 31.

17 See Aristotle, *Nicomachean Ethics*, 1145a15–33.

18 On Egeus' death, see Plutarch, *Theseus*, 22.1.

daughter's wedding to the man she loves. Once Theseus "over-bear[s]" (4.1.178) his will, Egeus—the only father in the play—says not another word and disappears with hardly a trace.

Shakespeare presents Theseus' overthrow of patriarchal authority as tantamount to his unification of the villages. The former points up the significance of the latter, for it turns Athens from a collection of sovereign fathers who, as in Rome, have absolute power over their family members to a union of families or households in which the city's power can reach family members.[19] By replacing command with consent, and fathers with families, as the fundamental principle and component of the city, Theseus' action lays the ground for the full development of democratic Athens, centuries later.[20]

Although Theseus deposes the ancestral gods, they are not simply replaced by the Olympian gods or gods of the city. In sharp contrast to Rome, where the Romans think of the gods in everything they do and thank them for everything they gain, the gods seem largely absent or irrelevant in Theseus' Athens. Theseus does not speak of any god when overruling Egeus' will, and his only hint of the gods in connection with the marriages is his saying that the weddings will take place "in the temple" (4.1.179). Theseus, in fact, never mentions a god in his own name after the opening scene, when he admonishes Hermia to think of her father as one and then threatens to punish her with a celibate life in the worship of Diana if she defies him (1.1.89). His only reference to an Olympian thus expressly associates piety with punishment, holiness with unhappiness (1.1.65–78). As one might expect, Cupid is mentioned far more frequently than any other god.

---

19   Thucydides, 2.15–16, Plutarch, *Theseus*, 24.1. On the contrast between Roman a Greek fathers, see Dionysius of Halicarnassus, *Roman Antiquities*, 2.26–27.

20   "Theseus was the first…who yielded to have a commonwealth or popular estate (as Aristotle says)" (Plutarch, *Theseus*, 25.2; North, 54). For his bringing democracy to Athens, see, further, Euripides, *The Suppliant Women*, 352–53, 404–5.

Venus comes second.[21] The two gods most often mentioned correspond directly to a human experience. Still, even these gods are not mentioned by anyone after Theseus overturns Egeus' authority. Once Theseus acts, humans speak of Greek gods only in the titles or the dialogue of the artisans' poetry or in profane, mock oaths.[22] The gods, existing now chiefly in fiction, seem to be expelled from Athens by love and replaced by art. Thus, while the virgin Athena is never mentioned, the only religious practice is the young lovers going into the woods early on a May morning "to observe / The rite of May" (4.1.131–32). After Theseus deposes the ancestral gods, only the fairies are said to follow a god: "[W]e fairies, that do run / By the triple Hecate's team" (5.1.369–70).[23]

The Athens we see in the play represents Athens at its peak as well as at its beginning. Unlike Shakespeare's Roman plays, which depict specific moments in Roman history, *MND* is entirely synchronic. The shifts from Theseus' brutal record of rape to his lawful marriage, and from his threat to enforce Athenian ancestral law to his overturning that law, are the most obvious, but not the only, examples of Shakespeare's coalescing different and even contradictory eras or times. Throughout the play, Shakespeare portrays—or parodies—the peak of Athens as present at its founding. His Thesean Athens is already a city of high art. The artisans, for example—"Hard-handed men that work in Athens here, / Which never labored in their minds till now" (5.1.72–73)— seek to trade their manual arts for an art of the mind. They hope— even confidently expect—to find fame and fortune, and become "made men" (4.2.18), thanks to their excellent theatrical performance. Right from the start, leisure has largely supplanted necessity in Athens. Exempt from the usual imperfections of the beginning

---

21   Cupid: 1.1.169, 235; 2.1.157, 161, 165; 3.2.102, 440; 4.1.72; Venus:
      1.1.171; 3.2.61, 107.
22   5.1.48, 52, 176, 273–74, 307–8, 323–28.
23   On Hermia's name confirming rather than confuting the general
      rule; see 2.2.55–59n.

of civic life, the earliest Athenians go beyond the needs of the body and pursue accomplishments of the high arts and mind.

Shakespeare treats Athens' transformation from barbaric to civilized, through a series of thematic substitutions. Beginning with Theseus' appearance with his hunting party in the May Day morning (4.1.102ff.), he compresses the development into a few key steps. First, Hippolyta, recounting the time she, Hercules, and Cadmus bayed bears with Spartan hounds in Crete, replaces the hunt itself with the "musical...discord" (4.1.117) of the hounds' gallant cry, which she acclaims as unequaled. Then, Theseus substitutes the melodious ("tuneable" [4.1.123]) sound of his own hounds for the discordant sound of the Spartan hounds. Although his are "bred out of the Spartan kind" (4.1.118), he praises them as superior. Where Spartan hounds are renowned for their courage and speed,[24] Theseus says that his are slow and extols them for their musical sound. The slow and the musical replace the fast and the fierce. And where Hippolyta praised the Spartan hounds in Crete for their "mutual cry" (4.1.116), Theseus lauds his for the harmony of their individual sounds ("matched in mouth like bells, / Each under each" [4.1.122–23]). The individual replaces the choral unison, as the Athenian exceeds the Spartan. Furthermore, owing to an art—the art of breeding—descendants exceed their ancestors. In Athens, the new surpasses the old. The excellence of art replaces the authority of age. Crete and Sparta, the oldest and most venerable Greek cities, whose fundamental principle, moreover, is reverence for age, and whose laws are traceable to Zeus and Apollo,[25] are surpassed by Athens, whose new principle is freedom and art. Accordingly, Theseus, next, hearing that the young women they have come upon are Egeus' daughter and "old Nedar's Helena" (4.1.129), orders that the four sleepers be awakened by the sound of horns: the music of human art replaces the musical sound of beasts. Then, learning that Demetrius once again loves Helena, Theseus summarily deposes

---

24   See 4.1.113n.
25   See Plato, *Laws*, 624al–6, 634al–2, 662c7; *Minos*, 31&1–3.

the ancient authority of Athenian fathers, allowing the lovers to marry as they choose (4.1.178–80). Finally, "the morning ...now something worn" (4.1.181), Theseus expressly "sets aside" the "purpos'd hunting" (4.1.182), so that the three couples can return to Athens for "a feast in great solemnity" (4.1.184)—a wedding celebration that takes the form of a dramatic performance. Act 4, Scene 1—Theseus' central scene—links the ferocity of ancient heroism on the one end and the civility of Athenian intellectual and democratic life on the other. The barbaric passes into the civilized.

Shakespeare's historical compression goes yet further. Not only does Hippolyta tell of hunting with Cadmus and Hercules in Crete, whose ancestors include Olympian gods.[26] Theseus mentions a song describing the battle in which his "kinsman" Hercules fought and defeated the centaurs (5.1.44–47).[27] Within the lifetime of Hippolyta and Theseus, Athens faced half-human, half-bestial foes, which are now present only in song.

---

26   Hesiod, *The Shield of Heracles*, 1–56; Apollodorus, *Library*, 2.4.8.
27   Diodorus Siculus, *Library*, 4.12.1–6; Apollodorus, 2.5.4; Virgil, *Aeneid*, 8.293–95.

LIST OF CHARACTERS

Theseus, Duke of Athens
Hippolyta, Queen of the Amazons, engaged to Theseus
Hermia, in love with Lysander
Helena, in love with Demetrius
Lysander, in love with Hermia
Demetrius, suitor of Hermia
Egeus, Hermia's father
Philostrate, Theseus' Master of the Revels
Oberon, King of the Fairies
Titania, Queen of the Fairies
Puck, or Robin Goodfellow, Oberon's jester and aide
Peaseblossom, Fairy serving Titania
Cobweb, Fairy serving Titania
Moth, Fairy serving Titania
Mustardseed, Fairy serving Titania
A Fairy serving Titania
Peter Quince, carpenter (Prologue in "Pyramus and Thisbe")
Nick Bottom, weaver (Pyramus)
Francis Flute, bellows-mender (Thisbe)
Tom Snout, tinker (Wall)
Snug, joiner (Lion)
Robin Starveling, tailor (Moonshine)
Other fairies serving their King and Queen
Lords and Attendants to Theseus and Hippolyta

Act One, Scene One

Enter Theseus, Hippolyta, and Philostrate,[1] with others.

Theseus: Now, fair Hippolyta, our nuptial hour
    Draws on apace.[2] Four happy days bring in
    Another moon.[3],[4] But, O, methinks how slow
    This old moon wanes![5] She lingers my desires[6]

---

1   S.D. 1. "*Theseus,…Philostrate*": Theseus' name means, in Greek, "He who Lays Down," indicating his legendary status as Athens' founder or perhaps alluding to his lifting the rock under which his father had hidden tokens of his paternity (see Plutarch, *Theseus*, 4.1). Hippolyta's name means "Of the Stampeding Horses." It refers to the Amazons' love of riding and their equestrian skill. On Philostrate's name, see Introduction, 2.

2   2. "Draws on apace": approaches soon.

3   3. "Another moon": A "new moon" is the first day of the Athenian month (see Aratos de Soles, *Visible Signs*, 733–35). Theseus, previously known for his ravishment and betrayal of women (see Introduction, 9–10; 2.1.78–80nn), now, showing surprising restraint, awaits, however impatiently, his wedding date; see, further, lines 1–4n.

4   3. "moon": The moon is mentioned often in *MND*. Like the moon itself, what is said about it changes completely from time to time. At times it is closely associated with chastity, coldness, and even perpetual celibacy (e.g., line 73; 2.1.156, 162). At other times it is just as closely associated with love, festivities, and the escape from patriarchal authority (e.g., lines 30, 209–10; 2.1.141, 5.1.136). Even though Diana, the goddess of chastity, is identified with the moon (see line 73n), Cupid is fully at home in its light (2.1.155–68).

5   1–4. "Now, … wanes": Theseus connects desire and time, as he will do, with even greater impatience, as his wedding nears. Desire involves a temporal gap between longing and fulfillment. Orienting us toward the future, it aims to turn the future into the present, the "not yet" into the "now." Theseus thus describes not only his desire but its satisfaction in temporal terms. Just as his wait is to be "four…days," his wedding is to be his "nuptial hour." As he will

5   Like to a stepdame or a dowager
       Long withering out[7] a young man's revenue.[8]
       Hippolyta: Four days will quickly steep themselves[9] in nights;
       Four nights will quickly dream away the time;
       And then the moon, like to a silver bow
10   New-bent in heaven, shall behold the night
       Of our solemnities.[10],[11]

---

later say, the "long age" of waiting—"the anguish of a torturing hour"—will finally end at "bed-time" (5.1.33, 34. 37).

6   4. "lingers my desires": delays the fulfillment of my desires.

7   6. "withering out": drying and shriveling up.

8   4–6. "She...revenue": Theseus likens the old moon to a father's widow who, while remaining alive, spends the money her stepson or son would otherwise inherit. Theseus will later overrule a father's authority in behalf of a daughter's love (see 4.1.178–80n). Here, thinking of his own love, he attacks a father's wife on behalf of a son's desire. Theseus in his first speech impugns age in the name of youth, piety in the name of pleasure. He impatiently waits for the rich old lady to die.

A "stepdame" is a stepmother. Theseus' stepmother is Medea, who sought not merely to wither out his revenue, but to murder him, fearing that he rather than her own son would become king (Plutarch, *Theseus*, 12.2–3; Ovid, *Metamorphoses*, 7.404–24). While there are no living mothers in *MND*, Medea, the first of four stepmothers, is paired with the last, Phaedra, whose presence is also by implicit allusion (see Coda, 197–198).

Dowager" is a legal term for "A widow endowed" (Thomas E. Tomlins, 1820, *The Law-Dictionary, s.v.* dowager).

9   7. "steep themselves": become absorbed (literally, soak themselves).

10 11. "solemnities": festive celebrations. In *MND*, "solemnity" always refers to a wedding or wedding celebration. In Plutarch, Shakespeare's principal source, the word refers to the "solemn oath" concluding the war between Theseus and Hippolyta's Amazons (Plutarch, *Theseus*, 27.5; North, 1:58). In Shakespeare's comedy, the marital replaces the martial.

11 7–11. "Four... solemnities": In contrast to Theseus, Hippolyta, the first Amazon to marry, stresses how quickly the time will pass. As Queen of the Amazons, she may not share Theseus' eagerness to

Theseus: Go, Philostrate,
   Stir up the Athenian youth to merriments.
   Awake the pert[12] and nimble spirit of mirth.
   Turn melancholy forth[13] to funerals;
   The pale companion[14] is not for our pomp.[15]   15

                      [Exit *Philostrate*.]

   Hippolyta, I wooed thee with my sword
   And won thy love doing thee injuries,[16]
   But I will wed thee in another key,
   With pomp, with triumph,[17] and with reveling.[18]

---

marry. The Amazons—"the daughters of Ares [Mars, in Latin]," the god of war (Isocrates, *Panegyricus*, 68)—are a mythological race of unwed warrior women, who conduct all the activities of war and government, while assigning the conventional domestic duties of women to the men among them (Diodorus Siculus, *Library*, 2.45). Note Hippolyta's simile of a "bow," and see, further, lines 16–17n.

12 13. "pert": lively, alert.
13 14. "forth": away.
14 15. "companion": fellow (contemptuous).
15 15. "pomp": splendid procession; see, further, line 19n.
16 16–17. "I wooed...injuries": The battle against the Amazons was the Athenians' first brave deed against foreigners (Pausanias, *Description of Greece*, 5.11.7). Theseus might mean that he wooed Hippolyta with his heroic prowess, that she fell in love with him because of his valiant victory over her. Or, more likely, he may be speaking hopefully, proleptically, or even euphemistically and apologetically: Hippolyta is his war prize, whose love he hopes to win despite his injuries to her. Throughout the play, Theseus uses terms of endearment for Hippolyta (1.1.1, 84, 122 [twice]; 4.1.105; 5.1.46, 87, 99). But she uses an affectionate term for him ("my Theseus" [5.1.1]) only once and only after they are married, and never says that she loves him or (apart from that term) anything like it. Her concluding phrase "our solemnities" is her only reference to their wedding.
17 19. "pomp,...triumph": "Pomp" and "triumph," particularly the latter, refer to the gloriously festive procession of a victorious general and his army; see, further, line 11n.
18 18–19. "But...reveling": Theseus, using a musical metaphor, stresses his shift from heroic to civic life and, in particular, from

Enter Egeus[19] and his daughter Hermia,[20]
and Lysander and Demetrius.[21]

20   *Egeus*: Happy be Theseus, our renowned Duke![22]
   Theseus: Thanks, good Egeus. What's the news with thee?

---

    martial victory to merry festivities. But Hippolyta, who never speaks with such passion or at such length as when recounting the time she bayed the bear with Hercules and Cadmus in Crete, will say that the "music" that most fills her heart is the "cry"— the "sweet thunder"—of the Spartan hounds on that hunt (4.1.111–17). She may still prefer the heroic to the civic. Hunting and war may still be this "warrior love['s]" (2.1.71) deepest passion.

19   S.D. 20. "*Egeus*": Egeus is the name of Theseus' father (see Plutarch, *Theseus*, 3.3–4; and Introduction, 10). Shakespeare elides the opening diphthong of the Greek spelling Aigeus into the long vowel "E." The Aegean Sea is named for him.

20   S.D. 20. "*Hermia*": Hermia is named after Hermes (Mercury, in Latin). On her resemblance to her namesake, see 2.2.55–59n.

21   S.D. 20. "*Lysander and Demetrius*". Lysander is the name of the Spartan military leader who destroyed the Athenian navy in 405 BC, forcing Athens to capitulate and ending the Peloponnesian War. Demetrius is the name of a Macedonian king who, among many other things, freed Athens from oligarchic rule in 307 BC and restored the democracy. Plutarch wrote *Lives* of Lysander and Demetrius as well as of Theseus. On Lysander and Demetrius, see, further, lines 104–5n.

22   20. "our...Duke": Egeus' appreciative description of Theseus points to the initial harmony between Theseus and the Athenian nobles. While the "poor people and private men" were "ready to follow [Theseus'] will" in unifying Attica, "the rich and such as had authority in every village [were] all against it." To mollify them, Theseus promised to share power with them, reserving to himself the command of the army and "the preservation of the laws" (Plutarch, *Theseus*, 24.2–4, 25.2; North, 1:52). Egeus has come to Theseus in his capacity as the promised preserver of the existing laws. The word "law" (*nomos*) for the Greeks has a wider meaning than for us. It includes custom. On the title Duke and Theseus' promise to avoid "the power of any sole prince," see Introduction, n4.

Egeus: Full of vexation come I, with complaint[23]
    Against my child, my daughter Hermia.[24],[25]
    Stand forth,[26] Demetrius. My noble lord,
    This man hath my consent to marry her.   25
    Stand forth, Lysander. And, my gracious Duke,
    This man hath bewitched the bosom of my child.
    Thou, thou, Lysander, thou hast given her rhymes[27]
    And interchanged love tokens with my child.
    Thou hast by moonlight at her window sung   30
    With feigning voice verses of feigning love[28]

---

23   22. "complaint": accusation (a legal term). The exchange with Egeus (lines 22–127), in effect a courtroom trial, teems with legal terminology.

24   23. "Against…Hermia": Although his anger seems directed against Lysander, Egeus must proceed against Hermia, for he has authority as a father over her and not over him. His authority is limited to his own; see, further, lines 41–42n.

25   22–23. "Full…Hermia": In Shakespeare's sources, Theseus' celebration of the conclusion of the Amazon war is interrupted by grieving Argive women, who beg him to make war on Creon, the king of Thebes. Following the civil war between Oedipus' sons, Creon, having taken the throne after the brothers killed each other for the crown, refused to allow the bodies of his dead enemies, including the suppliants' husbands, to be buried. Theseus, always generous in granting help when implored, immediately took his army to Thebes, defeated and killed Creon, and allowed all the dead to be buried (see, for example, Euripides, *The Suppliant Women*; Chaucer, *The Knight's Tale*, 1.893ff.). In *MND*, Egeus and Hermia replace the Argive suppliants. A dispute about marriage in Athens replaces the fratricidal war in Thebes; see, further, 4.1.131–35n, and 5.1.50–51n.

26   24. "Stand forth": A lawyer's courtroom language in a trial; see also line 26.

27   28. "rhymes": love poems.

28   31. "feigning…love": singing softly verses of pretended love. Egeus plays on the word "feign." In addition to meaning "pretend," the word in a now obsolete sense means "sing softly." "He feigneth to the lute marvelous[ly] sweetly" (Thomas Wilson, 1560, *The Arte of Rhetorique*, 67).

And stol'n the impression of her fantasy[29]
With bracelets of thy hair, rings, gauds, conceits,
Knacks,[30] trifles, nosegays, sweetmeats[31] (messengers
35 Of strong prevailment[32] in unhardened youth).[33]
With cunning hast thou filched my daughter's heart,
Turned her obedience (which is due to me)
To stubborn harshness.[34] And, my gracious Duke,
Be it so[35] she will not here before your Grace
40 Consent to marry with Demetrius,
I beg the ancient privilege of Athens:

---

29   32. "stol'n...fantasy": stealthily impressed yourself on her imagination/love ("fantasy" combines imagination and love). The image is of stamping an image in soft wax.

30   33–34. "gauds, ...Knacks": trinkets, fanciful articles, knick-knacks ("conceits" implies cunningly contrived).

31   34. "nosegays, sweetmeats": bunches of flowers, candied fruits.

32   35. "prevailment": power to influence.

33   28–35. "Thou...youth)": Egeus lists two sorts of seductive tricks: 1) words and songs, and 2) material "love-tokens" (line 29). He seems to consider the second more dangerous, because they are mere "messengers" (line 34). Working entirely upon the imagination (see line 32n), they can be taken to mean anything the recipient wishes. This is the first time that imagination and by implication artfulness are said to cause love or to steal one's heart; see, further, 192–93n. Egeus' "complaint" (line 19) is a forensic speech (lines 22–45), of which his enumeration of tricks is the rhetorical "proof;" see, further, lines 22–45n.

34   36–38 "With...harshness": Egeus' charge of theft is twofold. In robbing the daughter of her heart, Lysander has robbed the father of his due. To Egeus, the latter theft is more serious. As he repeatedly insists, Hermia is "my child" (lines 23, 27, 29), "my daughter" (lines 23, 36), and "[a]s she is mine, I may dispose of her" (line 42; see also lines 96–97). The charge that Lysander has deceived Hermia is largely beside the point. Whether or not Lysander has "feign[ed] love" (line 31), Egeus' complaint would be the same: Hermia has defied his paternal authority. And Lysander's true love would rob him of that as much as his false love. The question, for Egeus, concerns filial obedience, not true love.

35   39. "Be it so": if.

As she is mine, I may dispose of her,[36]
Which shall be either to this gentleman
Or to her death, according to our law
Immediately[37] provided[38] in that case.[39],[40]   45

---

36   41–42. "I...her": According to Egeus, "the ancient privilege of Athens" gives a father absolute authority over his offspring. His daughter is his paternal property, with whom he may do as he wishes; see, further, Introduction, 10–11.

37   45. "Immediately": 1) directly, expressly, 2) at once, without delay.

38   45. "provided": A legal term, used to conclude indictments of offenses against a law: "Contrary to the form of the statute in that case made and provided" (William L. Rushton, 1858, *Shakespeare a Lawyer*, 38).

39   41–45. "I beg...case": The fathers' "ancient privilege" crystallizes the state of affairs before Theseus' unification of Athens. Before then, families in Attica lived independently in small villages, each worshipping its own ancestors, and each governed by a sovereign father (Thucydides, 2.15–16; Plutarch, *Theseus*, 24.1). With the unification of Athens, the preservation of the law passed to Theseus (or to the city), and Athens became—or began to become—a union of families under civic law. Although Theseus does not overthrow the patriarchal law until later, we can see the initial effect of his promise to look after "the preservation of the laws." Egeus must petition him to support his "ancient privilege." His patriarchal power is no longer absolute. If his daughter must still consent to his choice, he nevertheless cannot punish her without Theseus' consent. The private is now at least partly subject to the public. "Case" is a legal term; see line 63n.

40   22–45. "Full...case": Proceeding as in a courtroom, Egeus delivers a judicial or forensic speech, claiming the support of "the ancient privilege" and "law" of Athens (lines 41. 44). His speech, using classical rhetoric anachronistically to appeal to pre-Thesean law, contains the four principal parts of a classical judicial speech: an introduction (*exordium* in Latin, *prooimion* in Greek), meant to catch the listener's attention while introducing the subject (lines 22–23), a narrative (*narratio*, in Latin, *diegesis* in Greek), briefly describing the facts in the case (lines 24–27), a proof (*confirmatio* in Latin, *pistis* in Greek), the main part of the speech arguing the case (lines 28–38), and a conclusion (*peroratio* in Latin, *epilogus* in Greek), summing up the argument and stirring the listener (lines 38–45). On

Theseus: What say you, Hermia? Be advised, fair maid.
    To you, your father should be as a god,
    One that composed your beauties, yea, and one
    To whom you are but as a form in wax
50   By him imprinted,[41] and within his power
    To leave the figure or disfigure it.[42]
    Demetrius is a worthy gentleman.[43]
Hermia: So is Lysander.
Theseus: In himself he is,
    But in this kind,[44] wanting your father's voice,[45]
55   The other must be held the worthier.[46]
Hermia: I would my father looked but with my eyes.[47]
Theseus: Rather your eyes must with his judgment look.

---

        the rhetorical tropes, see 4.1.153–58n. On judicial oratory, see Aristotle, *The Art of Rhetoric*, 1414a30–20b5; Cicero, *On Invention*, 1.20–109.

41   49–50, "but...imprinted": A cursory allusion to Aristotle's theory of sexual generation, in which the male, corresponding to a carpenter's tools, gives "the visible shape and the form" to material, which the female contributes (Aristotle, *Generation of Animals*, 730a34–b28).

42   47–51. "To you...disfigure it": As if explaining and supporting Egeus' claim, Theseus says that begetting implies absolute power over one's offspring and absolute obedience to one's begetter. A father may either sustain or destroy the life he has formed; see lines 49–50n, but see, further, line 52n.

43   52. "Demetrius ...gentleman": Having stated Egeus' premise in the starkest possible terms (see lines 47–51n), Theseus suddenly, if implicitly, abandons it. The issue is no longer Egeus' arbitrary power, but rather his good judgment, an issue that permits a reply.

44   54. "this kind": a matter of this sort.

45   54. "wanting...voice": lacking your father's approval.

46   55. "The other...worthier": the father's choice must be thought to be the worthier (regardless of the true worthiness of the man himself).

47   56. "I...eyes": Hermia introduces the key theme of love and sight. On the frequency of the word "eye[s]," see Introduction, n15. "[W]ould" means wish; "but" means 1) instead, 2) only.

Hermia: I do entreat your Grace to pardon me.
 I know not by what power I am made bold,
 Nor how it may concern my modesty   60
 In such a presence here to plead[48] my thoughts,[49]
 But I beseech your Grace that I may know
 The worst that may[50] befall me in this case[51]
 If I refuse to wed Demetrius.
Theseus: Either to die the death[52] or to abjure   65
 Forever the society of men.[53]
 Therefore, fair Hermia, question your desires,
 Know of[54] your youth, examine well your blood,[55]
 Whether (if you yield not to your father's choice)
 You can endure the livery of a nun,[56]   70
 For aye[57] to be in shady cloister mewed,[58]

---

48 61. "plead": A legal term for advocating a position in a court of law.

49 59–61. "I know...thoughts": Hermia says that she is unsure how her boldness in defying her father and submitting a plea to Theseus will suit ("concern") her modesty. By "modesty," she means being unassuming, showing no presumptuousness or impudence, observing the proprieties of her age, sex, and condition. On her view of modesty, see, further, 2.2.56–59n.

50 63. "may": can (according to the law).

51 63. "case": legal action, to be decided in a court of law (a legal term).

52 65. "die the death": be put to death by law (a solemn phrase).

53 65–66. "abjure...men": Theseus adds life-long celibacy as a second possible punishment. "Abjure," a legal term, means to forswear or renounce by oath; see Tomlins, *s.v.* abjuration.

54 68. "Know of": consult.

55 68. "blood": natural passions.

56 70. "livery...nun": The distinctive dress of a priestess (and, by extension, a priestess' way of life). "Nun" is not a Christian anachronism. "Egeus desiring...to know how he might have children, went to the city of Delphi to consult the oracle of Apollo, where by Apollo's nun that notable prophecy was given to him for an answer" (Plutarch, *Theseus*, 3.3; North, 1:31).

57 71. "aye": ever.

58 71. "mewed": caged, confined (often applied to hawks and poultry).

To live a barren sister all your life,
Chanting faint[59] hymns to the cold fruitless moon.[60]
Thrice-blessed they that master so their blood
75   To[61] undergo such maiden pilgrimage,[62]
But earthlier happy[63] is the rose distilled[64]
Than that which, withering on the virgin thorn,
Grows, lives, and dies in single[65] blessedness.[66]
Hermia: So will I grow, so live, so die, my lord,
80   Ere I will yield my virgin patent up
Unto his lordship whose unwished yoke
My soul consents not to give sovereignty.[67]

---

59   73. "faint": 1) passionless, 2) feeble, and 3) feigned, insincere.
60   73. "cold...moon": Sexless, childless Diana, the goddess of chastity, identified with the moon (see Cicero, *On the Nature of the Gods*, 3.51). The pious devotion to Diana is punishment for the impious disobedience to her father.
61   75. "To": as to (see Abbott, *Shakespearian Grammar*, §281).
62   75. "pilgrimage": long course of a pious life.
63   76. "earthlier happy": more earthly happy.
64   76. "distilled": made into perfume (with enduring sweetness).
65   78. "single": 1) unmarried, celibate, 2) thin, weak.
66   76–78. "But earthlier...blessedness": Although he grants that some people might consider such a life blessed (lines 74–75), Theseus says that blessedness is not the same as earthly happiness. Life's sweetness is his standard. As a single life resembles a rose that withers unplucked, a married life is like a rose that has been plucked so its fragrance can be distilled in perfume. Marriage—romantic love—sweetens human life. Theseus is silent about Hermia's obligation to Egeus. Her youth and passions, not her father's authority, are to decide whether she will carry out her daughterly duty.
67   79–82. "So...sovereignty": Hermia, describing marriage as a form of rule, speaks of a husband as a "lordship" possessing "sovereignty" (lines 81, 82). The husband rules the wife. But, contrary to the authority that her father claims, a husband's sovereignty over his wife is—or at least, in Hermia's view, ought to be—voluntary. It is based not on authority or command, but on choice or "consent" (line 82). The husband's sovereignty rests on the wishes of

Theseus: Take time to pause, and by the next new moon,
    The sealing day betwixt my love and me
    For everlasting bond of fellowship,[68]   85
    Upon that day either prepare to die
    For disobedience to your father's will,
    Or else to wed Demetrius, as he would,[69]
    Or on Diana's[70] altar to protest[71]
    For aye austerity and single life.   90
Demetrius: Relent, sweet Hermia, and, Lysander, yield
    Thy crazed title[72] to my certain[73] right.[74]
Lysander: You have her father's love, Demetrius.
    Let me have Hermia's. Do you marry him.
Egeus: Scornful Lysander, true, he hath my love;   95

---

    his wife. It is hierarchical rule based on a democratic foundation. Accordingly, Hermia uses a strictly legal term ("patent") for her exclusive right or privilege to her virginity. As legitimate sovereignty rests on consent, Hermia has sole title to the possession and disposal of her virginity. This is the only time she speaks in political or legal terms.

68   84–85. "sealing day…fellowship": Despite what ancient legends euphemistically describe as his own "marriages" (Plutarch, *Theseus*, 29.1–2; North, 1:58–59), Theseus characterizes marriage as an "everlasting bond of fellowship" (line 85). Much as Hermia suggested, it is a permanent union of similars or equals. "Seal" and "bond" are legal terms. "Seal" refers to the wax impressed by a device and attached to a document is to make it binding (Tomlins, s.v. seal). "Bond" is an agreement made binding on those who make it (Tomlins, s.v. bond).

69   88. "would": wishes, requires.

70   89. "Diana": This is Theseus' only explicit mention of an Olympian deity in his own name. He mentions the word "god" only when reminding Hermia that she should consider her father as one.

71   89. "protest": vow.

72   92. "crazed title": unsound, flawed claim.

73   92. "certain": undeniable.

74   92. "Thy…right": On Demetrius' tendency to juxtapose opposites, see 2.2.188–94n. His manner of speech corresponds to his adversarial view of courtship; see, further, lines 194–201n.

And what is mine my love shall render him.
And she is mine, and all my right of her
I do estate unto[75] Demetrius.[76]
Lysander: I am, my lord, as well derived[77] as he,
100   As well possessed.[78] My love is more than his;
My fortunes every way as fairly ranked
If not with vantage,[79] as Demetrius'.
And—which is more than all these boasts can be—
I am beloved of[80] beauteous Hermia.
105   Why should not I then prosecute my right?[81],[82]

---

75   98. "estate unto": bestow upon (a legal term; see Tomlins, *s.v.* estate).

76   95–98. "true,…Demetrius": Egeus, who used forensic rhetoric to accuse Lysander (see lines 22–45n), now answers him in the form of a syllogism, while emphasizing legal terminology:

    Major premise: My love shall give what is mine.
    Minor premise: She is mine.

    Conclusion: Therefore, I will give all my right to her to Demetrius, whom I love. As before, Egeus stresses what is his, referring to himself or what is his six times in four lines (and repeating his earlier "she is mine" [see line 42]). He twice mentions his love, but neither here nor anywhere else does he mention his love for Hermia.

77   99. "derived": descended.

78   100. "well possessed": wealthy.

79   102. "with vantage": better.

80   104. "beloved of": loved by.

81   105. "prosecute my right": pursue my legitimate claim (a legal phrase).

82   104–5. "I am…right": Lysander, adopting Demetrius' and Egeus' word (lines 92, 97), claims a right, though one based not on ancient law or paternity, but on Hermia's love. The suitors' rival claims agree with Plutarch's description of their historic namesakes. Telling how the Macedonian Demetrius came to be so great, Plutarch says:

    Demetrius' power and greatness fell unto him by inheritance from his father, Antigonus, who became the great-

Demetrius, I'll avouch it to his head,[83]
Made love to[84] Nedar's daughter, Helena,[85]
And won her soul; and she, sweet lady, dotes,
Devoutly dotes, dotes in idolatry,[86]
Upon this spotted[87] and inconstant man.   110
Theseus: I must confess that I have heard so much,
And with Demetrius thought to have spoke thereof;[88]
But, being overfull of self-affairs,[89]
My mind did lose it.[90] But, Demetrius, come,

---

est and mightiest prince of all the successors of Alexander [the Great] and had won the most part of Asia before Demetrius came of full age (Plutarch, *Comparison of Demetrius with Mark Antony*, 1.1.; North, 6:69; see also Plutarch, *Demetrius*; 3, 5–6, 18).

Lysander, by contrast, who "grew to be [a] great m[a]n, rising of [himself] through [his] own virtue," tried to overthrow the exclusive claim of two families to the Spartan throne,

Which [attempt]…, according to nature, doubtless seemed very just; that he which was the best among good men should be chosen king of that city, which was the chief over all Greece, not for her nobility [of birth], but for her virtue only (Plutarch, *Comparison of Sulla with Lysander*, 1, 2.1; North, 3:320, 321; see also Plutarch *Lysander*, 24–26).

The one owes his greatness to his inheritance; the other, to his nature or virtue. On Demetrius, see, further, 2.2.105–6n.

83   106. "avouch…head": declare it to his face, in his teeth.

84   107. "Made love to": wooed, courted; see, further, 4.1.170–71.

85   107. "Nedar's…Helena": On Helena's introduction by her patronymic, see 3.2.95n.

86   108–9. "dotes…idolatry": As Lysander underscores with lavish alliteration and repetition, to "dote," while also connoting becoming crazy or foolish, means to bestow love on someone extravagantly and uncritically. It is related to the noun "dotage"; see, further, line 225n.

87   110. "spotted": morally stained.

88   112. "spoke thereof": spoken about it.

89   113. "self-affairs": my own concerns (his upcoming wedding)

90   114. "My…it": it slipped my mind.

115 And come, Egeus; you shall go with me.
I have some private schooling[91] for you both.
For[92] you, fair Hermia, look you arm[93] yourself
To fit your fancies[94] to your father's will,
Or else the law of Athens yields you up
120 (Which by no means we may extenuate)[95]
To death or to a vow of single life.
Come, my Hippolyta. What cheer, my love?[96]
Demetrius and Egeus, go[97] along.
I must employ you in some business
125 Against[98] our nuptial and confer with you
Of something nearly that[99] concerns yourselves.[100]

---

91 116. "schooling": instruction, admonition. We cannot be sure what the lesson is or even whether Theseus ever delivers one. We never hear about it again, and neither Demetrius nor Egeus seems changed the next time they appear. Demetrius will still be pursuing Hermia and despising Helena (2.1.188ff.), and Egeus will still be demanding his patriarchal privilege under Athenian law (4.1.153–58); see, further, lines 123–26n.

92 117. "For": as for.

93 117. "arm": prepare.

94 118. "fancies": preference, taste.

95 120. "Which...extenuate": Although he uses the royal pronoun ("we") for the first time, Theseus suggests that his power is limited—that he must fully preserve and in no way mitigate the ancient privilege of Athenian fathers. He seems determined to live up to his promise to the nobles to see to "the preservation of the laws"; see, further, line 20n.

96 122. "What...love": Hippolyta, who has not said a word since replying to Theseus' opening speech (lines 6–11), has listened to Hermia's travail in silence. Theseus asks why she seems downcast, and she does not answer. Her look and silence likely show the disquiet of a matriarchal Amazon queen viewing the Athenian patriarchy's treatment of young women.

97 123. "go": come.

98 125. "Against": in preparation for.

99 126. "nearly that": that closely (see Abbott, §421).

100 123–26. "Demetrius...yourselves": The service ("business") of

Egeus: With duty and desire[101] we follow you.

Exit all but Hermia and Lysander.[102]

Lysander: How now, my love? Why is your cheek so pale?
How chance[103] the roses there do fade so fast?[104]
Hermia: Belike[105] for want of rain, which I could well   130
Beteem them[106] from the tempest of my eyes.[107]
Lysander: Ay me! For aught that I could ever read,
Could ever hear by tale or history,
The course of true love never did run smooth.[108]

Egeus, who will be with Theseus and Hippolyta when they go hunting on their wedding day (4.1.102ff.), presumably involves his helping to arrange the hunt, though this is never said. Demetrius' service, if any, is entirely unclear. Demetrius will soon flee Athens, and Theseus will never comment on his absence.

101   127. "duty and desire": ardent devotion (a hendiadys). Egeus' obeisant response is unwittingly ironic. The tension between duty and desire is just what marks his conflict with Hermia. She can do her putative duty only by renouncing her desire.

102   S.D. 128. "*Exit...Lysander*": Theseus's order to Egeus and Demetrius to go with him leaves Hermia and Lysander alone to plan their escape. If the effect is inadvertent (as seems most likely), the order is the first in a long series of happenstance and errors that will determine the action and the outcome of the play; see, further, 2.1.263–64n.

103   129. "chance": does it happen that, come about by chance that.

104   128–29. "How...fast?": Lysander's concern is not surprising, but his question surely is. He seems oblivious to the obvious. As his verb "chance" underscores (see line 129n), Lysander sees no connection between Hermia's miserable choice and her ashen face. Moreover, his lyrical tone is at odds with the grimness of her situation.

105   130. "Belike": probably, most likely.

106   130. "Beteem them": 1) grant them, allow them, 2) pour them down.

107   130–31. "Belike...eyes": Hermia latches onto Lysander's metaphor of fading roses and answers entirely figuratively. What is most likely ("Belike") is expressed as a likeness—a likely image of the truth.

108   132–34. "Ay...smooth": Lysander, seconding Hermia's suggestion, interprets their experience in the light of what he has learned from

135   But either it was different in blood—[109]
Hermia: O cross! Too high to be enthralled to low.
Lysander: Or else misgraffed[110] in respect of years—
Hermia: O spite! Too old to be engaged to young.
Lysander: Or else it stood upon[111] the choice of friends—[112]
140 *Hermia*: O hell! to choose love by another's eyes,[113]
Lysander: Or, if there were a sympathy[114] in choice,
      War, death, or sickness did lay siege to it,
      Making it momentany[115] as a sound,
      Swift as a shadow, short as any dream,
145   Brief as the lightning in the collied[116] night,
      That, in a spleen,[117] unfolds both heaven and earth,
      And, ere[118] a man hath power to say 'Behold!'

---

literature. Books and tales illuminate his love and his life. Lysander seems to regard both his knowledge and its source as absolute or comprehensive. "For aught...could ever read, / Could ever hear... / ...never did...." The general rule has no exceptions.

109 135. "blood": birth, rank.

110 137. "misgraffed": badly matched.

111 139. "stood upon": depended on.

112 139. "friends": The Folio reads "merit," which, among other difficulties, would not be paired with Hermia's response (line 140).

113 135–40. "But...eyes": Having stated his immutable conclusion (see lines 132–34n), Lysander goes on to survey specific types of examples of love's invariably unhappy course. Like his conclusion, his list, which he continues in his next speech, seems meant to be exhaustive: "But either it was.../ Or else.../ Or...." Hermia responds by echoing Lysander's lament in alternate lines, prefacing each repeated example with an emphatic interjection: "O cross!...O spite!...O hell!" The last example, of course, includes her own situation.

114 141. "sympathy": agreement, accord.

115 143. "momentany": momentary (an early form).

116 145. "collied": blackened (to "colly" is to blacken with coal-dust or soot).

117 146. "spleen": flash of anger or passion (metonymic: the spleen is the organ thought be the source of such outbursts).

118 147. "ere": before.

The jaws of darkness do devour it up.
So quick bright things come to confusion.[119],[120]
Hermia: If then true lovers have been ever crossed,[121]   150
It stands as an edict in destiny.
Then let us teach our trial patience[122]
Because it is a customary cross,
As due to love as thoughts and dreams and sighs,
Wishes and tears, poor fancy's[123] followers.   155
Lysander: A good persuasion. Therefore, hear me, Hermia:[124]

---

119   149. "confusion": destruction.
120   141–49. "Or...confusion": Lysander, declaring in mock tragic style
that even if lovers chose each other their love is always cut short
by causes beyond their control, describes love's brevity poetically.
Mimicking what he has read, he personifies the lightning and the
night, making the one angry and the other voracious, casts a
human spectator as witness to the act, suggests that the violent
event is cosmic in scope, and employs aphorism, alliteration,
wordplay, the historical present, and a series of repetitious, hyperbolic comparisons of equivalence. Inspired by love, the speech, describing the weakness of the bright in the world of darkness, is by
far Lysander's most poetic passage.
121   150. "ever crossed": always thwarted.
122   152. "teach...patience": teach ourselves patience. Hermia speaks
much like a Stoic. Since fate or "an edict in destiny" (line 151) de-
termines the outcome—since being thwarted is inevitably part of
love—patient resignation is called for.
123   155. "fancy's": love's.
124   156. "A good...Hermia": Lysander says that Hermia has per-
suaded him that her moral lesson is a good principle to adopt. But
then, stating the principle's further consequence ("Therefore..."),
he begins to propose a plan of escape (lines 157–68). He and Hermia can escape love's inescapable rule by escaping Athens.
Lysander's paradoxical conclusion reflects his tendency to see his
own life as literature. To the characters in a work of literature, their
actions and choices have the uncertainty and contingency that actions and choices in real life contain. But from the perspective of
the literary work itself, the events that seem contingent to the characters must seem inevitable to the readers in the end. The plot had
to end as it did. Thus, Lysander, observing his own life as letters,

I have a widow aunt, a dowager[125]
Of great revenue,[126] and she hath no child—
From Athens is her house remote[127] seven leagues[128]—
160   And she respects[129] me as her only son.
There, gentle Hermia, may I marry thee,
And to that place the sharp Athenian law
Cannot pursue us.[130] If thou lovest me, then
Steal forth thy father's house tomorrow night,

---

sees it from the outside and finds his fate inevitable. But observing it from within, he thinks he can escape that fate and change the ending. Seeing the outcome as both necessary and contingent, he views his situation with the double perspective of a literary work.

125 157. "dowager": See lines 4–6n.

126 158. "revenue": wealth.

127 159. "remote": located at a distance of.

128 159. "league": A league is roughly three miles.

129 160. "respects": regards.

130 157–63. "I…us": Because the aunt's house lies beyond Athens, Athens' patriarchal law does not apply there. Lysander, while reversing Theseus' opening complaint about step-mothers (see lines 4–6n), does not name "that place" (line 162). He says, however, that not only he and Hermia can marry there for love, but a childless widow can choose someone "as her…son" (love in marriage and parentage replaces birth, defeating both the authority of fathers and its basis, the power of natural generation).

Lysander's unnamed aunt's unnamed place seems to amount to an imaginary city—a city in thought or speech, in which the course of true love does indeed run smooth. Not unlike a philosophical utopia, it seems to be a place where the sole ruling compulsion is the inner power of reason and the love of the beautiful. Even the material conditions of a good life seem to be fully and easily provided there. Lysander and Hermia, however, never reach it. They lose their way while wandering in the woods, when Lysander forgets it (see 2.2.35n). Surpassing Athens, from which it is said to be refuge, the imaginary city or "place" seems to be, literally, a utopia: a "good place" (*eu topia*) which is at the same time a "no place" (*ou topia*) and is therefore unreachable (Thomas More, "Six Lines on the Island of Utopia," 123). Precisely because it abstracts from natural generation, it is a model impossible for any real city to achieve.

And in the wood a league without[131] the town   165
(Where I did meet thee once with Helena
To do observance to a morn of May),[132]
There will I stay for thee.
Hermia: My good Lysander,
I swear to thee by Cupid's strongest bow,
By his best arrow with the golden head,[133]   170
By the simplicity[134] of Venus' doves,[135],[136]
By that which knitteth souls and prospers loves,[137]
And by that fire which burned the Carthage queen
When the false Trojan under sail was seen,[138]

---

131 165. "without": outside, beyond.
132 167. "do…May": Lysander refers to their having observed the custom of going out into the woods early on May Day to celebrate the return of spring. While practiced by people of all ranks and ages (see 4.1.103n), the festive custom is associated especially with young people falling in love. Although May Day is an Elizabethan anachronism, the Athenians had corresponding holidays celebrating spring's arrival. On their special fondness for festivals, see Xenophon, *Constitution of the Athenians*, 3.2.
133 170. "arrow…head": Cupid, who is identified with Eros, has two arrows, one of gold to cause love, the other of lead to repel it (see Ovid, *Metamorphoses*, 1.468–71); see, further, lines 169–71n.
134 171. "simplicity": guilelessness (opposite of duplicity).
135 171. "Venus' doves": doves sacred to Venus, the goddess of love.
136 169–71. "by Cupid's…doves": When shooting his golden arrow, Cupid is sometimes driven by jealousy or spite, "fierce and cruel wrath" (Ovid, *Metamorphoses*, 1.452; Golding, 1.546), as when he caused Apollo to pursue Daphne (see 2.2.230–32n). Love and war may not be far apart (see, further, lines 16–17n, 2.2.338n). Cupid may not be as innocent or harmless as Venus' doves (see, further, 2.1.155–64n, 3.2.401–30n).
137 171–72. "doves…loves": Hermia, underscoring the intimacy that she vows, moves from blank verse to rhyming couplets. The rest of the scene, except line 179, is in couplets, as is their scene in the woods before Puck interferes (2.2.34–64).
138 173–74. "by…seen": Dido, the queen of Carthage, threw herself on a funeral pyre upon seeing the Trojan Aeneas sail away (see Virgil, *Aeneid*, 4.584–705).

175   By all the vows that ever men have broke
       (In number more than ever women spoke),
       In that same place thou hast appointed me,[139]
       Tomorrow truly will I meet with thee.[140]
Lysander: Keep promise, love. Look, here comes Helena.

Enter Helena.

180 *Hermia*: God speed, fair Helena. Whither away?[141]
     Helena: Call you me "fair"? That "fair" again unsay.[142]
       Demetrius loves your fair. O happy fair!
       Your eyes are lodestars[143] and your tongue's sweet air[144]
       More tunable[145] than lark to shepherd's ear
185   When wheat is green, when hawthorn buds appear.[146]

---

139   177. "appointed me": pointed out to me.
140   169–78. "by… thee": Hermia's oath, swearing to meet Lysander to-
      morrow at the designated place, playfully points to the weakness
      of such oaths. Her oath has two parts. In the first (lines 169–72),
      Hermia swears by the divinities of love; in the second (lines 173–
      76), by the betrayal of love and its tragic effect. As examples of the
      latter, she might have included Theseus' treatment of Perigouna,
      Aegles, Ariadne, and Antiopa (see 2.2.78–80nn).
141   180. "Whither away?": where are you going?
142   180–81. "God…unsay": Hermia greets Helena with a routine form
      of address ("fair Helena"). Helena, however, takes it in the strong
      sense of "beautiful" and painfully rejects the term as a description
      of herself. Helena, whose namesake—Helen of Troy—"far sur-
      passed all mankind in beauty" (Sappho, Frag. 16, lines 6–7), is in
      fact both literally and figuratively fair. Blond with light complex-
      ion in addition to being tall (see 3.2.291–98, 343), she is thought
      throughout Athens to be "fair" (1.1.227). All that matters to her,
      however, is what Demetrius finds fair. On the two Helens, see, fur-
      ther, 3.2.95n. On Helena's opening line, see line 243–45n.
143   183. "lodestars": "Guiding stars," that on which one's attention or
      hopes are fixed (a nautical term).
144   183. "air": music.
145   184. "tunable": melodious.
146   184–85. "than…appear": than the lark telling the shepherd that
      spring has arrived.

Sickness is catching. O, were favor[147] so!
Yours would I catch, fair Hermia, ere I go.
My ear should catch your voice, my eye your eye,[148]
My tongue should catch your tongue's sweet melody.
Were the world mine, Demetrius being bated,[149]   190
The rest I'd give to be to you translated.[150]
O, teach me how you look and with what art
You sway the motion of Demetrius' heart![151]
Hermia: I frown upon him, yet he loves me still.
Helena: O, that your frowns would teach my smiles such skill!   195
Hermia: I give him curses, yet he gives me love.
Helena: O, that my prayers could such affection move!
Hermia: The more I hate, the more he follows me.
Helena: The more I love, the more he hateth me.
Hermia: His folly, Helena, is no fault of mine.   200
Helena: None but your beauty. Would that fault were mine![152]

---

147   186. "favor": 1) attractive features, good looks, 2) the favor they bring.
148   188. "My…eye": The contrast is emphatic: "*Mine* is almost always found before 'eye,' 'ear,' etc. where no emphasis is intended. But where there is antithesis we have *my, thy*" (Abbott, §237).
149   190. "bated": excepted.
150   191. "translated": transformed.
151   192–93. "O, teach,…heart": Helena, like Egeus (see lines 28–35n), believes a cunning art can induce love. "My toil is pitched, and I have caught my pray" (Ovid, *The Art of Love*, 2.2; Heywood, 77). Attractiveness, she believes, can be taught or learned, and beauty alone, she also thinks, brings about love; see lines 194–201n.
152   194–201. "I frown…mine": Helena recognizes only perceived beauty as causing love. She fails to appreciate that the contrary ways that she and Hermia treat Demetrius—the one with disdain, the other with fervor—may produce his opposite responses to them; see, further, 2.1.240–42n. Love, for Demetrius, we shall see, proves to be a matter of challenge—of conquest of women and of rivalry with other men. For good reason, Puck will not remove the love juice from his eyes (see, further, 3.2.459–63n). The present exchange, in which one disputing character answers and partly repeats the other in alternate single lines of verse, exemplifies stichomythia, which originated in Greek tragedy.

Hermia: Take comfort: he no more shall see my face.
Lysander and myself will fly[153] this place.
Before the time I did Lysander see
205   Seemed Athens as a paradise to me.
O, then, what graces in my love do dwell
That he hath turned a heaven unto a hell![154]
Lysander: Helen, to you our minds we will unfold.
Tomorrow night when Phoebe[155] doth behold
210   Her silver visage[156] in the wat'ry glass,[157]
Decking with liquid pearl the bladed grass[158]
(A time that lovers' flights doth still[159] conceal),[160]
Through Athens' gates have we devised to steal.
Hermia: And in the wood where often you and I
215   Upon faint[161] primrose beds were wont to lie,
Emptying our bosoms of their counsel[162] sweet,
There my Lysander and myself shall meet

---

153 203. "fly": flee.

154 206–7. "O, then,…hell": Hermia, echoing Lysander (see lines 13–40), disabuses Helena of her assumption that mutual love makes for happiness. Regardless of the lovers' wishes or intentions, the attractiveness ("graces") that inspires love can bring misery ("a hell") when the law prevents the lovers from marrying.

155 209. "Phoebe": Another name for Diana, goddess of the moon; see, further, line 212n.

156 210. "visage": face.

157 210. "glass": mirror, reflection.

158 211. "Decking…grass": covering with dew the many-bladed grass. Dew was thought to fall from the moon: "[W]hen the moon is full, most dew falls" (Plutarch, *Table-Talk*, 3.10.3 (659b); see, further, 3.1.192n.

159 212. "still": always.

160 212. "(A…conceal)": Phoebe (Diana), the same goddess the perpetual virgin Hermia would have to worship (see line 73n), will provide a dark cover for her elopement. Phoebe will see her own reflection (lines 209–10), but no one will see the fleeing lovers. See, further, line 4n.

161 215. "faint": 1) pale colored, 2) slightly scented.

162 216. "counsel": confidences.

And thence from Athens turn away our eyes
To seek new friends and stranger companies.[163]
Farewell, sweet playfellow. Pray thou for us,   220
And good luck grant thee thy Demetrius![164]
Keep word, Lysander. We must starve our sight
From lovers' food[165] till morrow deep midnight.
Lysander: I will, my Hermia.

Exit Hermia.

Helena, adieu.
As you on him, Demetrius dote on you![166]   225

Exit Lysander.

Helena: How happy some o'er other some[167] can be![168]

---

163 218–19. "And…companies": Leaving Athens means starting a new
life in the company of strangers ("strange companies"). Hermia
speaks only of friends, not of family. As with Lysander's description of where his aunt lives, she speaks only of what one might
choose and ignores what birth imposes (see, further, lines 157–63n).

164 220–21. "Pray…Demetrius": Hermia asks Helena to "pray" for her
and Lysander, but only wishes Helena "good luck" in winning
back Demetrius. Their situations are converse. One woman has the
man she loves, but must start a new life in a new city. The other
keeps her life in Athens, but must gain the man she loves. Hermia
may think her own situation is more difficult than Helena's. Once
Hermia is gone, Demetrius is likely to return to Helena. But starting a life among strangers may require a prayer.

165 223. "lovers' food": the sight of each other.

166 225. "As…you": From his effusive and indignant description earlier (see lines 108–9n), one might think that Lysander finds fault
with causing someone to dote. As we now see, however, he objects
not to its excess, but to its one-sidedness in Helena's case. If the
doting is reciprocal, it is indeed to be wished for.

167 226. "o'er…some": in comparison with others.

168 226. "Happy…be": Helena, alone on stage, reflects on love and
judgment. Rejecting out of hand Hermia's talk of hell (see lines
206–7n), she begins by comparing Hermia's happiness to her own.
To Helena, Hermia is happy because she has Lysander's love. Mutual love, she thinks, assures happiness.

Through Athens I am thought as fair as she.
But what of that? Demetrius thinks not so.
He will not know what all but he do know.
230 And, as he errs, doting on Hermia's eyes,
So I, admiring of his qualities.[169]
Things base and vile,[170] holding no quantity,[171]
Love can transpose to form and dignity.[172]
Love looks not with the eyes but with the mind,[173]
235 And therefore is winged Cupid painted blind.
Nor hath Love's mind of any judgment taste.[174]
Wings, and no eyes, figure[175] unheedy haste.
And therefore is Love said to be a child
Because in choice he is so oft beguiled.[176]

---

169 229–31. "He…qualities": Helena takes no comfort from the fact that Demetrius is the only Athenian unaware of her beauty. So little do love and knowledge go together that she can recognize her own error in loving him and yet love him nonetheless.

170 232. "Things…base": even things base and vile (emphatic).

171 232. "holding no quantity": having no relation (to love's estimation).

172 233. "transpose…dignity": transform to beauty and worthiness.

173 234. "Love…mind": Love may lie in the eyes, as Hermia and Helena have already stressed (lines 56, 140, 202, 204, 222–23), but it looks with the imagination ("mind"), not with the eyes. Normally, when we perceive something, imagination connects our sensation and thought. It presents an interpreted sensation to the mind, which allows for thought (see, for example, Aristotle, *On the Soul*, 4127a16ff). Love alters the sequence. Instead of our senses informing our mind through the imagination, our imagination informs our mind with little or no benefit of our senses. Transforming its object by casting an imaginary form on what presents itself to the eyes, it is projective rather than receptive. It sees what it wishes to see or imagines.

174 236. "taste": a trace.

175 237. "figure": symbolize.

176 235–39. "And…beguiled": Helena, describing the traditional iconography of Cupid (Love) in painting and poetry, discusses art's apt image of love's unreason and folly. The illustration of Cupid's wings and blindness fitly represents love's heedless haste,

As waggish boys in game themselves forswear,   240
So the boy Love is perjured[177] everywhere.[178]
For, ere Demetrius looked on Hermia's eyne,[179]
He hailed down oaths that he was only mine;
And when this hail some heat from Hermia felt,
So he dissolved, and showers of oaths did melt.[180],[181]   245
I will go tell him of fair Hermia's flight.
Then to the wood will he tomorrow night
Pursue her. And, for this intelligence[182]
If I have thanks, it is a dear expense.[183]

---

while the depiction of Love as a child represents love's easy gulli-
bility (see, for example, Propertius, *Elegies*, 2.12; Ovid, *The Art of
Love*, 2.17–20). Like Lysander and Hermia (but unlike Demetrius),
Helena thinks of art and letters when thinking of her love-life.
Paintings and poetry explain her own situation to her.

177 241. "is perjured": perjures himself.
178 240–41. "As...everywhere": Not only is Love, a child, innocently
deceived (see lines 235–39n). Love himself, like prankish boys
making false oaths in jest, mischievously deceives. No vow of love
is to be trusted.
179 242. "eyne": eyes (archaic, used here for the rhyme).
180 244–45. "And...melt": Nothing else in the play indicates that Hermia deliberately encouraged Demetrius. It seems, rather, that Hermia's falling in love with Lysander was all the encouragement that
Demetrius needed. The heat he felt was rivalry or jealousy, not
love; see, further, lines 194–201n.
181 243–45. "He...melt": Helena seems to have expected that
Demetrius' vows not only were true when made, but would remain true forever. Notwithstanding her view that love defeats reason, she seems to have assumed that vows govern as well as
express love. It is perhaps a sign of her stress on words that Helena
is the most loquacious of the four young lovers (and of all the characters except Theseus and Bottom). She frequently uses verbs of
speech, most often emphasizing what has been said. Note the first
and last words of her first line ("Call...unsay" [line 181]).
182 248. "intelligence": information, news.
183 249. "dear expense": "Dear" means both bearing a high price and
cherished: 1) costly to Demetrius (because he hates Helena so much

250   But herein mean I to enrich my pain,
To have his sight thither and back again.[184]

Exit.

Act One, Scene Two

Enter Quince the carpenter, and Snug the joiner, and Bottom the weaver, and Flute the bellows-mender, and Snout the tinker, and Starveling the tailor.[185]

Quince: Is all our company here?
Bottom: You were best[186] to call them generally, man by man,[187]

---

it would pain him to thank her), 2) loved by Helena (because she loves him so much that any thanks from him would be cherished).

184 250–51. "But...again": Even if she gets no thanks, just the sight of Demetrius as he chases after Hermia will be her reward. In addition to illustrating love's folly, Helena gives no thought to betraying her friendship with Hermia for the sake of stealing a glimpse of her beloved (see, further, 3.2.309–13n).

185 S.D. 1. "*Enter...tailor*": Notwithstanding Athens' fame as the first democracy, the artisans are the only commoners in the play, and they have nothing directly to do with politics (but see 4.2.19–24n). Instead, they are doubly connected to art—artisans who attempt to perform a stage play. Although all are identified by their crafts, none ever explicitly says a word about his trade. All hope to make their fortunes by acting. In Theseus' Athens, even artisans think of themselves as artists.

     The names of all the artisans are metonymic, deriving from their crafts. "Quince" is a wooden wedge used by carpenters. "Snug" describes the close-fit a joiner aims to produce. "Bottom" refers to the wooden wheel or spool on which a weaver's wool is wound. "Flute" refers to the church organs which a bellows-mender repairs. "Snout," meaning a muzzle or a spout, suggests the kettles that a tinker mends. And "Starveling" refers to the proverbial leanness of tailors ("Nine tailors make a man," M.P. Tilley, *A Dictionary of Proverbs*, T23).

186 2. "You were best": it would be best for you (see Abbott, §230). Quince is at once producer, director, actor and author. Bottom,

42

according to the scrip.

Quince: Here is the scroll of every man's name which[188] is
    thought fit, through all Athens, to play in our interlude[189]   5
    before the Duke and the Duchess on his wedding
    day at night.[190]

Bottom: First, good Peter Quince, say what the play treats
    on,[191] then read the names of the actors, and so grow
    to a point.[192]   10

Quince: Marry, our play is "The most lamentable comedy,
    and most cruel death of Pyramus and Thisbe."[193]

Bottom: A very good piece of work, I assure you, and a

---

    however, tries to take charge right away, making corrections and
    giving directions.

187 2. "generally,...man": Although "generally" means without regard
    to individuals, Bottom means separately or individually. The arti-
    sans will often confuse whole and part, the collective and its indi-
    vidual members.

188 4. "which": who (refers to "man").

189 5. "interlude": short play, dramatic entertainment.

190 4–7. "Here...night": Quince claims that throughout all of Athens
    the artisans are thought fit to perform at Theseus' wedding. The
    artisans are greatly given to exaggerating their reputations and
    abilities as dramatic performers.

191 9. "on": of.

192 10. "grow...point": draw to a conclusion. It is not clear what con-
    clusion or sort of conclusion Quince might come to. No one, in-
    cluding Bottom, refers again to the suggestion. It may be little more
    than an inadvertent obscenity, which the artisans are also prone
    to.

193 11–12. "'The most...Thisbe'": "Pyramus and Thisbe," closely mir-
    roring Hermia and Lysander's furtive flight, is based on a tradi-
    tional tragic tale depicting the tension between the authority of
    fatherhood and the passion of love—the love of one's own and
    the love of the beautiful (see Ovid, *Metamorphoses*, 4.55–166;
    Chaucer, "The Legend of Thisbe"). Only their outcomes differ.
    The one, a tragedy, ends miserably in death; the other, a comedy,
    ends happily in marriage; see, further, Introduction, 7, Coda,
    198–199.

merry. Now, good Peter Quince, call forth your
15   actors by the scroll. Masters, spread yourselves.[194]
Quince: Answer as I call you. Nick Bottom, the weaver.
Bottom: Ready. Name what part I am for, and proceed.
Quince: You, Nick Bottom, are set down for Pyramus.
Bottom: What is Pyramus? A lover or a tyrant?[195]
20 *Quince*: A lover that kills himself, most gallant, for love.
Bottom: That will ask[196] some tears in the true performing of it.
        If I do it, let the audience look to their eyes.[197] I will
        move storms; I will condole[198] in some measure. To the
        rest[199]—yet my chief humor[200] is for a tyrant. I could
25   play Ercles[201] rarely, or a part to tear a cat in,[202] to make
        all split:[203]

---

194   15. "Masters,…yourselves": Addressing the actors as "masters," Bottom directs them to stand out as their names are called. "Master[s]" is Bottom's most frequent form of address. A term of respect or politeness, he uses it, with unknowing democratic irony, to give orders.

195   19. "A lover…tyrant": Bottom, who is not at all surprised to have a title role, imagines that it must be the part of a lover or a tyrant. He seems to assume that they are the only two leading roles or the only two he would want to play. Note that Bottom passed judgment on the play without knowing what Pyramus is (see line 13).

196   21. "ask": require.

197   22. "look…eyes": be careful that they don't cry themselves blind.

198   23. "condole": express grief, lament.

199   23–24. "To…rest": call the rest.

200   24. "humor": inclination.

201   25. "Ercles": Hercules, the most famous of all Greek heroes, whom Theseus emulated: "[T]he fame and glory of Hercules' noble deeds had long before secretly set [Theseus'] heart on fire" (Plutarch, *Theseus*, 6.6; North, 1:34–35); see, further, 5.1.2–23n. Hercules is Bottom's example of a tyrant; see, further, lines 36–37n.

202   25. "tear…in": rant and swagger. A burlesque allusion to the first of his Twelve Labors, in which Hercules strangled the Nemean lion with his bare hands, although it was thought to be invulnerable, and wore the lion's pelt as a trophy of his great feat (Apollodorus, 2.5.1).

203   25–26. "make all split": a nautical phrase for a ship splitting apart in a wreck.

> *The raging rocks*
> *And shivering shocks*
> *Shall break the locks*
> *Of prison gates.*   30
> *And Phibbus' car*[204]
> *Shall shine from far*
> *And make and mar*
> *The foolish Fates*

This was lofty.[205] Now name the rest of the players.   35
This is Ercles' vein, a tyrant's vein. A lover is more
condoling.[206]

Quince: Francis Flute, the bellows-mender?

Flute: Here, Peter Quince.

Quince: Flute, you must take Thisbe on you.   40

Flute: What is Thisbe? A wandering knight?[207]

Quince: It is the lady that Pyramus must love.

Flute: Nay, faith, let not me play a woman. I have a beard
coming.[208]

---

204 31. *"Phibbus' car"*: A mispronunciation of Phoebus, the Greek
sun god, who drives across the sky each day in his splendid,
bright-shining chariot (*"car"*) (Ovid, *Metamorphoses*, 2.107–
110).

205 35. "This was lofty": A reference to his lines, his performance,
or both. To demonstrate that he could play a tyrant's part
rarely, Bottom bursts into eight lines of bombastic doggerel
rhyme and exaggerated alliteration, describing destruction of
cosmic proportions. It is noteworthy that he is able to recite a
dramatic passage that he has committed to memory; see, further, 4.2.7–8n.

206 36–37. "This...condoling": A lover's manner of speech is pathetic;
a tyrant's is thundering. Bottom prefers a tyrant's part (line 24) because it permits or demands more ranting.

207 41. "wandering knight": knight errant (wandering in search of ad-
venture; a stock dramatic character).

208 43–44. "I...coming": Perhaps young Flute's wish; see, further, lines
70–73n

45　*Quince*: That's all one.[209] You shall play it in a mask,[210] and you
　　　may speak as small[211] as you will.

　　　Bottom: An[212] I may hide my face, let me play Thisbe too.
　　　I'll speak in a monstrous little voice: "Thisne,
　　　Thisne!"—"Ah Pyramus, my lover dear! Thy Thisbe

50　　　dear and lady dear!"[213]

　　　Quince: No, no, you must play Pyramus—and, Flute, you
　　　Thisbe.

　　　Bottom: Well, proceed.

　　　Quince: Robin Starveling, the tailor?

55　*Starveling*: Here, Peter Quince.

　　　Quince: Robin Starveling, you must play Thisbe's mother.
　　　Tom Snout, the tinker?

　　　Snout: Here, Peter Quince.

　　　Quince: You, Pyramus' father. Myself, Thisbe's father.[214]

60　　　Snug the joiner, you the lion's part. And I hope here
　　　is a play fitted.[215]

　　　Snug: Have you the lion's part written? Pray you, if it
　　　be, give it me, for I am slow of study.[216]

209　45. "That's…one": that makes no difference.

210　45. "play…mask": In Athenian as well as in Elizabethan drama,
　　　female parts were played by boys or young actors, who covered
　　　their faces with masks (See Julius Pollux, *Onomasticon*, 3.138–42).

211　46. "small": high-pitched (like a woman's voice). Flute's name sug-
　　　gests that he is fit for the role.

212　47. "An": if.

213　48–50. "Thisne…dear": Bottom, not at all adverse to playing a
　　　woman, wants to play both lovers. To show his qualification for
　　　playing the two parts at once, he breaks into a short, improvised
　　　dialogue between lovers. "Thisne" is a pet name for Thisbe.

214　56–59. "mother…father": None of these three characters appears
　　　in the play when performed. Even though it is a wedding celebra-
　　　tion, no parent appears in either the play-within-the-play or its on-
　　　stage audience. Instead of playing Pyramus' father, Snout will play
　　　the Wall (see, further, 5.1.131n).

215　61. "fitted": fitted out, equipped with what it needs.

216　63. "study": memorizing my lines (theater jargon).

Quince: You may do it extempore, for it is nothing but
    roaring.[217]   65
Bottom: Let me play the lion too. I will roar that I will do
    any man's heart good to hear me. I will roar that[218] I
    will make the Duke say, "Let him roar again. Let
    him roar again!"[219]
Quince: An[220] you should do it too terribly,[221] you would fright   70
    the Duchess and the ladies that[222] they would shriek,
    and that were enough to hang us all.
All: That would hang us, every mother's son.[223],[224]
Bottom: I grant you, friends, if you should fright the ladies
    out of their wits,[225] they would have no more discretion[226]   75

---

217 64–65. "You…roaring": In fact, Snug will have to speak eight lines of
prologue as Lion (5.1.214–21), which is more than he speaks otherwise.
Of Snug's 50 words apart from his role as Lion, only nine are longer
than four letters and only seven have two syllables. Snug has, suitably,
the shortest last name and is the only artisan lacking a first name.

218 67. "that": so that.

219 66–69. "Let…again!'": Bottom wants the Lion's part, too. Unlike
the roles of parents (lines 56–59), which he did not claim, the Lion's
part calls for a boisterous voice. Bottom wants the part so he can
show his excellence at roaring and affect the audience.

220 70. "An": if.

221 70. "too terribly": too terrifyingly.

222 71. "that": so that (see Abbott, §283).

223 73. "every mother's son": every one of us (proverbial: R.W. Dent,
Shakespeare's Proverbial Language, M1202).

224 70–73. "An…son": Bottom would be so good at imitating a lion that
the women would think he was a lion. His good acting would destroy
the dramatic illusion. Quince implicitly distinguishes between men
and women. Men would not be frightened (or perhaps deluded), but
all the women, including the Amazon queen, would be. Ironically, the
artisans express manly contempt for the women's fear just when they
fear for themselves and identify themselves as their mothers' offspring. Their manliness resembles Flute's beard (see lines 43–44n).

225 74–75. "fright…wits": Proverbial: Dent, W583.

226 75. "discretion": An official's judgment in exercising a court's
power in applying a punishment (a legal term).

but to hang us. But I will aggravate[227] my voice
so that I will roar you as gently as any sucking
dove.[228] I will roar you an 'twere[229] any nightingale.

Quince: You can play no part but Pyramus, for Pyramus

80   is a sweet-faced man, a proper[230] man as one shall see
in a summer's day, a most lovely gentleman-like
man. Therefore you must needs play Pyramus.

Bottom: Well, I will undertake it. What beard were I best to
play it in?[231]

85 *Quince*: Why, what you will.

Bottom: I will discharge[232] it in either your straw-color beard,
your orange-tawny beard, your purple-in-grain
beard, or your French-crown-color beard, your
perfect yellow.[233]

90 *Quince*: Some of your French crowns have no hair at all,
and then you will play barefaced.[234] But, masters,

---

227 76. "aggravate": He means "moderate," "mitigate."

228 77. "sucking dove": Bottom confuses "sitting dove" and "suckling
[weaning] lamb," both proverbially harmless (Tilley, D572, 573;
L33, 34).

229 78. "an 'twere": as if it were.

230 80. "proper": handsome.

231 83–84 "Well...it": Flattered that he has the looks for the leading man
(lines 79–82), Bottom immediately begins to think of the appearance
of his face and, particularly, of his beard. Beards, a mark of manliness (see, further, lines 43–44n), seem suitable for gallant lovers.

232 86. "discharge": perform.

233 86–89. "your...yellow": Bottom, as a weaver, is familiar with various dyes. "Orange-tawny" is dark yellow, "purple-in-grain" is
dyed with a fast purple, and "French-crown-color" is the light yellow of the French coin, the *écu*. "Your" is an impersonal pronoun,
referring to something the listener is familiar with.

234 90–91. "Some...barefaced": Quince picks up on the last of Bottom's
beard-colors. "French crowns" alludes to heads of French kings
that have become bald from the so-called "French disease"
(syphilis)—a stock joke. "Play" is a pun, meaning 1) to act one on
the stage, and 2) to have sexual intercourse. "[B]arefaced" means
1) beardless, and 2) brazen, without cover or disguise.

here are your parts, and I am to[235] entreat you, request
you, and desire you to con[236] them by tomorrow
night, and meet me in the palace wood, a mile without[237]
the town, by moonlight. There will we rehearse,   95
for if we meet in the city, we shall be dogged with
company,[238] and our devices[239] known. In the meantime
I will draw a bill of properties[240] such as our play
wants. I pray you fail me not.

Bottom: We will meet, and there we may rehearse most   100
obscenely[241] and courageously. Take pains. Be perfect.
Adieu.

Quince: At the Duke's Oak we meet.

Bottom: Enough. Hold or cut bowstrings.[242]

Exeunt.

---

235 92. "am to": must.

236 93. "con": learn

237 94. "without": outside.

238 97. "company": people.

239 97. "devices": plans.

240 98. "bill of properties": list of props. This is the first hint of the roles
of Moonshine and Wall. The props will take on a life of their own
and become full characters; see, further, 3.1.55–67n.

241 101. "obscenely": A malapropism if Bottom means "seemly," but
not if he means the word's literal and dramaturgical sense of "off
stage" or "in private," as Quince just suggested (lines 94–97).

242 104. "Hold...bowstrings": An uncertain archery phrase, probably
meaning "Keep your word or be disgraced." Forced by Quince's
stating where they will meet (line 103), Bottom, who thought he
had the final word ("Adieu" [line 102]), concludes with a phrase
which is, characteristically, at once confident and confused.

Act Two, Scene One

Enter a Fairy at one door and Robin Goodfellow
[or Puck] at another.[1]

Puck: How now, spirit? Whither wander you?[2]
Fairy: Over hill, over dale,[3]
               Thorough[4] bush, thorough brier,
          Over park, over pale,[5]
               Thorough flood, thorough fire,   5
          I do wander everywhere,
          Swifter than the moon's sphere.[6],[7]

---

1   S.D. 1. "*Enter...another.*" The scene shifts to the woods. The time is "tomorrow night" (1.1.164), the time of Lysander and Hermia's planned escape and the artisans' rehearsal (1.1.164, 209, 247; 1.2.93–94). But instead of seeing either the lovers or the artisans, we see a new group of characters—the fairies, who have come to celebrate Theseus and Hippolyta's wedding. The "doors" refers to those at opposite sides of the stage, not to doors represented in the scene itself.

2   1. "Whither...you?": The fairies frequently wander and cause others to wander, both literally and figuratively; see, further, lines 10–13n. The name of the fairies' king, Oberon, means "wander" in Latin.

3   2. "dale": valley.

4   3. "Thorough": through (alternative Elizabethan spelling).

5   4. "pale": enclosure (especially of a park).

6   7. "moon's sphere": An allusion to Ptolemaic astronomy, which holds that the heavenly bodies, including the moon, are each carried around the earth in a crystalline sphere—the moon in a day; see Ptolemy, *Almagest*, 9.1.

7   2–7. "Over...sphere": The Fairy, speaking in a rapid rhythm mimicking the celerity he describes, emphasizes his wandering's doubleness. Nowhere else in the play is every other word in a series of lines repeated not just once but twice. And while repeating every other word in the first four lines, the Fairy alternates these proposi-

51

And I serve the Fairy Queen,
To dew[8] her orbs[9] upon the green.
10   The cowslips tall her pensioners be,
In their gold coats spots you see;
Those be rubies, fairy favors;[10]
In those freckles live their savors.[11],[12]
I must go seek some dewdrops here,

---

tions with a list of nouns, which he (or she) immediately generalizes in a single word ("everywhere"). The general repeats while containing the particulars. Yet, the Fairy conflates antitheses and synonyms. The first and last pairs in his list (lines 2, 5) contain antitheses, while the middle two (lines 3, 4) contain synonyms, but the repeated prepositions ("Over" and "thorough") could be either antitheses or synonyms. The distinction between opposition and repetition, difference and sameness, loses force. Only the Fairy's swiftness seems to be expressed singly. But, stated as a comparison ("Swifter than... "), it is actually a suppressed double; see, further, lines 2–15n.

8   9. "To dew": by dewing (see Abbott, §356).
9   9. "orbs": fairy rings (darker or taller grass supposed to be a magic circle caused by fairies dancing hand-in-hand in a circle).
10   12. "favors": rich gifts.
11   13. "savors": fragrance.
12   10–13. "The cowslips...savor": The Fairy describes the queen's royal guard ("pensioners") as cowslips. Cowslips are deep yellow flowers, with red spots, produced in clusters in early spring. According to the Fairy, the cowslips are ("be") the queen's guard, not merely a resemblance of one. So, too, with the "rubies": the flowers' red spots are ("be") rubies, not merely an imitation of them. Yet, even as he implicitly denies the rubies' imitative character, the Fairy emphasizes it: "[The] spots you see; / Those be rubies." What Puck sees is something else. On the Fairy's lips, the doubleness of imitation strays into the singleness of identity, and the singleness of identity into the doubleness of imitation. The imitation and the imitated, the image and the imaged, are both different and the same. This ambiguity—of image and reality—will characterize nearly everything concerning the fairies. Titania and Oberon, the fairies' queen and king, will typically speak in doubles, both exact and inexact. For Titania, see, for example, lines 123–37n, and 81–114n; for Oberon, lines 148–74n.

And hang a pearl in every cowslip's ear.[13],[14]   15
Farewell, thou lob[15] of spirits. I'll be gone.
Our queen and all her elves[16] come here anon.
Puck: The King doth keep his revels here tonight.
Take heed the Queen come not within his sight,
For Oberon is passing fell and wrath[17]   20
Because that[18] she, as her attendant, hath
A lovely boy stolen from an Indian king[19]—
She never had so sweet a changeling.[20]
And jealous Oberon would have the child
Knight of his train, to trace[21] the forests wild.   25
But she perforce[22] withholds the loved boy,
Crowns him with flowers and makes him all her joy.
And now they never meet in grove or green,
By fountain clear or spangled starlight sheen,[23]

---

13   14–15. "I must…ear": The Fairy says he will adorn the pensioners
     with pearls in their ears, which come from dewdrops. According
     to Pliny, while pearls are "[t]he richest merchandise of all…
     throughout the whole world," they are generated by a "moist
     dew" and grow, "better or worse, great or small, according to the
     quality and quantity of dew which they received" (Pliny, *Natural
     History*, 9.106–7; Holland, 9.35 [160]).
14   2–15. "Over…ear": The Fairy's answer to Puck is the first of the
     fairies' virtually continual narratives throughout the scene. Story-
     telling is a favorite form of their speech.
15   16. "lob": big and clumsy (in comparison to the other fairies) (con-
     temptuous).
16   17. "elves": fairies.
17   20. "passing…wrath": exceedingly fierce and angry.
18   21. "Because that": because.
19   22. "Indian king": Oberon and Titania are associated with India;
     see, further, lines 69, 124, and 158n.
20   23. "changeling": "Changeling" normally refers to the ugly child
     fairies leave behind, not to the beautiful one they take. Puck inverts
     the word's usual sense (see *OED*, *s.v.* changeling, 3).
21   25. "trace": track, range over.
22   26. "perforce": by force.
23   29. "starlight sheen": shining light of the stars.

30   But they do square,[24] that[25] all their elves for fear
      Creep into acorn cups and hide them there.
   Fairy: Either I mistake your shape and making[26] quite,
       Or else you are that shrewd[27] and knavish sprite
      Called Robin Goodfellow.[28] Are not you he
35   That frights the maidens of the villagery,[29]
      Skim milk,[30] and sometimes labor in the quern[31]
      And bootless make the breathless huswife churn,[32]
      And sometime make the drink to bear no barm,[33]
      Mislead night wanderers, laughing at their harm?[34]
40   Those that "Hobgoblin" call you and "sweet Puck,"
      You do their work, and they shall have good luck.[35]
      Are not you he?

---

24   30. "But...square": without quarreling.

25   30. "that": so that.

26   32. "shape and making": outward appearance ("form and build").

27   33. "shrewd": mischievous.

28   34. "Robin Goodfellow": Goodfellow is not a family or proper name. It is a propitiatory term given to a spirit in the belief that such a laudatory term will conciliate him and win his favor; see, further, lines 40–41n.

29   35. "villagery": villages (collective term).

30   36. "skim milk": steal the cream.

31   36. "quern": a hand mill for grinding corn. Presumably Puck mischievously labors to cause the grinding to fail.

32   37. "bootless...churn": make the exhausted housewife work uselessly to turn cream into butter.

33   38. "drink...barm": stop the fermentation of ale.

34   35–39. "frights...harm": The Fairy describes six of Puck's pranks. All are domestic or homely, whose common element is causing frustrating emptiness or futility: false fears, vain efforts, and misdirected travel.

35   40–41. "Those...luck": Hobgoblin is another name for Robin Goodfellow, with "Hob" an alternative to Rob or Robin and "goblin" meaning a malevolent spirit. "Robin goodfellow, and Hob goblin were as terrible...as hags and witches be now" (Reginal Scot, *The Discovery of Witchcraft*, 7.2 [74]). Since "puck" is another term for a malicious spirit, "sweet Puck" is another propitiatory term (see line 34n). Puck benefits those who flatter him.

Puck: Thou speakest aright.
I am that merry wanderer of the night.
I jest to Oberon and make him smile
When I a fat and bean-fed horse beguile,   45
Neighing in likeness of a filly foal.[36]
And sometime lurk I in a gossip's[37] bowl
In very[38] likeness of a roasted crab,[39]
And, when she drinks, against her lips I bob[40]
And on her withered dewlap[41] pour the ale.   50
The wisest aunt,[42] telling the saddest[43] tale,
Sometime for three-foot stool mistaketh me;
Then slip I from her bum, down topples she
And "Tailor!"[44] cries and falls into a cough,
And then the whole choir[45] hold their hips and laugh   55
And waxen[46] in their mirth and neeze[47] and swear
A merrier hour was never wasted[48] there.[49]
But room,[50] fairy. Here comes Oberon.

---

36   45–46. "a fat…foal": arouse the sexual desire of a well-fed horse
       by neighing like a female foal. "Beguile" means trick.
37   47. "gossip's": old woman's.
38   48. "very": exact.
39   48. "crab": crab-apple (ingredient in a drink called Lambswool,
       consisting of hot ale mixed with the pulp of roasted apples, sugar,
       and spices).
40   49 "bob": bob up and down.
41   50. "dewlap": loose skin around the neck (used of cattle).
42   51. "aunt": old woman.
43   51. "saddest": most serious.
44   54. "Tailor!": Exact meaning uncertain; perhaps a pun on "tail" or
       backside.
45   55. "choir": company (laughing in concert like a chorus).
46   56. "waxen": wax, increase.
47   56. "neeze": sneeze.
48   57. "wasted": spent.
49   45–57. "when…there": The three pranks Puck describes all turn on
       his ability to assume any likeness and cause the likeness to be mis-
       taken for something real.
50   58. "room": make room, stand back.

Fairy: And here my mistress. Would that he were gone!

Enter Oberon the King of Fairies at one door, with his train, and Titania the Queen at another, with hers.[51]

60   *Oberon*: Ill met by moonlight, proud Titania.[52]
    Titania: What, jealous Oberon? Fairy, skip hence.[53]
     I have forsworn his bed and company.
    Oberon: Tarry, rash wanton.[54] Am not I thy lord?
    Titania: Then I must be thy lady.[55] But I know
65   When[56] thou hast stolen away from fairyland
     And in the shape of Corin sat all day
     Playing on pipes of corn and versing love
     To amorous Phillida.[57] Why art thou here,

---

51   S.D. 60. *"Enter...hers"*: With the entrance of Oberon and Titania, the dialogue shifts from rhyming couplets to blank verse.

52   60. *"Titania"*: The name is Latin for "daughter of Titans," pre-Olympian gods, who are the firstborn of Heaven (Uranus) and of Earth (Gaia). Prefiguring the story of Theseus and Egeus, just as the Titan Chronos (Time) overthrew his father Uranus, Zeus, his son, overthrew Chronos (Hesiod, *Theogony*, 132–8, 207–10, 389–96, 617–735, 807–140).

53   61. *"Fairy...hence"*: fairies, leave ("fairy" is a collective noun, which editors often emend to "fairies").

54   63. *"wanton"*: headstrong rebel.

55   63–64. *"Am...lady"*: Where Oberon asserts his authority as her husband, Titania turns his claim back against him: If he has the right to govern his wife, she has the right to expect him to be faithful. Their rights are reciprocal.

56   65. *"When"*: of times when.

57   65–68. *"When...Phillida"*: Corin and Phillida are traditional names in pastoral poetry for a lovesick shepherd and his beloved. The names come from Virgil, *Eclogues*, 2, 7, and, before that, from the first pastoral poet, Theocritus, *Idylls*, 4, 5.6. According to Titania, Oberon changed into Corin's shape and spent all day playing music on corn pipes and reciting his own love poem to the loving Phillida. As she tells it, love literally takes the form of literature. Oberon courts one stock character from poetry by imitating another. He imitates a poetic imitation of a lover (Corin), who is him-

Come from the farthest step[58] of India,
But that, forsooth, the bouncing[59] Amazon,   70
Your buskined[60] mistress and your warrior love,
To Theseus must be[61] wedded, and you come
To give their bed joy and prosperity?[62]
Oberon: How canst thou thus for shame,[63] Titania,
Glance at my credit with Hippolyta,[64]   75
Knowing I know thy love to Theseus?
Didst not thou lead him[65] through the glimmering night
From Perigouna, whom he ravished,[66]
And make him with fair Aegles break his faith,

---

self a poetic imitator ("versing love"), in pursuit of a poetic imitation of a beloved (Phillida). Love becomes wholly translated into
art. Note the pun on and parallel placement of Corin's identity and
musical instrument: "shape of Corin" and "pipes of corn" (lines
66, 67); see, further, lines 82–117n; see also 3.2.388–93n.

58 67. "farthest step": utmost reach.
59 70. "bouncing": bragging, swaggering.
60 71. "buskined": wearing hunting boots; see, further, 1.1.18–19n.
61 72. "must be": is to be (definite futurity; see Abbott, §314).
62 73. "To...prosperity": See, further, 5.1.377–82n.
63 74. "for shame": without shaming yourself. On the twin senses of
    shame, see, further, 3.2.285n.
64 75. "Glance...Hippolyta": indirectly attack my good name with
    Hippolyta.
65 77. "lead him": From all we can tell, Theseus knows nothing of any
    of the fairies, let alone of Titania. Fairies, to him, are mere fairy
    tales (see 5.1.3n). Yet, as seems true of Puck and all the fairies, Ti-
    tania's effect may be unknown to those she affects. The power of
    imagination may conceal itself in the object of desire; see, further,
    1.1.234n.
66 78. "Perigouna,...ravished": "[Theseus] killed another [cruel rob-
    ber] called Sinnis...This Sinnis had a goodly fair daughter called
    Perigouna, which fled away when she saw her father slain....The-
    seus, finding her, called her, and swore by his faith he would use
    her gently and do her no hurt....Upon which promise she came
    out of the bush, and lay with him...Afterwards Theseus married
    her to one Deioneus" (Plutarch, *Theseus*, 8.2; North, 1:36).

80   With Ariadne[67] and Antiopa?[68],[69]
Titania: These are the forgeries of jealousy:
        And never, since the middle summer's spring,[70]
        Met we on hill, in dale, forest, or mead,
        By paved[71] fountain or by rushy brook,
85   Or in[72] the beached margent[73] of the sea,
        To dance our ringlets[74] to[75] the whistling wind,
        But with thy brawls[76] thou hast disturbed our sport.[77]

---

67 79–80. "Aegles...Ariadne": "[S]ome say that Ariadne hung herself for sorrow, when she saw that Theseus had cast her off....[Others] think that Theseus left her, because he was in love with another, as by these verses should appear: 'Aegles, the nymph, was loved of Theseus, / which was the daughter of Panopeus'" (Plutarch, *Theseus*, 20.1; North, 1:47).

68 80. "Antiopa": "[Some] hold opinion that [Theseus] went thither with Hercules against the Amazons, and that to honor his valiantness, Hercules gave him Antiopa the Amazon....But Bion...the Historiographer says...that Theseus enticed her to come into his ship,...and so soon she was aboard, he hoisted his sail, and so carried her away" (Plutarch, *Theseus*, 26.1–2; North, 1:55).

69 78–80. "From...Antiopa": All of these notorious encounters with women occurred in the context of Theseus' heroic feats: 1) Perigouna: his cleansing the countryside of monsters, evildoers, and bandits, on his way to Athens, in emulation of Hercules' courageous deeds, 2) Ariadne: his slaying the Minotaur in Crete, and 3) Antiopa: his defeat of the Amazons. Oberon and Titania present each other as loving the pre-civilized, heroic Theseus and Hippolyta.

70 82. "the middle...spring": the beginning of mid-summer ("spring" means beginning: "what mid-summer springs from"; it does not name the season).

71 84. "paved": with stone or pebbly bottom.

72 85. "in": on.

73 85. "margent": margin, shore.

74 86. "ringlets": circular dances (fairies typically dance hand-in-hand in circles; see, further, line 9n).

75 86. "to": to the sound of.

76 87. "brawls": A pun: 1) quarrels, 2) dances.

77 87. "sport": enjoyment.

Therefore the winds, piping to us in vain,
As in revenge have sucked up from the sea
Contagious[78] fogs, which, falling in the land,   90
Hath every pelting[79] river made so proud
That they have overborne their continents.[80]
The ox hath therefore stretched his yoke[81] in vain,
The plowman lost his sweat, and the green corn[82]
Hath rotted ere his[83] youth attained a beard.   95
The fold[84] stands empty in the drowned field,
And crows are fatted with the murrain flock.[85]
The nine-men's-morris is filled up with mud,
And the quaint mazes in the wanton green,[86]
For lack of tread, are undistinguishable.[87]   100

---

[78]   90. "Contagious": poisonously infectious.
[79]   91. "pelting": paltry.
[80]   92. "overborne...continents": overflowed their banks.
[81]   93. "stretched his yoke": pulled its plow.
[82]   94. "corn": grain.
[83]   95. "his": its (old form of the genitive of "it": see Abbott, §228).
[84]   96. "fold": sheep-pen.
[85]   97. "murrain flock": flock infected with murrain, a disease of sheep and cattle.
[86]   99. "wanton green": luxuriant grass.
[87]   98–100. "nine-men's-morris...undistinguishable": Contrasting pastimes, each involving imitation. "Nine-men's-morris" imitates the dancers in a "morris." Its figure consists of a square within a square within a square, whose corners are joined by straight lines. It can be played on a board or, as indicated here, on a lawn. "Men" refers to the number of pieces each of the two players starts with (see Cecil J. Sharp and Herbert C. Macilwaine, *The Morris Book*). "[T]he quaint mazes," on the other hand, refer to a dance which Theseus danced in Delos with the youths he had saved from the Minotaur. The dance, called the Crane, is an imitation of the "many turns and returns...of the Labyrinth," which was still danced in Plutarch's day (Plutarch, *Theseus*, 21.1; North, 1:49). Its figure is an intricate maze. While the "morris" figure has been covered over by too much mud, the Crane path has become indistinguishable for the lack of people to trample it down.

The human mortals want their winter cheer.[88]
No night is now with hymn or carol[89] blessed.
Therefore the moon, the governess of floods,[90]
Pale[91] in her anger, washes[92] all the air,
105   That[93] rheumatic[94] diseases do abound.
And thorough this distemperature[95] we see
The seasons alter: hoary-headed frosts
Fall in the fresh lap of the crimson rose,
And on old Hiems'[96] chin[97] and icy crown
110   An odorous chaplet[98] of sweet summer buds
Is, as in mockery, set. The spring, the summer,
The childing[99] autumn, angry winter, change
Their wonted liveries,[100] and the mazed[101] world

---

88   101. "want…cheer": lack their usual winter festivities. "Cheer" is a common emendation for "here," which would be a weaker way to formulate the same meaning.

89   102. "hymn or carol": A hymn is an ode or song of praise or honor of a deity; a carol is a ring-dance.

90   103. "of floods": of tides.

91   104. "Pale": shining dimly through the contagious fog.

92   104. "washes": moistens, wets.

93   105. "that": so that.

94   105. "rheumatic": watery or mucous secretions, from the eyes, nose, or mouth, as in colds and coughs.

95   106. "distemperature": A pun: 1) (Oberon's) bad temper, 2) (the air's) distempered conditions, and 3) (the seasons') disordered temperatures; see, further, lines 81–114n.

96   109. "Hiems": winter personified.

97   109. "chin": Commonly emended to "thin." However, in Golding's translation, Ovid describes Winter as "Forladen with the Icicles that dangled up and down / Upon his gray and horary beard and snowy frozen crown" (Ovid, *Metamorphoses*, 2,30; Golding, 2.38–39); see, further, lines 82–117n.

98   110. "chaplet": garland.

99   112. "childing": fruitful.

100 112–13. "change…liveries": exchange their accustomed apparel.

101 113. "mazed": bewildered (a strong word).

By their increase[102] now knows not which is which.[103]
And this same progeny of evils comes   115
From our debate,[104] from our dissension;
We are their parents and original.[105],[106]

---

102 114. "increase": 1) (seasonal) product , 2) aggrandizement.

103 81–114. "These...which": The bulk of Titania's narrative—the longest speech in the play—contains two major parts, each introduced by the word "Therefore." The first (lines 88–102) describes the effects of the wind's revenge; the second (lines 103–114), of the moon's anger. Both parts emphasize antitheses, the former between the empty and the full, the latter between the winter cheer that humans want and the rheumatic diseases that abound. In both, the contrast is between what is absent and what is present. Titania's account of the moon's anger, however, inverts her account of the wind's revenge. Whereas the winds sucked up contagious fogs from the sea, which then fell back to earth and produced floods, the moon, by contrast, caused floods, which then produced the unhealthy air. In the one account, the pestilent fogs caused the disastrous floods; in the other, the inundating floods produced the rheumatic air. Although both are introduced by the word "Therefore," they reverse cause and effect. While the causal link between the flooding rivers and the flooded fields is obvious, the causal connection between the rheumatic air and the seasons' disorder rests merely on a pun; see line 106n.

The speech brims with linguistic doubles. Titania echoes her own words (lines 88 and 93, 99 and 101, 104 and 112, 99 and 113, and 114), puns (lines 87, 106), contrasts and combines contraries (lines 83, 84, 89–90, 91, 108–9), personifies the wind, rivers, corn, moon, seasons (see also lines 115–17n), describes a seasonal change as resembling "mockery" (line 111) and Oberon's charges as "forgeries" (line 81), names two contrasting mimetic pastimes (lines 98–99), and will conclude with a pair of redundancies (lines 116–17).

104 116. "debate": constant quarreling.

105 115–17. "And...original": This is the only to reference Titania and Oberon's offspring. The fairy king and queen have a child only in a figurative sense. While its cause is said to be a living "child" (lines 24, 122), their only "progeny" is an offspring of the imagination. While they claim to have the power to bless the children

Oberon: Do you amend it, then. It lies in you.
Why should Titania cross her Oberon?
120 I do but beg a little changeling boy
To be my henchman.[107]
Titania: Set your heart at rest:
The Fairyland buys not the child of me.[108]
His mother was a votress[109] of my order,
And in the spiced Indian air by night
125 Full often hath she gossiped[110] by my side
And sat with me on Neptune's[111] yellow sands,
Marking th'embarked traders[112] on the flood,
When we have laughed to see the sails conceive
And grow big-bellied with the wanton[113] wind;

---

of others (lines 72–73, 4.1.89, 5.1.391–400), the fairy king and queen generate directly only in the imagination and generate children only indirectly through the imagination's effect on lovers. They are always at least one remove from procreation.

106 82–117. "And...original": Although Oberon never questions Titania's description, nowhere else in the play is there even a hint of such disorders. Apart from the fog that Puck produces (3.2.355–59), there are no fogs, floods, or famine, and no sign of winter in summer. Nor does anyone seem to be at all concerned with such things; see, further, Introduction, 7–8. But at the same time that Titania's narrative seems detached from the world around it, it borrows heavily, sometimes word for word, from Arthur Golding's translation of Ovid's *Metamorphoses*—his accounts of Deucalion Flood, Ceres' curse on Sicily, the Plague of Aegina, and the seasons (Golding, 1.285, 312–40; 2.33–39; 7.678–702; 15.233–35). Titania, taking the imaginary as the real, sees the natural world as the world described in Ovid's poetry (see, further, 1.1.132–34n; lines 65–68n, 109n).

107 121. "henchman": a young high-ranking male attendant of someone of royal or noble rank.

108 122. "The...me": I would not trade the boy for all of Fairyland.

109 123. "votress": one who has taken a vow.

110 125. "gossiped": passed the time in intimate, personal talk.

111 126. "Neptune": god of the sea.

112 127. "traders": trading ships.

113 129. "wanton": lustful (metaphorical).

Which she, with pretty and with swimming gait,[114]   130
Following[115] (her womb then rich with my young squire),
Would imitate and sail upon the land
To fetch me trifles and return again,
As from a voyage, rich with merchandise.[116]
But she, being mortal, of that boy did die,   135
And for her sake do I rear up her boy,
And for her sake I will not part with him.[117],[118]

---

114   130. "pretty...gait": pretty, smooth gliding motion (a hendiadys).
115   131. "Following": copying.
116   123–34. "His mother...merchandise": A votress of Diana wears the
      habit of a nun, lives in isolation, remains a virgin, and chants pas-
      sionless hymns to the passionless moon (see 1.1.73n). A votress of
      Titania, by contrast, besides being a mother, lives a life of intimacy,
      laughter, and sensual pleasure. As seems fitting for a votress of Ti-
      tania, imitation or mimicry marks the woman herself. As she and
      Titania would laugh at her pregnant belly as a metaphor for the
      ships' full sails, she would copy ("[f]ollow") the ships and "imitate"
      their movement at sea with her movement on land. She would
      mimic what mimicked her. She and the ships were reciprocal
      metaphors, each a figure for the other. See, further, lines 123–37n.
117   135–37. "But...him": Titania is the third stepmother in the play. Al-
      though Puck said that the boy had been stolen from an Indian king
      (line 22), Titania suggests that she adopted him at his mother's
      death. It is not clear whether the twin accounts are complementary
      parts of a single story or rival versions of events.
118   123–37. "His mother...him": Like her previous narrative (see lines
      81–114n), Titania's description of the woman is suffused with lin-
      guistic doubles. She pairs "child" and "mother" (lines 122, 123),
      the ship's "sails" on the water and the woman's "sail[ing]" on the
      land (lines128, 132), her own refusal to trade the child ("buys not"
      [line 122]) and "traders" embarked on the sea (line 127), the
      woman's "[f]ollowing" and "imitate[ing]" the ships (lines 131,
      132), the woman's womb "rich with [Titania's] young squire" and
      the ships "rich with merchandise" (lines 131, 134), and her
      "fetch[ing]...and return[ing] again" (line 133). In addition to re-
      peating, or half-repeating, words and phrases, Titania uses a hen-
      diadys (see line 130n), anaphora (lines 136–37), and alliteration
      (line 128–32) as well as metaphors and explicit comparison. She

Oberon: How long within this wood intend you stay?[119]
Titania: Perchance till after Theseus' wedding day.
140   If you will patiently dance in our round[120]
And see our moonlight revels, go with us.
If not, shun[121] me, and I will spare[122] your haunts.
Oberon: Give me that boy and I will go with thee.
Titania: Not for thy fairy kingdom. Fairies, away.
145   We shall chide[123] downright if I longer stay.

Exeunt Titania and her fairies.

Oberon: Well, go thy way. Thou shalt not from[124] this grove
Till I torment thee for this injury.[125]
My gentle Puck, come hither. Thou rememb'rest
Since[126] once I sat upon a promontory
150   And heard a mermaid on a dolphin's back
Uttering such dulcet[127] and harmonious breath[128]
That the rude[129] sea grew civil[130] at her song
And certain stars shot madly from their spheres[131]
To hear the sea-maid's music.[132]

---

also stresses the antithesis of land and sea (lines 126–34), sitting and moving (lines 126, 130–340), seeing and hearing (lines 125–29), and conception and death (lines 128–31, 135). In fact, the boy's birth is the mother's death. The two are one and the same.

119   138. "stay": to stay (see Abbott, §349).
120   140. "round": simple circular dance.
121   142. "shun": avoid.
122   142. "spare": stay away from.
123   145. "chide": quarrel.
124   146. "from": depart from.
125   147. "injury": insult, affront.
126   149. "Since": the time when (see Abbott, §132).
127   151. "dulcet": sweet.
128   151. "breath": voice, song.
129   152. "rude": rough.
130   152. "civil": calm, well behaved.
131   153. "spheres": orbits; see line 7n.
132   152–54. "That...music": The mermaid's song affected both the sea

Puck: I remember.

Oberon: That very time I saw (but thou couldst not),   155
    Flying between the cold moon[133] and the earth,
    Cupid all armed.[134] A certain[135] aim he took
    At a fair vestal,[136] throned by[137] the west,
    And loosed[138] his love-shaft[139] smartly[140] from his bow
    As it should[141] pierce a hundred thousand hearts.   160
    But I might[142] see young Cupid's fiery shaft
    Quenched in the chaste beams of the watery moon,
    And the imperial votress[143] passed on
    In maiden meditation, fancy-free.[144],[145]

---

    and the stars, but in opposite ways. It calmed the rough sea, but disordered the well-ordered stars.

133 156. "cold moon": cold because 1) gives no heat, 2) is identified with Diana, the goddess of chastity (see 1.1.73n).

134 157. "all armed": armed with his usual weapons ("all" is an intensifier); see 1.1.170n.

135 157. "certain": sure, exact.

136 158. "vestal": virgin (originally, one of the priestesses, vowed to virginity, who had charge of the sacred fire in the temple of Vesta at Rome; see Livy, *History*, 1.20.3).

137 158. "by": in the region of (Oberon is from the far reaches of India, in the east; see line 69).

138 159. "loosed": shot, let fly (a technical term of archery).

139 159. "love-shaft": golden arrow (see 1.1.170n).

140 159. "smartly": strongly.

141 160. "As it should": that it could.

142 161. "might": was able to, could (see Abbott, §312).

143 163. "imperial votress": votress of the goddess Diana; see, further, 1.1.73n

144 164. "fancy-free": free from thoughts of love.

145 155–64. "That very...fancy-free": Oberon's account of Cupid's action contains the play's most extensive description of a god's action. It is no surprise that the god is Cupid, but it may be surprising that Oberon describes the god's failure. Despite taking sure aim and shooting his golden arrow strongly, Cupid missed his target—a virgin under a vow of chastity to Diana, whose chaste moon beams were able to quench the power of love. Piety and virginity are not always helpless against Cupid, though they may need divine help (see, further, 4.1.72–73n).

165   Yet marked I where the bolt[146] of Cupid fell.
It fell upon a little western flower,
Before, milk-white, now purple[147] with love's wound,
And maidens call it "love-in-idleness."[148]
Fetch me that flower; the herb I showed thee once.
170   The juice of it on sleeping eyelids laid
Will make or[149] man or woman madly dote
Upon the next live creature that it sees.[150]
Fetch me this herb, and be thou here again
Ere the leviathan[151] can swim a league.[152]

---

146 165. "bolt": arrow.

147 167. "purple": the color of blood.

148 168. "'love-in-idleness'": "[This flower is called] Hart's easy, Pansy, Love in Idleness" (John Gerard, 1597, *Herbal*, 853). The aphrodisiac's name is a play on the proverbial "Idleness begets lust" (Tilley, I9). "Pansy" means "thought" in French.

149 171. "or": either.

150 172. "The juice...sees": Cupid's loss was Oberon's gain. The god's errant arrow passed its power on to the wounded flower, whose juice—a reification of the imagination in love—permitted Oberon to acquire the magical power of love; see, further, 1.1.234n.

151 174. "leviathan": imaginary sea-monster.

152 148–74. "Thou...league": Oberon's account of the love juice resembles Titania's story of the Indian boy and mother, to which it responds. Titania and Oberon both sat on the edge of the land, looking out at the sea (lines 126–27, 149–54). The one tells of a mother who was her "votress," the other of a virgin who was Diana's "votress" (lines 123, 163). Both speak of the motion of the sea (lines 127, 130–34, 150, 174) and of the sea itself (lines 127, 152). Both mention "swim[ming]," Titania metaphorically (line130), Oberon implicitly and literally (lines 150, 174). And both mention someone returning (lines 133, 173–74). Both also emphasize antitheses, stressing sitting and moving, seeing and hearing. But where Titania tells of birth and death, Oberon tells of love and virginity. Both, however, distinguish sharply between the past and the present (lines 135–36, 167). As Titania's tale ends with a woman's death and Titania's acquiring her child, Oberon's ends with a god's failure and Oberon's acquiring his power. And where Titania describes the woman and the ships imitating each other,

Puck: I'll put a girdle round about the earth 175
    In forty minutes.[153]

[Exit.]

Oberon: Having once[154] this juice,
    I'll watch Titania when she is asleep
    And drop the liquor of it in her eyes.
    The next thing then she, waking, looks upon
    (Be it on lion, bear, or wolf, or bull, 180
    On meddling monkey, or on busy ape)
    She shall pursue it with the soul of love.[155]

Oberon describes a flower duplicating the power of Cupid's arrow.

Moreover, like Titania's narrative, Oberon's account is replete with linguistic doubles, both exact and inexact. He uses "sea," "west[ern]," and "maiden[s]" once each as an adjective and once as a noun (lines 152, 154; 158, 166; 164, 168), "certain" meaning "some" one time and "sure" another (lines 153, 157), the homonyms "sea" / "see" (lines 152, 161), and numerous synonyms, including "breath" and "song" (lines 151, 152), "mermaid" and "sea-maid" (lines 150, 154), "love-shaft," "fiery-shaft" and "bolt" (lines 159, 161, 165), "maiden meditation" and "fancy-free" (line 164), and "flower" and "herb" (lines 166, 169).

Oberon, moreover, frames his tale by beginning with a mermaid on a dolphin's back and concluding with a leviathan swimming a league (lines 150, 174). Besides prompting Puck's memory (lines 148, 154) and then tells him partly what Puck already knows and partly what he has not heard before, Oberon speaks of the intended and unintended results, the contrasting changes in the sea and the stars, what he but not Puck could see, both Cupid and his arrow flying between the moon and earth, a fiery shaft quenched by the watery moon, the change in the flower, the contrast between the changed flower and the unchanged virgin, and his love juice duplicating Cupid's arrow.

153 175–76. "I'll...minutes": The Fairy boasted of his ability to circle the earth in a day (see line 7n). Puck will do it in 40 minutes.
154 176. "Having once": once I have.
155 182. "soul of love": 1) essence of love, 2) full intensity of love. The essence of love, Oberon seems to mean, is naturally unrestrained

And ere I take this charm from off her sight
(As I can take it with another herb),
185   I'll make her render up her page to me.[156]
But who comes here? I am invisible,
And I will overhear their conference.[157]

Enter Demetrius, Helena following him.

Demetrius: I love thee not, therefore pursue me not.
Where is Lysander and fair Hermia?
190   The one I'll slay; the other slayeth me.[158]
Thou told'st me they were stol'n unto this wood,
And here am I, and wood within this wood[159]

---

in intensity even when indiscriminate in its object. Its madness is not simply metaphorical.

156   183–85. "And…me": It is hard to see why Oberon's plan would work. Why would Titania give up something she wants (the boy) in order to rid herself of something she madly desires (her love)? Oberon will suggest that Titania will "[l]ove and languish" when her love is not returned (2.2.28). But, as the lovelorn young lovers will soon show, the very power of love would seem to work against her wanting to get rid of the passion. Oberon's plan will in fact work, but only for a completely unexpected and accidental reason.

157   186–87. "I…conference": By chance, the two plots—that of the royal fairies and that of the young lovers—converge. Oberon chooses to make himself "invisible" so he can overhear the young Athenians. As he could see what is invisible (lines 155ff.), he can also make himself invisible. Without the former he would not possess the love juice; without the latter he would not affect the lovers. On imagination's ability to render itself invisible, see line 77n.

158   190. "The…me": The sentence, organized around a strong break in the middle of the line ("medial caesura"), balances "the one" and "the other," while the rest of the sentence forms a chiasmus, varying the same word ("slay" / "slayeth") and reversing subject and object.

159   191–92. "wood…wood": A triple pun: 1) wooed, 2) madly frantic (from the Old English *wód* = senseless, mad, raging), 3) in a forest.

Because I cannot meet my Hermia.[160]
Hence,[161] get thee gone, and follow me no more.[162]
Helena: You draw me, you hard-hearted adamant![163]   195
But yet you draw not iron, for my heart
Is true as steel.[164] Leave you[165] your power to draw,
And I shall have no power to follow you.
Demetrius: Do I entice you? Do I speak you fair?[166]
Or rather do I not in plainest truth   200
Tell you I do not, nor I cannot[167] love you?[168]
Helena: And even for that do I love you the more.
I am your spaniel, and, Demetrius,

---

160   193. "my Hermia": Demetrius speaks as though his love for Hermia, not hers for him, makes her his. Even as he bemoans not having what he desires, he speaks as though he already possesses it. At least in speech, love may tend to fuse longing and fulfillment.

161   194. "Hence": While a synonym for "therefore," the word is command, both spatial ("away from here") and temporal ("from now on"). It is at once a conclusion and a consequent command.

162   188–94. "I...more": Demetrius juxtaposes pairs or opposites in four sentences, as he characteristically does throughout the play; see, further, 1.1.92n. In addition to five balanced breaks (lines 188, 189, 190, 192, 194) and a pair of repeated last words in successive phrases (lines 188, 191–92), he plays on double, triple, and quadruple meanings (see, further, lines 190n, 191–92n, 194n).

163   195. "adamant": 1) magnet, 2) hardest metal: Demetrius both draws and resists her.

164   196–97. "iron...steel": Steel is much harder, but steel is true: "As true as steel" (Dent, S840). Contrasting their hearts, Helena assures Demetrius that her heart is not hard, like iron (and his), but tender and true as steel.

165   197. "Leave you": give up ("leave off").

166   199. "speak you fair": speak kindly to you.

167   201. "nor I cannot": A common double negative (see Abbott, §406).

168   199–201. "Do...you": Demetrius seems to assume that only words can attract ("entice") love and plain words of rejection must repel. Love cannot be aroused unless it is returned. Demetrius seems to have forgotten Hermia's treatment of him.

The more you beat me I will fawn on you.[169]
205 Use me but as your spaniel: spurn me, strike me,
Neglect me, lose me; only give me leave
(Unworthy as I am) to follow you.
What worser place can I beg in your love—
And yet a place of high respect with me[170]—
210 Than to be used as you use your dog?[171]
Demetrius: Tempt not too much the hatred of my spirit,
For I am sick when I do look on thee.[172]
Helena: And I am sick when I look not on you.[173]
Demetrius: You do impeach[174] your modesty too much
215 To leave[175] the city and commit yourself
Into the hands of one that loves you not,
To trust the opportunity of night
And the ill counsel of a desert[176] place
With the rich worth of your virginity.[177]

---

169 203–4. "I…you": Proverbial: "The spaniel, that fawns when he is beaten, will never forsake his master" (Tilley, S705). See, further, 1.1.194–201n.
170 209. "high…me": highly regarded by me.
171 202–10. "And…dog": Love will do anything—even thoroughly debase itself—to win its beloved.
172 212. "I…thee": This may not be simply a figure of speech. Unwanted love may induce physical as well as moral disgust; see, further, lines 213–14n.
173 213–14. "For…you": Helena, repeating Demetrius' words, turns them against him with a different meaning. He means nauseated; she means languishing. Note that throughout their exchange Helena uses the respectful pronoun "you," but Demetrius alternates from speech to speech between "you" and the scornful "thee." Only his last speech (lines 235–37) breaks the pattern.
174 214. "impeach": call into question, discredit.
175 215. "To leave": by leaving.
176 218. "desert": deserted, uninhabited.
177 214–19. "You…virginity": Spending the night in the woods with a man who does not love her would expose Helena to reproach by making her appear to think that her virginity is worth little. By "modesty," Demetrius means reputation; see, further, 2.2.56–59n.

Helena: Your virtue is my privilege.[178] For that[179]   220
    It is not night when I do see your face,
    Therefore I think I am not in the night.
    Nor doth this wood lack worlds of company,
    For you, in my respect,[180] are all the world.
    Then, how can it be said I am alone   225
    When all the world is here to look on me?[181]
Demetrius: I'll run from thee and hide me in the brakes[182]
    And leave thee to the mercy of wild beasts.[183]
Helena: The wildest hath not such a heart as you.[184]
    Run when you will. The story shall be changed: 230
    Apollo flies and Daphne holds[185] the chase;
    The dove pursues the griffin;[186] the mild hind[187]
    Makes speed to catch the tiger. Bootless[188] speed

---

178   220. "Your…privilege": your special quality is my immunity from such a reproach.

179   220. "For that": because.

180   224. "in my respect": in my eyes.

181   220–26. "For…me": Helena answers that Demetrius' special qualities ("virtue") give her immunity ("privilege") from his warning or reproach: seeing his face turns night into day, and being with him is being with the whole world. Helena, who may not mean quite what she says, qualifies both points: "I think…" (line 222), "in my respect" (line 224). Yet, recognizing the disparity between what is and what she thinks may not matter or may only strengthen her conviction (see, further, 1.1.229–31n).

182   227. "brakes": thickets.

183   228. "mercy…beasts": Notwithstanding what Oberon (lines 180–81) and Demetrius say, the woods around Athens seem remarkably free of dangerous animals or other threats to human life, though not to fairies; see 2.2.2–7n.

184   229. "The…you": Helena again turns Demetrius' words around; see, further, lines 213–14n.

185   231. "holds": pursues.

186   232. "griffin": A fabulous creature: "griffins are beasts like lions, but with the beak and wings of an eagle" (Pausanias, 1.24.6).

187   232. "hind": doe (female deer).

188   233. "Bootless": useless.

When cowardice pursues and valor flies![189]

235   *Demetrius*: I will not stay thy questions.[190] Let me go,
       Or if thou follow me, do not believe
       But[191] I shall do thee mischief in the wood.
Helena: Ay, in the temple, in the town, the field,
       You do me mischief.[192] Fie, Demetrius!
240   Your wrongs do set a scandal on my sex.
       We cannot fight for love as men may do.
       We should be wooed and were not made to woo.[193],[194]

                                                    [*Demetrius exits.*]

---

189   230–34. "Run...flies": Helena views her own situation in the light
       of a "story" (line 230)—the myth of Apollo and the nymph
       Daphne. She, however, exchanges the roles of Apollo and Daphne,
       and depicts love as reversing the natural effects of speed and
       courage. She omits mentioning that Daphne was transformed into
       a laurel before Apollo could embrace her (see Ovid, *Metamorphoses*,
       1. 452–567).

190   235. "stay thy questions": stay for you to talk. "Question" com-
       monly means "conversation." The plural, here, probably refers
       to Helena's repeated attempts to get Demetrius to talk to her. On
       the contrast between Demetrius and the other young lovers in
       tending to see their own loves through literature, see 1.1.235–
       39n.

191   237. "But": but that (see Abbott, §122).

192   237–39. "But...mischief": Helena once more turns Demetrius'
       words back on him while shifting their sense. He meant deliberate
       harm or evil, she means being forced to act in a scandalous way;
       see, further, 240–42n.

193   240–42. "Your...woo": Helena says that Demetrius has forced her
       to act like a man. She seems to assume that a woman may do noth-
       ing proper to attract or win a man. Not able or allowed to fight or
       to woo, women must be entirely passive or else become shameful
       mimics of men. Helena's helplessness is every woman's fate; see,
       further, 1.1.194–201n.

194   241–42. "do...woo": Except for lines 247–48, the rest of the scene
       is in couplets.

I'll follow thee[195] and make a heaven of hell
To die[196] upon the hand I love so well.[197]

Helena exits.

Oberon: Fare thee well, nymph.[198] Ere he do leave this grove,   245
Thou shalt fly[199] him, and he shall seek thy love.

Enter Puck.

Hast thou the flower there? Welcome, wanderer.
Puck: Ay, there it is.
Oberon: I pray thee give it me.
I know a bank where the wild thyme[200] blows,[201]
Where oxlips[202] and the nodding violet grows,   250
Quite overcanopied with luscious woodbine,[203]

---

195   243. "thee": This is the first time Helena addresses Demetrius as "thee." She does it in his absence.

196   244. "To die": in dying (see Abbott, §356).

197   244. "I'll...well": Helena appears to take Demetrius' warning of violence (line 237) at face value. She speaks of following him and dying by his hand. Although echoing Hermia's complaint of being in hell, she inverts what Hermia said (see 1.1.206–7n). Hermia spoke of turning "a heaven into hell"; Helena, of making "a heaven of hell." For Hermia, being unable to marry the man she loves has transformed Athens from a heaven into a hell. For Helena, being killed by the man she loves would transform her hell into a heaven. Death, she seems to say, is her only hope; see, further, 3.2.243–44n.

198   245. "nymph": Nymphs in classical mythology are beautiful female deities inhabiting all the regions of earth and water (Hesiod, *Theogony*, 130). While it came to be a courtly way of addressing a young woman, the term, in Greek, means "bride" (see Homer, *Iliad*, 18.492).

199   246. "fly": flee.

200   249. "thyme": herb with fragrant leaves.

201   249. "blows": blooms.

202   250. "oxlips": cross between cowslips and primroses.

203   251. "woodbine": common honeysuckle, a climbing shrub with pale yellow fragrant flowers.

With sweet muskroses,[204] and with eglantine.[205]
There sleeps Titania sometime of the night,[206]
Lulled in these flowers with dances and delight.
255 And there the snake throws[207] her enameled skin,
Weed[208] wide enough to wrap a fairy in.
And with the juice of this I'll streak her eyes
And make her full of hateful fantasies.[209]
Take thou some of it, and seek through this grove.
260 A sweet Athenian lady is in love
With a disdainful youth. Anoint his eyes,
But do it when the next thing he espies[210]
May be the lady. Thou shalt know the man
By the Athenian garments he hath on.[211]
265 Effect it with some care, that he may prove
More fond[212] on her than she upon her love.
And look thou meet me ere the first cock crow.[213]
Puck: Fear not, my lord. Your servant shall do so.

Exeunt.

---

204 252. "muskroses": climbing roses, with musk-scented flowers.
205 252. "eglantine": sweet-briar, a kind of rose. "The eglantine or wild-brier rose, more commonly called sweet-brier, ...is not loved for its fair delicate blooms only; but its fragrant leaves, which...entitle it to its frequent association with the woodbine or honeysuckle" (Frances S. Osgood, *The Poetry of Flowers and the Flowers of Poetry*, 178–79).
206 253. "sometime...night": sometimes during the night (see Abbott, §176).
207 255. "throws": throws off, casts.
208 256. "Weed": garment.
209 258. "hateful fantasies": repulsive mental images.
210 262. "espies": sees.
211 263–64. "Thou...on": Oberon, who takes great care in telling Puck how to apply the juice (lines 261–63, 265–66), should know that his description of Demetrius is insufficient. He heard Demetrius say that Lysander had "stol'n unto this wood" (2.1.191). Much of what happens to the young lovers will result from Oberon's careless error; see, further, S.D. 1.1.128n.
212 266. "fond": doting ("fond" implies "folly").
213 267. "And...crow": On Oberon's need to avoid the full light of day, see 3.2.388–93n.

Act Two, Scene Two

Enter Titania, Queen of Fairies, with her train.

Titania: Come, now a roundel and a fairy song,[214]
Then, for the third part of a minute,[215] hence—
Some to kill cankers[216] in the muskrose[217] buds,
Some war with reremice for their leathern wings[218]
To make my small elves coats, and some keep back   5
The clamorous owl that nightly hoots[219] and wonders
At our quaint[220] spirits.[221] Sing me now asleep.
Then to[222] your offices[223] and let me rest.

---

214 1. "roundel…song": A "roundel" is a circular dance, like other fairy
       dances (see 2.1.9n, 86n, 140n). Titania's train join hands and dance
       around her, while singing a song. The song is also called a "rondel"
       ("roundelay"), a short song with a refrain. In this instance, the song
       is a lullaby, consisting of two quatrains, each followed by a six-line
       refrain (lines 9–23).
215 2. "third…minute": The brevity of time fits the fairies' diminutive
       world. Their world is at once speeded up and (mostly) pared
       down.
216 3. "cankers": canker-worms (caterpillars).
217 3. "muskrose": see 2.1.252n.
218 4. "reremice…wings": "The *rere-mouse*, or bat, alone of all creatures
       that fly,…hath wings made of… thin skins " (Pliny, 10.168; Hol-
       land, 10.61 [301]).
219 6. "The clamorous…hoots": "[H]e is the very monster of the night,
       neither crying nor singing out clear, but uttering a certain heavy
       groan of doleful mourning" (Pliny, 10.34; Holland, 276).
220 7. "quaint": unusual in appearance.
221 2–7. "hence…spirits": The fairies are not without natural enemies.
       They must "kill" canker-worms to protect the roses they love, and
       make "war" on bats to provides the coats they need. And their un-
       usual appearance provokes the threat of dangerous owls; see, fur-
       ther, lines 9–23n.
222 8. "to": go to.
223 8. "offices": various duties.

Fairies sing.

1ˢᵀ Fairy:	*You spotted snakes with double[224] tongue,*
10	*Thorny hedgehogs,[225] be not seen.*
	Newts and blindworms,[226] do no wrong,
	Come not near our Fairy Queen.
Chorus:	*Philomel,[227] with melody*
	Sing in our sweet lullaby.
15	*Lulla, lulla, lullaby, lulla, lulla, lullaby.*
	Never harm, nor spell, nor charm
	Come our lovely lady nigh.[228]
	So good night, with lullaby.
1ˢᵀ Fairy:	*Weaving spiders,[229] come not here.*
20	*Hence, you long-legged spinners,[230] hence!*
	Beetles black, approach not near.
	Worm nor snail, do no offence.[231]
Chorus:	*Philomel, with melody (etc.)[232]*

---

224 9. *"double"*: forked.

225 10. *"Thorny hedgehogs"*: "[The hedge-hog is] beset and compassed all over with sharp thorny hairs" (Edward Topsell, *The History of Four-Footed Beasts*, 217).

226 11. *"Newts and blindworms"*: Both are poisonous. Newts, which are small lizards, have a "venomous nature." Blindworms, also called slow-worms, have a "poison" that is "very strong" (Topsell, 744, 764).

227 13. *"Philomel"*: Philomel—whose name in Greek means "love of lyric song"—was transformed into a nightingale to escape her sister's murderous husband who had torn out her tongue after raping her to keep her from revealing his crime (Ovid, *Metamorphoses*, 6.424–614).

228 17. *"nigh"*: near.

229 19. *"spiders"*: "All spiders are venomous, but yet some more, and some less" (Topsell, 769).

230 20. *"long-legged spinners"*: daddy-long-legs spiders.

231 22. *"offence"*: harm.

232 9–23. *"You...melody (etc.)"*: The fairies' song is meant to sing Titania to sleep and to protect her while sleeping. It is a charm to ward off evil as well as a lullaby. The two quatrains are consequently couched entirely in the negative.

                                   Titania sleeps.

2ⁿᵈ Fairy: Hence, away! Now all is well.
                 One aloof stand sentinel.[233]   25

                             Exeunt Fairies.

Enter Oberon [and squeezes the flower on Titania's eyelids].

Oberon: What thou seest when thou dost wake
                 Do it for thy true love take.[234]
                 Love and languish[235] for his sake.
                 Be it ounce,[236] or cat,[237] or bear,
                 Pard,[238] or boar with bristled hair,[239]   30
                 In thy eye that shall appear
                 When thou wak'st, it is thy dear.
                 Wake when some vile thing is near.

                               [Exit.]

        Enter Lysander and Hermia.

Lysander: Fair love, you faint with wand'ring in the wood.

---

233 25. "One…sentinel": let one sentinel stand not far away from Titania.

234 27. "take": receive, believe, accept willingly.

235 28. "Love and languish": Oberon is sure that Titania's passion will not be returned. Beasts by nature desire only members of their own kind.

236 29. "ounce": "The Ounce [lynx]…is a most cruel beast,…his face and ears like to a Lion's, his body, tail, feet, and nails like a Cat's, of a very terrible aspect, his teeth…strong and sharp" (Topsell, 440).

237 29. "cat": wildcat.

238 30. "Pard": "[T]he Panther, Pardal, Libbard, and Leopard are all but one beast, called by diverse names" (Topsell, 448).

239 30. "boar…hair": "[The Boar] is brutish, stubborn,…wrathful, and furious…. [N]either are there any beasts so clothed with hair as Lions and Boars, wherefore both of them are of a like fierce and angry nature" (Topsell, 540). All five animals that Oberon names are known for ferocity.

35   And, to speak troth,[240] I have forgot our way.[241]
       We'll rest us, Hermia, if you think it good,[242]
       And tarry[243] for the comfort of the day.
   Hermia: Be it so, Lysander. Find you out a bed,
       For I upon this bank will rest my head.
40   *Lysander*: One turf shall serve as pillow for us both;
       One heart,[244] one bed, two bosoms, and one troth.[245]
   Hermia: Nay, good Lysander. For my sake, my dear,
       Lie further off yet. Do not lie so near.
   Lysander: O, take the sense, sweet, of my innocence![246]
45   Love takes the meaning in love's conference.[247]
       I mean that my heart unto yours is knit,
       So that but one heart we can make of it;
       Two bosoms interchained[248] with[249] an oath—
       So then two bosoms and a single troth.
50   Then by your side no bed-room me deny,
       For lying so, Hermia, I do not lie.[250]

---

240 35. "troth": truth (old spelling). No one speaks of truth nearly as often as Lysander, who mentions "troth" thrice in this exchange (also lines 41, 49).

241 35. "I...way": Lysander may not be suffering simply a failure of memory. There may well be no "way" to "no place"; see, further, 1.1.157–63n. Neither of the lovers ever again mentions their original destination in fleeing Athens (see 4.1.150–52).

242 36. "if...good": Lysander does not command, but seeks Hermia's consent.

243 37. "tarry": wait.

244 41. "One heart": one in mutual love.

245 41. "two...troth": two in body, one in faithful vows.

246 44. "take...innocence": understand my innocent meaning.

247 45. "Love...conference": love understands a lover's words.

248 48. "interchained": The Quarto's reading. The Folio reads "interchanged."

249 48. "with": by.

250 46–51. "I...lie": Lysander, who repeats more strongly what Hermia did not want him to say (line 42), tries, by playing on the two senses of "lie," to turn the question to that of his truthfulness: since he does not lie, they should lie together.

Hermia: Lysander riddles very prettily.[251]
　　Now much beshrew[252] my manners and my pride
　　If Hermia meant to say Lysander lied.
　　But, gentle[253] friend, for love and courtesy,[254]　　　　55
　　Lie further off in human modesty.
　　Such separation, as may well be said,
　　Becomes a virtuous bachelor and a maid.
　　So far be[255] distant,[256] and good night, sweet friend.[257]
　　Thy love ne'er alter till thy sweet life end!　　　　60
Lysander: Amen, amen to that fair prayer, say I,
　　And then end life when I end loyalty![258]

251　52. "Lysander…prettily": Hermia, complimenting Lysander on his charmingly clever wordplay, tops him by turning his twin meanings of "lie" into a play on his name.

252　53. "much beshrew": A curse upon (meant lightly).

253　55. "gentle": noble, well-bred.

254　55. "courtesy": politeness, good manners.

255　59. "be": A wish (subjunctive used optatively; see Abbott, §365).

256　56–59. "Lie…distant": By "human modesty," Hermia means a sense of self-restraint springing from an appreciation of what is proper or seemly; see, further, 3.2.285n. Although "modesty" is often thought to be limited to women (see 2.1.214–19n), Hermia says that "human modesty" sets off, or graces, "a virtuous bachelor" as well as "a maid." "[H]uman modesty," in her view, is human in its application as well as in its fundamental source.

257　55–59. "But…friend": Throughout the play, but particularly here, Hermia lives up to her name. In addition to being a god of speech and of dreams, Hermes, after whom she is named, is the god of travelers, and hence is both the transgressor and the preserver of boundaries. He both crosses and respects borderlines. Where Dionysus, his rival, blurs and dissolves limits, Hermes maintains hierarchies and distinctions, even as he traverses them (see Anonymous, *Hymn to Hermes*). Hermia, like him, defies her father's authority and yet preserves her own modesty. Though she contravenes boundaries, she keeps her restraint intact.

258　60–62. "Thy…loyalty": Hermia offers a prayer for Lysander's unchanged love until his death, which he then seconds and offers a vow. Neither of them thinks that Hermia's love needs a prayer or a vow. Except for Titania (under the influence of the love juice), it

Here is my bed. Sleep give thee all his rest!
Hermia: With half that wish the wisher's eyes be pressed![259]

They sleep.

Enter Puck.

65   *Puck*:   Through the forest have I gone,
But Athenian found I none
On whose eyes I might approve[260]
This flower's force in stirring love.
Night and silence! Who is here?[261]
70   Weeds[262] of Athens he doth wear.
This is he[263] my master said
Despised the Athenian maid.
And here the maiden, sleeping sound
On the dank and dirty ground.
75   Pretty soul, she durst[264] not lie
Near this lack-love, this kill-courtesy.[265]
Churl,[266] upon thy eyes I throw
All the power this charm doth owe.[267]

---

      is men, not women, whose loves are inconstant in the play; see, further, 3.2.134n.

259   64. "pressed": pressed with sleep. Lysander's eyes will of course be pressed, ironically, with Oberon's love juice as well as with sleep.

260   67. "approve": try, test.

261   69. "Night…here": Puck juxtaposes the absence of light and sound in his fruitless search with the abrupt, apparent presence of what he has been seeking.

262   70. "Weeds": garments.

263   71. "he": he who.

264   75. "durst": dared.

265   76. "kill-courtesy": Puck mistakes not only Lysander for Demetrius, but practicing modesty for suffering discourtesy. Courtesy means nothing to him.

266   77. "Churl": discourteous boor.

267   78. "owe": own, possess.

When thou wak'st, let love forbid
Sleep his seat on thy eyelid.[268]   80
So, awake when I am gone,
For I must now to Oberon.

Exit.

Enter Demetrius and Helena, running.

Helena: Stay, though thou[269] kill me, sweet Demetrius.
Demetrius: I charge[270] thee, hence, and do not haunt[271] me thus.
Helena: O, wilt thou darkling[272] leave me? Do not so.   85
Demetrius: Stay, on thy peril. I alone will go.

Exit.

Helena: O, I am out of breath in this fond[273] chase.
The more my prayer, the lesser is my grace.[274]
Happy is Hermia, wheresoe'er she lies,
For she hath blessed and attractive eyes.[275]   90
How came her eyes so bright? Not with salt tears.
If so, my eyes are oftener washed than hers.
No, no, I am as ugly as a bear,

---

268   79–80. "let…eyelid": Oberon told Puck to make the man fonder of
      the woman than the woman of him (2.1.265–66). Puck, indignant,
      goes further. He will punish the "lack-love" by making him fall so
      much in love that he will be unable to sleep.
269   83. "thou": Unlike earlier, Helena uses familiar pronouns in ad-
      dressing Demetrius to his face (also line 85).
270   84. "charge": order.
271   84. "haunt": follow, hang around.
272   85. "darkling": in the dark.
273   87. "fond": 1) doting, 2) foolish.
274   88. "grace": favor (quibble on "prayer").
275   88–90. "The more…eyes": Although she sees that the more she
      pursues him the less Demetrius wants her, Helena still fails to rec-
      ognize the connection between the two. She still attributes her own
      unhappiness to her looks, not to her actions; see, further, 1.1.194–
      201n.

For beasts that meet me run away for fear.[276]

95   Therefore no marvel though Demetrius

Do as[277] a monster fly my presence thus.

What wicked and dissembling glass[278] of mine

Made me compare with Hermia's sphery eyne?[279],[280]

But who is here? Lysander, on the ground!

100   Dead or asleep? I see no blood, no wound.

Lysander, if you live, good sir, awake.

Lysander: [*waking up*] And run through fire I will for thy sweet sake![281]

Transparent Helena! Nature shows art,

That through thy bosom makes me see thy heart.[282]

---

276 93. "No,…fear": No longer distinguishing between the ways Demetrius and the rest of Athens see her (see 1.1.229–31n), Helena now thinks that he is right—even beasts run away from her for fear of her ugliness.

277 95–96. "no marvel…as": it is no wonder that Demetrius should do as though I were.

278 97. "glass": mirror.

279 98. "sphery eyne": starry eyes.

280 97–98. "What…eyne": Helena blames her mirror for showing a false reflection of her own eyes that made her think herself equal to ("compare with") Hermia. Although she blames the mirror for deceiving her, she takes for granted that she can know herself only by comparing herself to another. Beauty, for her, is always a matter of comparison (see 1.1.181–201, 226–29; 3.2.232–34n). In this important respect, she and Demetrius form a pair. For her, beauty, for him, love, are essentially rooted in rivalry. Comparisons are everything. On Demetrius, see 1.1.194–201n.

281 102. "And…sake": Love speaks in perpetual hyperbole.

282 103–4. "Transparent…heart": Lysander uses "transparent" to mean both brilliant and diaphanous. The blond Helena is gloriously radiant and entirely ingenuous. While her outward looks radiate beauty, her inner goodness is wholly visible to Lysander's eyes. Lysander, while supposing art to be superior to nature, at once states and cancels their usual antithesis. Bodies, by nature, are impenetrable to sight. Art, however, reveals the inside by means of the outside. It exhibits its characters' natures by imitating or representing their actions and words (Aristotle, *Poetics*, 1449b37–

Where is Demetrius? O, how fit a word   105
Is that vile name to perish on my sword![283]
Helena: Do not say so. Lysander, say not so.
What though he love your Hermia? Lord, what though?[284]
Yet Hermia still loves you. Then be content.
Lysander: Content[285] with Hermia? No, I do repent   110
The tedious minutes I with her have spent.[286]
Not Hermia, but Helena I love.
Who will not change a raven for a dove?[287]

50a7). With Helena, however, nature shows directly what art shows indirectly. It allows at least the loving Lysander to see her heart right through her opaque body ("bosom").

283 105–6. "O, how…sword": Just as art is his standard for nature (see lines 103–4n), Lysander confuses Demetrius and his name. He speaks as though what stands for the man is the man, and to kill the "word" or the "name" is to kill the man himself. Lysander, accordingly, calls Demetrius' name "vile." Plutarch explains that he wrote the *Life of Demetrius* because young men should see what is base as well as noble—not only the "arts [of] temperance, justice, and wisdom…, but…the nature and effects of lewdness, corruption, and damage" (Plutarch, *Demetrius*, 1.2; North, 5:372). The bookish Lysander seems to have studied Plutarch's cautionary tale all too well. Once again seeing books as life, he confuses Plutarch's character and Helena's scornful beloved. Taking the namesake for the original, he not only finds the name vile, but thinking it equivalent to what it names, he wants to strike the name as the man himself.

284 108. "what though": what difference does that make? Helena of course does not realize that Lysander threatens Demetrius, not for loving Hermia, but for hurting Helena—not for being his rival for Hermia, but for not being his rival for Helena.

285 110. "Content": A shift in meaning: Helena meant "calm" (line 109); Lysander, who rhymes the word twice (lines 110–11), means "satisfied."

286 111. "The…spent": If love distorts what it sees in a present beloved, it no less distorts what it remembers of a past one; see, further, lines 140–41.

287 113. "raven…dove": Hermia, dark-haired and of dark complexion (see 3.2.257n, 263n), is a raven, a bird proverbial for its blackness

115   The will[288] of man is by his reason swayed,
And reason says you are the worthier maid.
Things growing are not ripe until their season:
So I, being young, till now ripe not[289] to reason.
And touching now the point of human skill,[290]
Reason becomes the marshal to my will[291]
120   And leads me to your eyes, where I o'erlook[292]
Love's stories written in love's richest book.[293]
Helena: Wherefore[294] was I to this keen mockery born?[295]
When at your hands did I[296] deserve this scorn?

---

and known for its noisy, aggressive omnivorousness (see Dent, R32.2; Pliny, 10.32–33). Helena, blonde and of fair complexion (see 1.1.180–81), is a dove, a bird proverbial for its whiteness and its harmless innocence (see Dent, D572, D573.2). Having fallen in (and out of) love for no reason other than the love juice, the love-smitten Lysander believes that the most superficial aspect of the women's appearances reveals the inner qualities that make them lovable or unlovable; see, further, lines 103–4n.

288 114. "will": desire.
289 117. "ripe not": having not ripened, matured ("ripe" is a verb).
290 118. "touching...skill": having now reached the peak of human judgment.
291 114–19. "The will...will": Lysander, concluding that reason fully guides his desire, attempts to set forth his explanation in a fully rational or logical manner. Twice he first states a general principle and then its particular instance (lines 114–15, 116–17). Then, continuing his formal argument, he offers the obverse of his combined general principles with a positive predicate (lines 118–19). Lysander, who mentions reason four times in these six lines and nowhere else, is never less rational than when claiming to be nothing but rational. His claim to reason amounts to love's mockery of reason. See, further, 3.2.134n.
292 120. "o'erlook": look over, read through.
293 120–21. "And...book": Lysander, yet again confounding love and letters, says that while Helena's eyes offer "Love's stories," she herself is "love's richest book." Helena becomes a love story.
294 122. "Wherefore": why, on account of what.
295 122. "Wherefore...born": Helena takes Lysander's words as mockery—as a derisive imitation of love.
296 123. "When...I": what did I do to you to.

Is't not enough, is't not enough, young man,
That I did never, no, nor never[297] can   125
Deserve a sweet look from Demetrius' eye,
But you must flout my insufficiency?[298]
Good troth, you do me wrong, good sooth,[299] you do,
In such disdainful manner me to woo.[300]
But fare you well. Perforce[301] I must confess   130
I thought you lord of more true gentleness.[302]
O, that a lady of[303] one man refused
Should of another therefore be abused!

Exit.

Lysander: She sees not Hermia.[304] Hermia, sleep thou there,
And never mayst thou come Lysander near.   135
For, as a surfeit of the sweetest things
The deepest loathing to the stomach brings,
Or as the heresies that men do leave
Are hated most of those they did deceive,[305]

---

297 125. "nor never": double negative for emphasis (in context, a quadruple negative).

298 127. "flout my insufficiency": jeer at my unattractiveness.

299 128. "Good troth,…good sooth": Two expletives meaning "indeed," "in truth."

300 129. "In…woo": Love's hyperbolic speech may be (unintentionally) comic when meant (see, for example, line 102), but insulting when not meant. The professed praise becomes mockery, ridiculing as absent the very qualities it pretends to praise as present.

301 130. "Perforce": of necessity.

302 131. "gentleness": good breeding, gentlemanly conduct.

303 132. "of": by (same in line 133).

304 134. "She…Hermia": Lysander explains to himself that Helena mistook his love because she failed to see Hermia asleep on the ground. Had she seen her, Helena would have realized that he no longer loves Hermia. Lysander apparently imagines that Helena—or anyone else—would view Hermia as he now does and recognize that he does not love her any more.

305 138–39. "Or…deceive": as the heresies that men reject are hated most by those they had deceived.

140   So thou, my surfeit and my heresy,
           Of all be hated, but the most of me![306]
           And, all my powers, address[307] your love and might
           To honor Helen and to be her knight.

Exit.

Hermia: [*waking up*] Help me, Lysander, help me! Do thy best
145   To pluck this crawling serpent from my breast.
           Ay me, for pity! What a dream was here!
           Lysander, look how I do quake with fear.
           Methought a serpent ate my heart away,
           And you sat smiling at his cruel prey.[308],[309]
150   Lysander! What, removed? Lysander, lord!
           What, out of hearing? Gone? No sound, no word?
           Alack, where are you? Speak, an if[310] you hear.

---

306   140–41. "So,…me": Lysander says that everyone should loath and hate what he loathes and hates, though he most of all. Love, it seems, may not simply fade or disappear, but rather change into its equally strong opposite. And while a lover does not want everyone to love what he loves, a former lover may want, even expect, everyone to hate what he hates. Love is exclusive; hatred and loathing are not.

307   142. "address": apply, direct.

308   149. "prey": act of preying.

309   144–49. "Help,…prey": Hermia's dream points up that a dream's deception lies in the dreamer's mistaking a resemblance for what it resembles, an appearance for a reality. When we dream, we become literal-minded and take a likeness for the thing itself. It is only after waking that we recognize the dream as a dream, as Hermia does here. Hermia's dream was a likeness in two respects—an image that was only figuratively true. Hermia did not dream that Lysander renounced his love and declared his love for someone else. She dreamt that a serpent ate her heart and Lysander did nothing but sit and smile at the snake's preying upon her. It was an image that was only metaphorically true.

310   152. "an if": if indeed (emphasizes the uncertainty; see Abbott, §105).

Speak, of all loves![311] I swoon almost[312] with fear.
No? Then I well perceive you are not nigh.[313]
Either death or you I'll find immediately.[314]   155

Exit.

---

311 153. "of all loves": for the sake of love (expresses a strong appeal
     or entreaty).
312 153. "swoon almost": almost swoon (see Abbott, §29).
313 154. "nigh": near.
314 155. "Either…immediately": Hermia's desperate thought is uncer-
     tain. She may mean death by her own hand or death by her loss
     and pain. Whichever the case, unlike Helena, who also talked of
     dying (see 2.1.244n), she seems to mean what she says.

Act Three, Scene One

[The wood. Titania still asleep.]
Enter the Clowns: [Quince, Bottom, Snout, Starveling, Snug, and Flute].

Bottom: Are we all met?
Quince: Pat, pat.[1] And here's a marvelous convenient place
    for our rehearsal. This green plot shall be our stage,
    this hawthorn brake our tiring-house,[2] and we will
    do it in action[3] as we will do it before the Duke.[4]   5
Bottom: Peter Quince!
Quince: What sayest thou, bully Bottom?[5]
Bottom: There are things in this comedy[6] of Pyramus and
    Thisbe that will never please. First, Pyramus must
    draw a sword to kill himself, which the ladies cannot   10
    abide.[7] How answer you that?
Snout: By'r lakin,[8] a parlous[9] fear.
Starveling: I believe we must leave the killing out, when all is done.[10]

---

1   2. "Pat, pat": on the dot, punctually.
2   4. "hawthorn…tiring-house": hawthorn thicket our dressing room.
3   5. "do…action": act it out fully.
4   5. "do…Duke": Nothing they practice is what they later perform.
    Their "rehearsal" (line 3) does not rehearse the play.
5   7. "bully Bottom": "Bully" is a term of friendly endearment and a
    familiar form of address. It is often prefixed to the name of the per-
    son addressed. On the name Bottom, see S.D. 1.2.1n.
6   8. "comedy": Before Act 5, the players always refer to "Pyramus
    and Thisbe" as a comedy; in Act 5, always as a tragedy. The differ-
    ence may be lost on them, who seem to care only about what
    pleases the audience. But see, further, Coda, 198–199.
7   11. "abide": stand, endure.
8   12. "By'r lakin": by our lady (a tame oath).
9   12. "parlous": perilous.
10   13–14. "I…done": Such a change would, of course, destroy the plot
    and rob the play of any meaning. To Starveling, it seems, a play is

15 *Bottom*: Not a whit.[11] I have a device to make all well. Write
    me[12] a prologue, and let the prologue seem to say we
    will do no harm with our swords and that Pyramus
    is not killed indeed. And, for the more better[13] assurance,
    tell them that I, Pyramus, am not Pyramus,
20 but Bottom the weaver.[14] This will put them out of[15]
    fear.
    Quince: Well, we will have such a prologue, and it shall be
    written in eight and six.[16]
    Bottom: No, make it two more. Let it be written in eight and
25 eight.[17]
    Snout: Will not the ladies be afeard of the lion?[18]
    Starveling: I fear it, I promise you.[19]
    Bottom: Masters, you ought to consider with yourself, to[20]
    bring in (God shield us!) a lion among ladies is a

---

not a coherent whole with a beginning, middle, and end, but a heap
of episodes or parts any of which can be dropped for any reason.

11 15. "Not a whit": not in the least.
12 15–16. "Write me": write (a colloquialism).
13 18. "more better": double comparative for greater emphasis (see Abbott, §11).
14 19–20. "I,...weaver": Bottom garbles his assurance. He means to distinguish himself from his character and say that he is merely playing the part of Pyramus. Instead, he says both that he is and that is not Pyramus, first identifying himself with his part ("I, Pyramus") and then distinguishing himself from his part ("am not Pyramus"). Afraid that the women will mistake his personation for what he personates, he repeats the very confusion he attempts to remove.
15 20. "out of": free from the effects of.
16 23. "eight and six": alternating lines of eight and six syllables, the common meter for ballads (see, for example, lines 120–23).
17 24–25. "No...eight": Bottom, as usual, wants more. "More" is nearly his most frequent word. He says it 11 times (and "most" five times). No one says "more" (or "most") more often than he.
18 26. "Will...lion": Quince originally raised this concern in the casting scene (see 1.2.70–72).
19 27. "I promise you": let me tell you.
20 28. "to": that to.

most dreadful thing.[21] For there is not a more fearful 30
wildfowl[22] than your lion living, and we ought to
look to't.

Snout: Therefore another prologue must tell he is not a
lion.

Bottom: Nay, you must name his name, and half his face 35
must be seen through the lion's neck, and he himself
must speak through, saying thus, or to the same
defect:[23] "Ladies," or "Fair ladies, I would wish you,"
or "I would request you," or "I would entreat you,
not to fear, not to tremble: my life for yours![24] If you 40
think I come hither as a lion, it were pity of my life.[25]
No, I am no such thing. I am a man as other men
are." And there indeed let him name his name and
tell them plainly he is Snug the joiner.[26]

Quince: Well, it shall be so. But there is two hard things: 45
that is, to bring the moonlight into a chamber, for
you know Pyramus and Thisbe meet by moonlight.

Snout:[27] Doth the moon shine that night we play our play?

Bottom: A calendar, a calendar! Look in the almanac. Find
out moonshine, find out moonshine! 50

Quince: Yes, it doth shine that night.[28]

---

21   29–30. "lion...thing": For the sexual quibble on "lion," see 5.1.281n.
22   30–31. "fearful wildfowl": A "wildfowl" is normally a wild bird,
such as a duck or a goose, caught for game. Bottom misapplies the
term to a fearsome beast.
23   38. "defect": He means "effect."
24   40. "my...yours": I fear for my life if you fear for yours.
25   41. "pity...life": my life would be in danger ("of," here, means "regarding": see Abbott, §174).
26   35–44. "Nay,...joiner": Bottom tries, as always, to be resourceful. He
fears that the ladies, confusing the actor with his character, would not
realize that the actor addressing them is human; see, further, 5.1.214n.
27   S.H. 48. "*Snout*": In early editions, the speech heading is "*Sn.*,"
which could refer also to Snug, who is otherwise silent in the scene.
28   48–51. "Doth...night": No one thinks of looking up to the moon above
them (see, further, 5.1.300–2n). Instead, Bottom calls for a calendar,

Bottom: Why, then, may you leave a casement[29] of the great
　　chamber window, where we play, open, and the
　　moon may shine in at the casement.
55　*Quince*: Ay, or else one must come in with a bush of thorns[30]
　　and a lantern and say he comes to disfigure[31] or to
　　present[32] the person of Moonshine.[33] Then there is
　　another thing: we must have a wall in the great
　　chamber, for Pyramus and Thisbe, says the story,
60　　did talk through the chink of a wall.
　Snout: You can never bring in a wall. What say you,
　　Bottom?
　Bottom: Some man or other must present Wall. And let him
　　have some plaster, or some loam, or some roughcast[34]
65　　about him to signify wall, or let him hold his
　　fingers thus, and through that cranny shall Pyramus
　　and Thisbe whisper.[35]

---

　　and Quince, who for some reason has an almanac on hand, consults
　　its calendar and reports the moon will shine that night. The young
　　lovers are not the only bookish Athenians. Quince's report, however,
　　is puzzling. The moon does not shine on a new moon (see 1.1.3n).

29　52. "casement": hinged frame, forming part of a window.
30　55. "bush of thorns": According to some legends, the man in the
　　moon is the figure of a human, carrying a bundle ("bush") of sticks
　　on his back. The "thorns" are said to indicate that he has been sent
　　there as punishment; see, for example, William Dunbar Henryson,
　　The Testament of Cresseid, 260–64. See, further, 5.1.247–49n.
31　56. "disfigure": figure, represent.
32　57. "present": personate.
33　52–57. "Why,…Moonshine": The players apparently think that the
　　possibilities for presenting the moon are limited to either the moon
　　itself or an actor explicitly personating a personified symbol of the
　　moon ("the man in the moon"). Both possibilities would destroy
　　dramatic illusion, the one by presenting the real thing, the other
　　by expressly announcing the imitation as an imitation.
34　64. "roughcast": a mixture of lime, water and fine gravel, used to
　　plaster the outside of buildings.
35　55–67. "Ay, or…whisper": The players will personate the play's
　　props or scenery as well as its characters.

Quince: If that may be, then all is well. Come, sit down,
  every mother's son,[36] and rehearse your parts. Pyramus,
  you begin. When you have spoken your speech,   70
  enter into that brake, and so everyone according to
  his cue.[37]

  Enter Puck [invisible to those onstage].

Puck: What hempen homespuns[38] have we swaggering here,
  So near the cradle[39] of the Fairy Queen?
  What, a play toward?[40] I'll be an auditor.[41]   75
  An actor too perhaps, if I see cause.
Quince: Speak, Pyramus. Thisbe, stand forth.
Bottom: *Thisbe, the flowers of odious savors sweet—*
Quince: Odors, "odorous!"[42]

---

36   69. "every…son": everyone (proverbial; see 1.2.73n).

37   68–72. "Come,…cue": Quince proceeds as if there were no changes
      in the script. Yet, three new characters—Prologue, Moonshine, and
      Wall—have been added and the part of Lion greatly expanded.
      The players overlook their own changes.

38   73. "hempen homespuns": coarse rustics dressed in homespun
      cloth of hemp.

39   74. "cradle": bed (suggests diminutive size).

40   75. "toward": in preparation.

41   75. "auditor": hearer, listener, audience.

42   79. "Odors, 'odorous!'": The Quarto's reading. The Folio reads
      "Odors, odors." The Quarto's reading seems preferable. It suggests
      that Quince is insistently explaining his correction of Bottom's mal-
      apropism, by indicating how the correct adjective is formed, which
      Bottom then proceeds to misunderstand (line 79). Some editors
      emend to "Odorous, odorous."
          Malapropisms, to which the artisans are prone, go together with
      their literalism. The one, a blunder of speech, the other a blunder
      of thought, mistake similarity for sameness. Literalism takes an
      image for that of which it is an image, while a malapropism re-
      places one word with another which is similar in sound but inap-
      propriate in meaning. Both errors join what should be kept apart.
      The artisans seem to model their dramatic art on their productive
      arts (carpenter, joiner, weaver, bellows mender, tinker, tailor; see

Bottom: *Odors savors sweet.*
80   *So hath thy breath, my dearest Thisbe dear.*
        But hark, a voice! Stay thou but here awhile,
        And by and by[43] I will to thee appear.[44],[45]

                                                        Exit.

Puck: A stranger Pyramus than e'er played here.[46]

                                                        Exit.

Flute: Must I speak now?
85 Quince: Ay, marry, must you, for you must understand
        he goes but to see a noise that he heard[47] and is to
        come again.
    Flute: *Most radiant Pyramus, most lily-white of hue,*
        Of color like the red rose on triumphant[48] brier,

S. D. 1.2.1n), all of which involve some manner of joining. They do
inappropriately with words and drama what is appropriate to do
with their hands in their trades.

43   82. *"by and by"*: soon, in a moment.

44   78–82. *"Thisbe,…appear"*: While the second and fourth lines of
      Pyramus' quatrain rhyme (*"dear"* / *"appear"*), the first and third
      do not (*"sweet"* / *"awhile"*). The faulty rhyme pattern is evidently
      unique in a Shakespeare dialogue (see Alexander Schmidt, in Fur-
      ness, 119).

45   81–82. *"But…appear"*: Quince's plot, requiring Pyramus to
      leave suddenly and promise to return right away, alters the
      traditional Pyramus and Thisbe story, in which the lovers
      leave one another only to meet in the woods near Ninus' tomb
      (Ovid, *Metamorphoses*, 4.83–92). To permit the departure,
      Quince relies on the lame theatrical expedient of having the
      character hear an unexpected noise nearby. Quince's needless
      change in the story's plot becomes Puck's opportunity; see line
      83n.

46   83. *"A stranger…here"*: Quick-witted Puck thinks of the trick that
      he intends to play on Bottom and therefore exits here.

47   86. *"see…heard"*: Quince confuses hearing and seeing; see, further,
      4.1.209–12n; and cp. 3.2.177–83n.

48   89. *"triumphant"*: noble.

Most brisky juvenal[49] and eke[50] most lovely Jew,[51]   90
As true as truest horse, that yet would never tire.
I'll meet thee, Pyramus, at Ninny's tomb.[52]
Quince: "Ninus' tomb,"[53] man! Why, you must not speak that
   yet. That you answer to Pyramus. You speak all
   your part at once, cues and all.[54]   95
   Pyramus, enter. Your cue is past. It is "never tire."
Flute: O—As true as truest horse, that yet would never tire.

   Enter Puck, and Bottom as Pyramus with the ass-head [on].

---

49   90. "*brisky juvenal*": brisk youth.
50   90. "*eke*": also (archaism).
51   90. "*Jew*": 1) an abbreviation of "*juvenal*," with which it forms a jin-
   gle, 2) a desperate rhyme with "*hue*."
52   88–92. "*Most...tomb*": The paucity of Quince's poetry is evi-
   dent. Thisbe's first four lines, which apostrophize and describe
   her beloved, contain seriatim superlatives ("*Most...*" four
   times, "*truest*" once), unsuited modifiers and comparisons (a
   "*triumphant*" wild rose, a love as "*true*" as an unwearied
   horse), conflicting colors (*most lily-white of hue, / Of color like
   the red rose*), affected poetic diction ("*briskly*," "*juvenal*"), and
   an archaism ("*eke*"). The verses are also stretched with idle
   fillers (the needless "*eke*," "*brisky*" for "brisk," "*juvenal*" for
   "youth") and hopeless attempts to rhyme ("*Jew*" with "*hue*,"
   "*tire*" with "*brier*"). So, too, with the storyline. Although Pyramus just told her to stay here and he will soon return, Thisbe
   announces, in the spirit of complete faithfulness, that she will
   leave to meet him at Ninny's tomb. This inconsistency returns
   Quince's play to the traditional story (see Ovid, *Metamorphoses*, 4.88–89).
53   92–93. "*Ninny's...tomb*": "Ninny" means fool. Ninus, king of the
   Assyrians (c. 2,000 BC), is said to be the first of the Asian kings to
   achieve great deeds (Diodorus Siculus, 2.1.4). Nineveh, his cele-
   brated capitol, is named after him.
54   94–95. "*You...all*": Quince's correction is incorrect. A cue, which is
   the concluding word(s) of a speech, signaling another actor to
   enter or to begin his speech (see 5.1.182–83), is meant to be read.
   Bottom, however, has missed his cue, and Flute has read two of
   Thisbe's speeches as one; see line 96.

Bottom: If I were fair, Thisbe, I were only thine.[55]

Quince: O monstrous! O strange! We are haunted.[56] Pray,

100   masters, fly, masters! Help!

          Quince, Flute, Snout, Snug, and Starveling exeunt.

Puck: I'll follow you. I'll lead you about a round,[57]

     Through bog, through bush, through brake, through brier.

     Sometime a horse I'll be, sometime a hound,

     A hog, a headless bear, sometime a fire,

105   And neigh and bark and grunt and roar and burn,

     Like horse, hound, hog, bear, fire, at every turn.[58]

                        Exit.

Bottom: Why do they run away? This is a knavery[59] of them

     to make me afeard.

                Enter Snout.

Snout: O Bottom, thou art changed! What do I see on

110   thee?

---

55   98. *"If…thine "*: if I were handsome ("fair"), Thisbe, I would still be only yours. The mispunctuated line should be, "If I were [true], fair Thisbe, I were [= would be] only thine."

56   99. "haunted": Reginal Scot, describing setting an ass's head on a man's neck and shoulders, says that someone doing it "shall be thought a witch" (Scot, 13.19 [179]).

57   101. "about a round": 1) roundabout, 2) circular dance (see, further, 2.1.140n).

58   101–6. "I'll…turn": Puck's stanza, while conflating what he will "be" and be "[l]ike," echoes what he said of his ability to assume any likeness (see 2.1.45–57n). In addition to directly repeating the Fairy's "through bush, through brier" (2.1.30), the stanza echoes itself, with its combination of repeated alliteration and frequent reiteration of first words, its contrasting combinations of present and absent connecting particles, and, covering more than half its lines, a series of five nouns, followed by a series of their five corresponding verbs, followed by the original series of five nouns. Puck's mimetic diction mimics his mimetic action.

59   107. "knavery": malicious trick.

Bottom: What do you see? You see an ass-head of your own,[60] do you?

[*Exit Snout.*]

Enter Quince.

Quince: Bless thee, Bottom, bless thee! Thou art translated![61]

Exit.

Bottom: I see their knavery. This is to make an ass of me, to   115
fright me,[62] if they could. But I will not stir from this
place, do what they can. I will walk up and down
here, and I will sing, that[63] they shall hear I am not
afraid.

[*Sings.*]   *The ouzel cock,[64] so black of hue,*   120
With orange-tawny bill,
The throstle[65] with his note so true,
The wren with little quill[66] —

Titania: [*Waking up*] What angel wakes me from my flowery bed?

Bottom: [*Sings*] *The finch, the sparrow, and the lark,*   125
The plainsong cuckoo[67] gray,
Whose note full many a man doth mark
And dares not answer "nay"[68] —

---

60   111. "You…own": you pretend to see only what your own asinine
heads have made up to scare me (proverbial: see Dent, A388).

61   114. "translated": transformed.

62   115–16. "make…me": Bottom believes that the others want to do to
him figuratively what, unbeknownst to him, is now true of him literally and has always been true of him figuratively. His new body,
also a pun on his name, reveals rather than transforms his true form.

63   118. "that": so that.

64   120. "ouzel cock": male blackbird.

65   122. "throstle": song thrush.

66   123. "little quill": small pipe (shrill voice).

67   126. "plainsong cuckoo": cuckoo who sings a simple, repetitive song.

68   126–28. "The plainsong…'nay'": Both the name and the call of the
cuckoo sound like "cuckold," a derisive name for the husband of
an unfaithful wife. Any a man, Bottom sings, hearing the bird's

for, indeed, who would set his wit to so foolish a

130   bird? Who would give a bird the lie though he cry
"cuckoo" never so?[69]

Titania: I pray thee, gentle[70] mortal, sing again.
Mine ear is much enamored of thy note,
So is mine eye enthralled to thy shape,

135   And thy fair virtue's force perforce doth move me[71]
On the first view to say, to swear, I love thee.

Bottom: Methinks, mistress, you should have little reason[72] for
that. And yet, to say the truth, reason[73] and love
keep little company together nowadays. The more

140   the pity that some honest[74] neighbors will not make
them friends.[75] Nay, I can gleek[76] upon occasion.

Titania: Thou art as wise as thou art beautiful.

Bottom: Not so neither; but if I had wit enough to get out of

---

    mocking cry that his wife is unfaithful, dares not say that she is
not; see, further, lines 129–31n.

69   129–31. "for,...so": Bottom explains that no one would use his intelligence to confute a foolish mocking beast. He seems to miss the
point of the song.

70   132. "gentle": noble.

71   135. "thy...me": the force of your beautiful excellence does necessarily move me. "Virtue" refers to a superiority or excellence in a
particular sphere, not necessarily a moral quality. The word, derived from the Latin word for "man" (*vir*), often means "strength"
or "force": hence, the comically redundant "virtue's force perforce."

72   137. "reason": cause.

73   138. "reason": good sense.

74   140. "honest": honorable.

75   137–41. "Methinks...friends": Bottom, speaking with an air of
gravity and worldly wisdom, makes a surprising reply. Emphasizing "reason" and generalizing, he denies that anyone brings reason and love together nowadays. His sensible-sounding reply
implicitly contradicts Lysander's claim that reason guides his love
for Helena (see 2.2.114–19n).

76   141. "gleek": make a satirical joke.

this wood, I have enough to serve mine own turn.[77]
Titania: Out of this wood[78] do not desire to go.   145
    Thou shalt remain here whether thou wilt or no.
    I am a spirit of no common rate.[79]
    The summer still doth tend upon my state,[80]
    And I do love thee. Therefore go with me.
    I'll give thee fairies to attend on thee,   150
    And they shall fetch thee jewels from the deep[81]
    And sing while thou on pressed flowers dost sleep.
    And I will purge thy mortal grossness so
    That thou shalt like an airy spirit go.[82]
    Peaseblossom, Cobweb, Moth, and Mustardseed![83]   155

---

77   137–44. "Methinks…turn": Bottom, continuing to sound sensible, speaks with an uncharacteristic mien of modesty. By "wood," he seems to mean madness: if he had enough intelligence to get out of his present mad confusion, he could take care of himself. Titania misunderstands him; see line 145n.

78   145. "wood": 1) forest, 2) wooed; cp. lines 143–44; for the pun on "wood," see 2.1.191–92n.

79   147. "rate": rank.

80   148. "The summer…state": the summer always waits upon (serves) my exalted status.

81   151. "jewels…deep": such as pearls and corals.

82   153–54. "purge…go": No one mentions mortality so much as Titania does. It is nearly her first word to Bottom (3.1.132), it is at the heart of her description of her Indian votress (2.1.135) and of the effects of her quarreling with Oberon (2.1.101), and it is her only word to describe the young lovers (4.1.101). Apart from Titania, only Peaseblossom, echoing her (line 168), and Puck, remarking on human beings as fools (3.2.115), use the word. Titania, however, says not that she will purge Bottom of his mortality, but of his living body's grossness. She promises that he will move "like an airy spirit," not that he will become one.

83   155. "Peaseblossom,…Mustardseed": Titania's four fairy-servants have British names, like Robin Goodfellow (Puck) and the artisans. Those in the play who serve have British names; those who rule or belong to the noble class have classical names. The fairy-ser-

Enter four Fairies [Peaseblossom, Cobweb, Moth, and Mustardseed].

Peaseblossom: Ready.
Cobweb: And I.
Moth: And I.
Mustardseed: And I.
All: Where shall we go?
Titania: Be kind and courteous to this gentleman.
 Hop in his walks and gambol in his eyes;[84, 85]
 Feed him with apricocks and dewberries,[86]
160 With purple grapes, green figs, and mulberries.
 The honey-bags steal from the humble-bees,[87]
 And for night-tapers crop their waxen thighs
 And light them at the fiery glowworms' eyes
 To have my love to bed and to arise;[88]

---

vants' names are all common nouns and, except for Peaseblossom ("Blossom of a pea plant"), name things that are insubstantial, tiny, or tenuous. "Moth," which is a common spelling of "mote" and was pronounced much the same, seems intended to name a speck of dust rather than an insect. Moth says next to nothing on his own (two speeches, three words) and, unlike the other three fairies, is never described or discussed in the dialogue.

84 158. "in his eyes": before him
85 158. "Hop...eyes": The fairies move in highly stylized ways. Just as they typically speak with lyrical diction and in narrative form, they "skip" (2.1.61), "gambol" (line 158), "hop" (line 158, 5.1.380), "trip" (4.1.95), "trip away" (5.1.407), and, most notably, dance (2.1.86, 140; 2.2.1, 254; 4.1.88; 5.1.382). Mere walking and running are largely left to humans (see, further, 5.1.339n). As poetry differs from ordinary speech, the fairies' movement differs from that of humans.
86 159. "apricocks and dewberries": apricots (old spelling) and blackberries.
87 161. "humble-bees": bumblebees.
88 162–64. "crop...arise": cut off their wax-packed thighs and light them at glowworms' eyes, so as to be his tapers when he comes to bed and arises. The fire of glowworms comes, in fact, not from their eyes, but from "the brightness of their sides and tails" (Pliny, 11.98; Holland, 326).

And pluck the wings from painted butterflies   165
To fan the moonbeams from his sleeping eyes.[89]
Nod to him, elves, and do him courtesies.[90]
Peaseblossom: Hail, mortal![91]
Cobweb: Hail!
Moth: Hail!   170
Mustardseed: Hail!
Bottom: I cry your worships mercy,[92] heartily. I beseech your
    worship's name.
Cobweb: Cobweb.
Bottom: I shall desire you of more acquaintance,[93] good   175
    Master Cobweb. If I cut my finger, I shall make bold
    with you.[94] Your name, honest[95] gentleman?
Peaseblossom: Peaseblossom.
Bottom: I pray you, commend me[96] to Mistress Squash, your
    mother, and to Master Peascod, your father.[97] Good   180
    Master Peaseblossom, I shall desire you of more
    acquaintance too. Your name, I beseech you, sir?
Mustardseed: Mustardseed.

---

89   161–66. "The honey-bags...eyes": The fairies seem to have no def-
    inite size. They are large enough to feed Bottom full-sized fruits
    and yet small enough to steal the honey-bags of bees.
90   158–67. "Hop...courtesies": Titania's instructions are a series of ten
    end-stopped verses, repeating a single rhyme, whose repetition
    supports the speech's lyrical effect.
91   168. "mortal": See lines 153–54n.
92   172. "I...mercy": I beg your honors' pardon (for asking your
    names).
93   175. "you ...acquaintance": to be better acquainted with you.
94   176–77. "If...you": Cobwebs were used to stop bleeding.
95   177. "honest": honorable.
96   179. "commend me": give my regards.
97   179–80. "Mistress...father": Bottom's attempt at urbane wit turns
    bawdy. While the mother of Peaseblossom ("Blossom of a pea
    plant") is Squash, the father is Peascod—a quibble on "codpiece,"
    its syllables reversed, and a punning reference to male genitals
    (scrotum).

Bottom: Good Master Mustardseed, I know your patience
185   well. That same cowardly, giantlike ox-beef hath
      devoured many a gentleman of your house.[98] I
      promise you, your kindred hath made my eyes water
      ere now.[99] I desire you of more acquaintance, good
      Master Mustardseed.
190 *Titania*: Come, wait[100] upon him. Lead him to my bower.[101]
      The moon,[102] methinks, looks with a watery eye,
      And when she weeps, weeps every little flower,[103]
      Lamenting some enforced[104] chastity.[105]
      Tie up my lover's tongue. Bring him silently.[106]

Exunt.

---

98   184–86. "I…house": Mustardseed has shown his patience in enduring the loss of kinsmen, who have been devoured as mustard
by those eating beef.

99   187–88. "your…now": my eyes have 1) teared in sympathy, 2)
smarted from the pungency of the mustard which I ate.

100 190. "wait": attend.

101 190. "bower": shady retreat, overarched with branches of trees,
shrubs, or other plants.

102 191." The moon": Diana, the goddess of chastity (see 1.1.73n).

103 192. "when…flower": "[T]he Moon imprints her moisture in the
earth, & is cause of …dew therein, as *Ambrose* says, and he calls
the Moon mother of dew" (Bartholomew the Englishman, *On the
Properties of Things*, 11.6); see, further, 1.1.211n.

104 193. "enforced": violated.

105 191–93. "The moon…chastity": These are her first words since
awakening which are not spoken to or regarding Bottom and the
only ones of the sort she will speak until Oberon removes the effect
of the love juice (4.1.75ff.). Yet, the difference may be largely apparent. Love compels Titania to sound like as well as to celebrate
her beloved. Thus she repeats (and elevates) Bottom's mention of
watering eyes (line 187); see, further, 4.1.186–98n.

106 194, "Tie…silently": Despite her strong love, Titania may no longer
be so sure that Bottom is wise (see line 142). She will praise his
amiable cheeks, smooth head, and large ears (see 4.1.1–4), but
never again praise his wisdom; see, further, 1.1.229–31.

Act Three, Scene Two

Enter Oberon, King of Fairies.

Oberon: I wonder if Titania be awaked;
   Then what it was that next came in her eye,
   Which she must dote on in extremity.

Enter Puck.

   Here comes my messenger. How now, mad spirit?
   What night-rule[107] now about this haunted grove?   5
Puck: My mistress with a monster is in love.
   Near to her close[108] and consecrated[109] bower,
   While she was in her dull and sleeping hour,
   A crew of patches,[110] rude mechanicals,[111]
   That work for bread upon Athenian stalls,[112]   10
   Were met together to rehearse a play
   Intended for great Theseus' nuptial day.
   The shallowest thick-skin[113] of that barren sort,[114]
   Who Pyramus presented[115] in their sport,[116]
   Forsook his scene[117] and entered in[118] a brake.   15

---

107 5. "night-rule": conduct of the night, revelry, activities.
108 7. "close": 1) secluded, 2) secret.
109 7. "consecrated": sacred.
110 9. "patches": fools, clowns.
111 9. "rude mechanicals": rough, uneducated workingmen.
112 10. "upon…stalls": in the workshops of Athens.
113 12. "thick-skin": blockhead, dunce. "Some…suppose creatures are brutish, more or less, according as their skin is thicker or thinner" (Pliny, 11.226; Holland, 346).
114 13. "barren sort": stupid group.
115 14. "presented": acted.
116 14. "sport": entertainment.
117 15. "scene": stage.
118 15. "in": into (see Abbott, §159).

When I did him at this advantage take,
An ass's noll[119] I fixed on his head.
Anon[120] his Thisbe must be answered,
And forth my mimic[121] comes. When they him spy,

20 As[122] wild geese that the creeping fowler[123] eye,
Or russet-pated choughs, many in sort,[124]
Rising and cawing[125] at the gun's report,
Sever themselves[126] and madly sweep the sky,
So at his sight away his fellows fly,

25 And, at our stamp,[127] here o'er and o'er one falls.
He "Murder" cries and help from Athens calls.[128]
Their sense thus weak, lost with their fears thus strong,
Made senseless things begin to do them wrong.
For briers and thorns at their apparel snatch,

30 Some sleeves, some hats, from yielders[129] all things catch.[130]
I led them on in this distracted fear

---

119   17. "noll": noodle, head.
120   18. "Anon": presently, soon.
121   19. "mimic": actor, player (contemptuous term).
122   20. "As": like.
123   20. "fowler": bird-hunter.
124   21. "russet-pated...sort": gray-headed jackdaws, in a flock.
125   22. "cawing": making the bird's raucous cry.
126   23. "Sever themselves": scatter.
127   25. "at our stamp": A disputed phrase. Presumably, "our" is a jocular use of the royal "we," and "stamp" refers to Puck's activity. The preposition "at" connotes both the timing and the origin or cause.
128   19–26. "When...calls": In the spirit of mock-heroic narrative, Puck uses a double simile—what one sort of bird saw and the other heard. The mingling of the senses matches the players' confusion. This is Puck's only simile until nearly the close of the play (5.1.372).
129   30. "yielders": those fleeing from fear.
130   27–30. "Their...catch": The terrified players not only tripped and fell. They also believed that their various hindrances were deliberate wrongs. Fear needs a particular object and will therefore imagine one if its object is unknown. Fear also tends to personify its object, accusing it of deliberate harm. Fear of the unknown thus

And left sweet Pyramus translated[131] there.
When in that moment, so it came to pass,
Titania waked and straightway loved an ass.[132]
Oberon: This falls out better than I could devise.   35
    But hast thou yet latched[133] the Athenian's eyes
    With the love juice, as I did bid thee do?
Puck: I took him sleeping—that is finished, too—
    And the Athenian woman by his side,
    That,[134] when he waked, of force[135] she must be eyed.   40

Enter Demetrius and Hermia.

Oberon: Stand close.[136] This is the same Athenian.
Puck: This is the woman, but not this the man.

[They stand aside.]

Demetrius: O, why rebuke you[137] him that loves you so?[138]

---

    ultimately transforms even "senseless things"—briars and
    thorns—into moral beings capable of intending the fear they cause
    and the harm they seem to threaten, and hence of committing in-
    justice or "wrong"; see, further, 5.1.22–23n.
131 32. "translated": transformed.
132 31–34. "I...ass": Although fear and love are contraries, the two top-
    ics of Puck's report—the artisans' fear of the unknown and Tita-
    nia's falling in love with an ass—depend crucially on imagination
    for their objects and the shaping of their objects (see 5.1.22–23n).
    Fear of the unknown and the love juice are mirror images of each
    other.
133 36. "latched": 1) caught, 2) moistened.
134 40. "That": so that.
135 40. "of force": of necessity.
136 41. "close": concealed, out of sight.
137 43. "you": Throughout the exchange (lines 43–81), Demetrius ad-
    dresses Hermia with the respectful "you," while she replies with
    the contemptuous "thou."
138 43. "why...so": The last time we saw Demetrius he was spurning
    his lover, who was chasing him (2.2.83–86). Now he is chasing his
    beloved, who is spurning him. Not surprisingly, the irony of the
    reversal seems entirely lost on him. Helena thought she could win

Lay breath[139] so bitter on your bitter foe!
45 *Hermia*: Now I but chide, but I should use thee worse,
For thou, I fear, hast given me cause to curse.
If thou hast slain Lysander in his sleep,
Being o'er shoes[140] in blood, plunge in the deep
And kill me too.
50 The sun was not so true unto the day
As he to me. Would he have stolen away
From sleeping Hermia? I'll believe as soon
This whole[141] earth may be bored, and that the moon
May through the center[142] creep and so displease[143]
55 Her brother's[144] noontide[145] with th'Antipodes.[146]
It cannot be but[147] thou hast murdered him.
So should a murderer look, so dead,[148] so grim.[149]

Demetrius' love by declaring her love for him. Demetrius, despite
having rejected Helena's love, now thinks he can win Hermia's
love by declaring his love for her (cp. 2.1.188–201).
139   44. "breath": speech.
140   48. "o'er shoes": in so deep (proverbial: Tilley, S379).
141   53. "whole": solid.
142   54. "center": center of the earth.
143   55. "displease": by bringing night with it.
144   55. "Her brother's": the sun's.
145   55. "noontide": the time of noon.
146   52–55. "I'll… th'Antipodes": Hermia, stating intentionally impossible conditions, says that she will not believe that Lysander chose to
leave her until the moon could tumble through the center of the
earth and bring night at noon to the opposite side of the world. The
"Antipodes" —"those "stand[ing] one against another, Foot to Foot"
(Pliny, 2.65; Holland, 104)—are dwellers directly on the opposite
side of the earth. The term shows Hermia's learning. Pliny, in the
same passage, says, "There is …debate between learned men and…
the ignorant multitude" on "whether there be any [Antipodes],"
with the learned supporting and the ignorant denying that the earth
is a globe and hence that it is possible that Antipodes exist.
147   56. "cannot be but": can only be (a double negative for emphasis).
148   57. "dead": deadly pale.
149   57. "grim": harsh, cruel.

Demetrius: So should the murdered look, and so should I,
    Pierced through the heart with your stern cruelty.
    Yet you, the murderer, look as bright, as clear,   60
    As yonder Venus[150] in her glimmering sphere.[151],[152]
Hermia: What's this to[153] my Lysander? Where is he?
    Ah, good Demetrius,[154] wilt thou give him me?
Demetrius: I had rather give his carcass to my hounds.
Hermia: Out, dog! Out, cur! Thou driv'st me past the bounds   65
    Of maiden's patience. Hast thou slain him, then?
    Henceforth be never numbered among men.[155]
    O, once[156] tell true! Tell true, even for my sake![157]
    Durst thou[158] have looked upon him, being awake?
    And hast thou killed him sleeping? O brave touch![159]   70
    Could not a worm,[160] an adder, do so much?
    An adder did it, for with doubler tongue[161]

---

150 61. "Venus": the planet (named after the goddess of love, Venus).

151 61. "sphere": crystalline sphere or orbit in which the plant moves (see, further, 2.1.7n).

152 58–61 "So…sphere": Demetrius, seizing upon Hermia's comparison, turns her words around. By denying Demetrius her love, Hermia murders him with cruelty. However, to Demetrius, Hermia does not resemble her own description of a murderer. She is not pale, but bright, not grim, but cheerful. She may be distraught with the thought of Lysander's murder, but to Demetrius' loving eyes she is as beautiful and sparkling as the brightest object in the nighttime sky after the moon.

153 62. "to": to do with.

154 63. "good Demetrius": Wheedling rather than rebuking him, Hermia now addresses him as "good Demetrius," something she calls him nowhere else.

155 67. "Henceforth…men": An implicit threat.

156 68. "once": once and for all.

157 68. "even…sake": An appeal to his love for her.

158 69. "Durst thou": did you dare to.

159 70. "O brave touch": noble deed (ironic, adding the charge of cowardice to that of murder).

160 71. "worm": snake.

161 72. "doubler tongue": 1) forked tongue, 2) more duplicitous speech.

Than thine, thou serpent, never adder stung.[162]

Demetrius: You spend[163] your passion[164] on a misprised mood.[165]

75   I am not guilty of Lysander's blood,

Nor is he dead, for aught that I can tell.

Hermia: I pray thee, tell me then that he is well.

Demetrius: An if[166] I could, what should I get therefor?[167]

Hermia: A privilege never to see me more.

80   And from thy hated presence part I so.

See me no more, whether he be dead or no.

Exit.

Demetrius: There is no following her in this fierce vein.[168]

Here, therefore, for a while I will remain.

So[169] sorrow's heaviness doth heavier grow[170]

85   For debt that bankrupt sleep doth sorrow owe,[171]

Which now in some slight measure it will pay,

If for his tender[172] here I make some stay.[173],[174]

---

162   72–73. "An adder...stung": Hermia concludes that a snake did, and did not, kill Lysander. A metaphorical snake—namely, Demetrius—did it, for no literal snake, even with a forked or duplicitous tongue, would ever do it. Demetrius is more murderous than a treacherous snake.

163   74. "spend": 1) expend, 2) waste.

164   74. "passion": emotion.

165   74. "misprised mood": mistaken anger.

166   78. "An if": even if (emphatic).

167   78. "therefore": for that, in return.

168   82. "vein": mood.

169   84. "So": thus (as I now feel).

170   84. "sorrow's...grow": while my sadness makes me drowsy, my drowsiness makes me sadder (a play on "heavy").

171   85. "For...owe": because of the sleeplessness that sorrow causes, sleep cannot pay with the rest it owes.

172   87. "his tender": sleep's offer (legal term for an offer to discharge a debt; see Henry Campbell Black, *A Law Dictionary, s.v.* tender).

173   87. "make...stay": wait awhile.

174   84–87. "So...stay": Demetrius uses the mercenary and legalistic

He lies down and sleeps.

Oberon: What hast thou done? Thou hast mistaken quite[175]
  And laid the love juice on some true-love's sight.
  Of thy misprision[176] must perforce ensue[177]   90
  Some true-love turned,[178] and not a false turned true.[179]
Puck: Then fate[180] o'er-rules, that,[181] one man holding troth,[182]
  A million fail, confounding oath on oath.[183,184]
Oberon: About the wood go swifter than the wind,
  And Helena of Athens[185] look thou find.   95

---

    metaphor of bankruptcy and legal repayment for his sorrow and sleeplessness. His most elaborate metaphor apart from when he wakes up influenced by the love juice (see 3.2.137–42), the trope transforms the language of love into the language of borrowed money.

175 88. "quite": completely.

176 90. "Of thy misprision": because of your mistake (of one thing for another).

177 90. "must...ensue": must unavoidably follow.

178 91. "turned": changed.

179 91. "false...true": The love juice may produce true as well as false love. For Oberon, it seems, true love is not so much love that is constant or returned as love of the proper person. It is true in its suitability at least as much as in its constancy, reciprocity, or source.

180 92. "fate": what usually occurs, what agrees with human nature.

181 92. "that": in that (see Abbott, §284).

182 92. "troth": faith.

183 93. "confounding...oath": breaking oath upon oath.

184 92–93. "Then...oath": According to Puck, faithless love is the virtually invariable rule; faithful love, the rare exception. Puck may have erred, but his mistake, he says, making light of it, fully comports with human nature.

185 95. "Helena of Athens": The name "Helena of Athens" strongly suggests Helen of Troy, who surpassed all others in beauty (see 1.1.180–81n). Oberon, who somehow knows Helena's name without having heard it, will, in effect, turn Helena of Athens into Helen of Troy. He will make her, in Demetrius' eyes, the most beautiful woman of Greece (see 4.1.169–70). Both Helens are identified by their fathers' names. As ancient writers call

All fancy-sick[186] she is and pale of cheer[187]
With sighs of love that costs[188] the fresh blood dear.[189]
By some illusion see thou[190] bring her here.
I'll charm his eyes against[191] she do appear.

100 *Puck*: I go, I go, look how I go!
Swifter than arrow from the Tartar's bow![192]

Exit.

Oberon: [*applying the juice to Demetrius' eyelids.*]
Flower of this purple dye,
Hit with Cupid's archery,
Sink in apple of his eye.[193]
105 When his love he doth espy,
Let her shine as gloriously

Helen of Troy by her patronymic "Tyndaris," "daughter of Tyn-darus" (see Homer, *Odyssey*, 24.199; Ovid, *Metamorphoses*, 15.233), Shakespeare introduces Helena as "Nedar's daughter, Helena" (1.1.107; see also 4.1.129). Both women are poor at choosing husbands.

186 97. "fancy-sick": lovesick.
187 96. "cheer": face, look.
188 97. "costs": Singular because a collective verb; also affected by "love" intervening between subject and verb. Common in Shakespeare; see Abbott, §247.
189 97. "sighs…dear": Sighing was thought to consume the heart's blood. "I will… breathe out mine [blood] / In sighs…" (George Chapman, *The Revenge of Bussy D'Ambois*, 1.1).
190 98. "see thou": make sure that you.
191 99. "against": in preparation for when (used metaphorically to express time; see Abbott, §142).
192 101. "Swifter…bow": "[Atalanta] Did fly as swift as arrow from a Turkey bow" (Ovid, *Metamorphoses*, 10.588; Golding, 10.687). The Tartars, made up of Turkic and Mongol elements, were fierce warriors famous for their powerful bows. Europeans often identified them as Turkey.
193 104. "apple…eye": 1) pupil, 2) what he most cherishes; see, further, 4.1.168–70n. On the omission of "the," see Abbott, §89.

As the Venus of the sky.[194]
When thou wak'st, if she be by,
Beg of her for remedy.

Enter Puck.

Puck:	Captain of our fairy band,	110
	Helena is here at hand,	
	And the youth, mistook by me,	
	Pleading for a lover's fee.[195]	
	Shall we their fond pageant[196] see?	
	Lord, what fools these mortals be![197]	115
Oberon:	Stand aside. The noise they make	
	Will cause Demetrius to awake.	
Puck:	Then will two at once woo one.	
	That must needs be sport alone.[198]	
	And those things do best please me	120
	That befall preposterously.[199]	

[They stand aside.]

---

194   107. "Venus...sky": The planet Venus is the brightest object in the sky other than the sun and the moon. Oberon borrows Demetrius' words of love for Hermia (see line 61n). In Demetrius' eyes, his new love may merely replace his old love, as happened before (see 1.1.106–10, 242–45). Helena may become Hermia "translated" (1.1.191).

195   113. "fee": reward, recompense.

196   114. "fond pageant": foolish spectacle ("pageant," a theatrical term, often refers to a stage play performed on the street).

197   115. "what...be": It is not hard to see why Puck identifies love and folly. But it is less obvious why he appears to limit the foolishness to mortals. He seems to overlook Titania's mad love of Bottom, which he has just recounted (lines 6–34).

198   119. "sport alone": 1) amusing in itself, 2) amusing above all else (see Abbott, §18).

199   121. "preposterously": 1) literally, when front and rear are reversed, 2) more generally, when things happen contrary to proper order.

Enter Lysander and Helena.

Lysander: Why should you think that I should woo in scorn?
    Scorn and derision never come in[200] tears.
    Look when[201] I vow, I weep; and vows so born,
125   In their nativity all truth appears.[202]
    How can these things in me seem scorn to you,
    Bearing the badge of faith[203] to prove them true?
Helena: You do advance[204] your cunning more and more.
    When truth kills truth, O devilish holy fray![205]
130   These vows are Hermia's. Will you give her o'er?[206]
    Weigh oath with oath and you will nothing weigh.[207]
    Your vows to her and me, put in two scales,[208]
    Will even[209] weigh, and both as light as tales.[210]
Lysander: I had no judgment when to her I swore.[211]

---

200   123. "in": with.
201   124. "when": whenever.
202   124–25. "vows…appears": vows born in tears are proved completely true by their tears. "[A]ll truth" means "nothing but truth."
203   127. "badge of faith": namely, tears (a "badge" is a distinguishing sign or mark). Lysander speaks as though tearfulness is always truthfulness in love.
204   128. "advance": show, exhibit.
205   129. "When…fray": Two vows amount to no vows. Lysander's vows to Helena, if true, destroy the truth of his vows to Hermia, and vice versa. One truth destroys the other, in a conflict ("fray") that is "holy" because it involves truths, but "devilish" because it destroys both truths.
206   130. "give her o'er": give her up.
207   131. "Weigh…weigh": balance your oaths to her and to me, and you will be balancing nothing against nothing (the image of a balance scale, with a balanced beam and two pans).
208   132. "scales": pans; see lines 131n.
209   133. "even": evenly.
210   133. "tales": pure fictions.
211   134. "I…swore": As when first declaring his love for her, Lysander unwittingly makes Helena's present point. Then, he said that reason guides his love (2.2.115). He was silent about his earlier vow to Hermia

Helena: Nor none, in my mind, now you give her o'er.   135
Lysander: Demetrius loves her, and he loves not you.[212]
Demetrius: (*waking up*) O Helen, goddess, nymph, perfect, divine![213]
    To what, my love, shall I compare thine eyne?[214]
    Crystal is muddy. O, how ripe in show[215]
    Thy lips, those kissing cherries, tempting grow!   140
    That pure congealed white, high Taurus' snow,
    Fanned with the eastern wind,[216] turns to a crow[217]
    When thou hold'st up thy hand. O, let me kiss
    This princess of pure white,[218] this seal of bliss![219]
Helena: O spite! O hell! I see you all are bent   145
    To set against me[220] for your merriment.
    If you were civil[221] and knew courtesy,[222]

---

    that "then end life when I end loyalty" (2.2.62). A vow promises to
    bind the future. By appealing then to reason and now to judgment for
    loving Helena, Lysander implicitly cancels not only his vow to Hermia,
    but vows as such. "[T]hen end life" becomes "unless reason says I
    made a mistake." Vows on Lysander's lips may be canceled by reason.
212 136. "Demetrius…you": Ironically, on his own principle, Lysander
    should love Hermia and not Helena, for the one but not the other
    loves him.
213 137. "O, Helen,…divine": Love's idealization rises to deification.
214 138. "eyne": eyes (archaic).
215 139. "ripe in show": full and red in appearance.
216 141–42. "high…wind": Taurus is a high mountain range in Asia,
    famously snowy (see Appian, *The Civil Wars*, 1.97). On the "blasts
    of the eastern wind" (Eurus) in that region, see Ammianus Mar-
    cellinus, *History*, 18.9.2.
217 142. "turns…crow": looks black (by contrast).
218 144. "princess…white": surpassing all others in whiteness
    ("princess" = "paragon").
219 144. "seal of bliss": promising to marry (by giving her hand).
    Under the influence of love juice, this "spotted and inconstant
    man" (1.1.110) no sooner falls in love than his hope turns to mar-
    riage, which he thinks of as bliss.
220 146. "set…me": attack me.
221 147. "civil": civilized, fit to live with others.
222 147. "courtesy": good manners.

You would not do me thus much injury.[223]
Can you not hate me, as I know you do,

150   But you must join in souls[224] to mock me too?
If you were men, as men you are in show,
You would not use a gentle[225] lady so,
To vow and swear and superpraise[226] my parts,[227]
When, I am sure, you hate me with your hearts.

155   You both are rivals and love Hermia,
And now both rivals to mock Helena.
A trim[228] exploit, a manly enterprise,
To conjure tears up[229] in a poor maid's eyes
With your derision! None of noble sort[230]

160   Would so offend a virgin and extort
A poor soul's patience,[231] all to make you sport.

Lysander: You are unkind, Demetrius. Be not so,
For you love Hermia—this you know I know.
And here with all goodwill, with all my heart,

165   In Hermia's love I yield you up my part
And yours of Helena to me bequeath,[232]
Whom I do love and will do till my death.

Helena: Never did mockers waste more idle[233] breath.

Demetrius: Lysander, keep thy Hermia. I will none.[234]

---

223   148. "do…injury": insult me so.
224   150. "in souls": 1) heartily, 2) together.
225   152. "gentle": 1) well born, 2) kind.
226   153. "superpraise": praise excessively.
227   153. "parts": qualities.
228   157. "trim": fine (ironical).
229   158. "conjure…up": bring tears up (as by a malevolent charm).
230   159. "sort": quality.
231   160–61. "extort…patience": torture a poor soul by forcing her to endure suffering.
232   166. "bequeath": transfer, yield.
233   168. "idle": 1) useless, 2) foolish.
234   169. "I will none": I do not want her.

If e'er I loved her, all that love is gone.[235]   170
My heart to her but as guest-wise sojourned,[236]
And now to Helen is it home returned,
There to remain.
Lysander: Helen, it is not so.
Demetrius: Disparage not the faith thou dost not know,
    Lest to thy peril thou aby it dear.[237]   175
    Look where thy love comes. Yonder is thy dear.[238]

Enter Hermia.

Hermia: Dark night, that from the eye his[239] function takes,
    The ear more quick of apprehension makes.
    Wherein it doth impair the seeing sense,
    It pays the hearing double recompense.   180
    Thou art not by mine eye, Lysander, found;
    Mine ear, I thank it, brought me to thy sound.
    But why unkindly didst thou leave me so?[240]

---

235   170. "If…gone": Despite having single-mindedly pursued Hermia, Demetrius now seems unsure that he ever loved her. As Lysander previously demonstrated (see 2.2.111n), a present love tends to obscure the memory of a past love.

236   171. "to her…sojourned": visited merely as a guest to her.

237   175. "aby it dear": pay for it dearly ("aby" is a shortening of "abye," that is, "to pay a price (for something)."

238   176. "thy dear": A shift in the sense of "dear" from "costly" (line 175) to "beloved"; see 1.1.249n. Lysander will pay dear by losing his dear.

239   177. "his": its (see 2.1.95n).

240   177–83. "Dark…so": Hermia, despite the urgency of her asking Lysander why he left her (see 2.2.155n), prefaces her one-line question with four lines describing the general tendency of one sense to make up for another and two lines on how that allowed her to find Lysander in the dark. Where Quince confounded the object of seeing and hearing (see 3.1.86n), Hermia, mentioning them in six alternate lines, carefully distinguishes the two senses according to their perceptional organs and their proper activities. Unlike for Quince (and Bottom), the unity does not destroy the plurality of the senses; see, further, 4.1.209–12n.

Lysander: Why should he stay whom love doth press to go?[241]

185　*Hermia*: What love could press Lysander from my side?

Lysander: Lysander's love, that would not let him bide,[242]

　　　　Fair Helena, who more engilds[243] the night

　　　　Than all yon fiery oes and eyes[244] of light.

　　　　Why seek'st thou me? Could not this make thee know

190　　　The hate I bear thee made me leave thee so?[245]

Hermia: You speak not as you think. It cannot be.

Helena: Lo, she is one of this confederacy!

　　　　Now I perceive they have conjoined all three

　　　　To fashion this false sport in spite of me.[246]

195　　　Injurious[247] Hermia,[248] most ungrateful maid,

241　184. "press to go": Hermia's last word to Lysander, responding to his vow to "end life when I end loyalty" (2.2.62), was "pressed": "with half that wish the wisher's eyes be pressed" (2.2,64). Lysander's eyes were soon pressed, however, by the love juice, and love now presses him to break his vow and leave. Hermia repeats the word in the next line.

242　186. "bide": remain.

243　187. "engilds": brightens with golden light.

244　188. "oes and eyes": stars. Notwithstanding Hermia' point about darkness (see lines 177–83), some things are more easily seen at night: the night's darkness adds to their brightness. Lysander, however, seems to confound seeing and its object. While "eyes" are organs of sight, "oes" are round ornamental spangles. In keeping with his tendency to see his life and love as letters (see 1.1.1.56n), Lysander puns on the letters "o" and "i."

245　189–90. "Could...so": Lysander does not say that he left Hermia because he loves Helena, but that he left her because he hates her. To Lysander, a past love is a present hate (see, further, 2.2.140–41n). Lysander also seems to think that his new passion speaks for itself, that Hermia should know it without his saying so much as a word (see, further, 2.2.134n).

246　194. "in...me": to spite me, in scorn of me.

247　195 "Injurious": insulting (see line 148n)

248　195. "Injurious Hermia": The rest of Helena's speech—the loquacious Helena's longest—is directed entirely to Hermia. Its subject is friendship. While prefaced by the accusation that Helena's

Have you conspired, have you with these[249] contrived,[250]
To bait[251] me with this foul derision?
Is all the counsel[252] that we two have shared,
The sisters' vows, the hours that we have spent
When we have chid the hasty-footed time   200
For parting us—O, is all forgot?[253]
All school-days' friendship, childhood innocence?
We, Hermia, like two artificial gods,[254]

---

friends are conspiring against her (lines 192–94), the speech is the play's fullest discussion of the union or oneness of friends. It has three parts. The first (lines 195–97) and last (lines 215–19) deal with the present and contain Helen's accusation that Hermia has joined the men in tormenting her. The second (lines 198–214) deals with the past and recounts the togetherness of the two women. While the opening and closing sections emphasize the opposition of "you" and "me," the central section, claiming that the women were once one, uses no singular pronoun and repeatedly speaks, instead, of "we," including "we two," "us," "our," and "both," particularly, "both one." Thematically, the crux of the speech lies in the natural ambiguity of the pronoun "we" (see, further, lines 208–14n). On "our" in the third section, see lines 215–19n.

249 196. "these": Helena never names either of the men anywhere in her speech. Earlier, she included them in "all three" (line 193). Here, she refers to them by the demonstrative pronoun "these." Later, she will be even less specific in using the generic "men" (line 216). Only the two women matter.

250 196. "contrived": plotted.

251 197. "bait": torment (as dogs attack a chained animal).

252 198. "all the counsel": all the confidences. Where Helena emphasized words prefixed by the connective "con" when describing the three conspirators (lines 192, 193, 196 [twice]), she now stresses the intimate word "counsel" in describing what she and Hermia had shared (see also 1.1.216, and line 308). And as she emphasized "all" in describing the three conspirators (line 193), she thrice stresses the word in describing what the women had shared (lines 198, 201, 202).

253 201. "all forgot": Friendship as well as love can be forgotten.

254 203. "artificial gods": The phrase has both an active and a passive meaning: 1) highly skilled in art, 2) made by art (see Abbott, §3).

Have with our needles created both one flower,
205 Both on one sampler,[255] sitting on one cushion,
Both warbling of one song, both in one key,[256]
As if our hands, our sides, voices, and minds
Had been incorporate.[257] So we grew together
Like to a double cherry, seeming parted,
210 But yet an union in partition,
Two lovely berries molded on one stem,
So with two seeming bodies but one heart,
Two of the first, like coats in heraldry,
Due but to one, and crowned with one crest.[258],[259]
215 And will you rent[260] our ancient love asunder,
To join with men in scorning your poor friend?

The sequel (lines 204–14), claiming that the girls came to resemble
what they did, illustrates the twin senses.
255 205. "sampler": piece of embroidery.
256 206. "in one key": in mental accord (their minds as well as their
voices were in the same key; see "voices, and minds," line 207).
257 208. "incorporate": one body.
258 213–14. "Two...crest": Helena uses terms of heraldry. "First" in
heraldic jargon refers to the color first mentioned in the formal description of a coat-of-arms. It is the "field" or the background of
the coat-of-arms. "Two of the first" means that the shield is divided
into equal halves of the first color, yet in another sense the shield
is not really divided because it is granted or belongs to one person:
"Due but to one, and crowned with one crest."
259 208–14. "So...crest": Helena, emphasizing their union, their oneness, depicts their separateness as only "seeming" (lines 209, 212;
cp. lines 201, 207). Yet she cannot emphasize their union without
at the same time acknowledging their separateness, their twoness.
She does, and does not, distinguish between one and two. Nor can
she. "We" implies both "union" and "partition"—both one and
two. The union is a union of parts, which must remain parts in
order for them to be parts of the union. The parts' pairing presupposes their apartness. Notwithstanding the inseparability that Helena tries to stress, "we"—"we two"—always means "you and I."
The pronoun is plural.
260 215. "rent": rend, tear.

It is not friendly, 'tis not maidenly.
Our sex, as well as I, may chide you for it,
Though I alone do feel the injury.[261]
Hermia: I am amazed[262] at your passionate words.   220
　　I scorn you not. It seems that you scorn me.
Helena: Have you not set Lysander, as in scorn,
　　To follow me and praise my eyes and face,
　　And made your other love,[263] Demetrius,
　　Who even but now[264] did spurn me with his foot,[265]   225
　　To call me goddess, nymph, divine and rare,
　　Precious, celestial? Wherefore speaks he this[266]
　　To her he hates? And wherefore doth Lysander
　　Deny your love,[267] so rich[268] within his soul,
　　And tender me, forsooth,[269] affection,   230
　　But by your setting on, by your consent?[270]
　　What though I be not so in grace[271] as you,
　　So hung upon with love,[272] so fortunate,
　　But miserable most, to love unloved?[273]

261　215–19. "And...injury": Helena, in the speech's final section, continues to group Hermia and herself, though differently now. Using "our" to opposite effects, she allies "Our sex" with herself ("I") in opposition to "you" in chiding Hermia for tearing "our ancient love" asunder. "Our" both unites and sets the women apart. Hermia is at once inside and outside the circle of "our."

262　220. "amazed": dumbfounded, stupefied (a very strong term).

263　224. "your...love": he who loves you.

264　225. "even but now": just now.

265　225. "spurn...foot": As she had asked him to do (see 2.2.205).

266　227. "Wherefore...this": why would he speak this.

267　229. "your love": his love for you.

268　229. "rich": plenteous, abundant.

269　230. "forsooth": truly, certainly (contemptuous).

270　231. "by your consent": as you wish, as you instigated.

271　232. "in grace": in favor.

272　233. "hung...love": clung to lovingly.

273　232–34. "What...unloved": Helena, once again, understands herself and her situation as a matter of comparison; see 2.2.97–98n.

235   This you should pity rather than despise.
   Hermia: I understand not what you mean by this.
   Helena: Ay, do. Persever,[274] counterfeit sad[275] looks,
      Make mouths upon[276] me when I turn my back,
      Wink at each other, hold the sweet jest up.[277]
240   This sport, well carried, shall be chronicled.[278]
      If you have any pity, grace,[279] or manners,
      You would not make me such an argument.[280]
      But fare you well. 'Tis partly my own fault,
      Which death or absence soon shall remedy.[281]
245 *Lysander*: Stay, gentle Helena. Hear my excuse,[282]
      My love, my life, my soul, fair Helena![283]
   Helena: O excellent!
   Hermia: Sweet, do not scorn her so.
   Demetrius: If she cannot entreat,[284] I can compel.

---

274 237. "Persever": persevere (stress on second syllable; see Abbott, §492).
275 237. "sad": serious.
276 238. "Make...upon": make jeering faces at.
277 239. "hold...up": keep up the trick you enjoy so much.
278 240. "This... chronicled": this performance, if you can keep it up, will be written up in history.
279 241. "grace": good will.
280 242. "such an argument": subject of such mockery.
281 243–44. "'Tis...remedy": Helena, abruptly stopping herself and bidding farewell, admits her partial blame for the mockery and makes what seems intended as an ominous threat or prediction. She does not specify her fault. Nor does she leave. Instead, she stays for another 100 lines (see lines 314–17n, and S.D. line 343), making one wonder whether her foreboding words are mere histrionics. A person who constantly cares about appearances, she is not above putting on a show. This is not the first time she has spoken of dying for love; see 2.2.243n
283 245. "my excuse": reason for you to excuse me.
284 246. "My...Helena": These are stronger terms of love than he ever used for Hermia; cp. 1.1.128, 179; 2.2.34.
284 248. "cannot entreat": prevail by entreating.

Lysander: Thou canst compel no more than she entreat.
Thy threats have no more strength than her weak prayers.[285] 250
Helen, I love thee. By my life, I do.
I swear by that which I will lose for thee,
To prove him false that says I love thee not.[286]
Demetrius: I say I love thee more than he can do.
Lysander: If thou say so, withdraw and prove it too.[287]   255
Demetrius: Quick, come!
Hermia: Lysander, whereto tends all this?
Lysander: Away, you Ethiope![288]
Demetrius: No, no. He'll
Seem[289] to break loose.[290] [*To Lysander.*] Take on as you would follow,
But yet come not.[291] You are a tame man, go![292]

---

285   250. "prayers": Editors commonly emend the texts' "praise," as needed by the antithesis to "threats," to match the preceding line's antithesis of "compel" and "entreat."

286   251–53. "Helen,…not": A triple negative: swearing as strongly as he can, Lysander swears by that which he will lose for Helena that he will loses it to prove him wrong who says he does not love her. His willing loss measures his love.

287   255. "withdraw…too": A challenge to prove it by dueling: Men may "fight for love" (2.1.241).

288   257. "Ethiope": As when he first fell in love with Helena, Lysander not only prefers the blonde to the brunette, but identifies the brunette with her looks and exaggerates them in extreme (see, further, 2.2.113n). The brunette Athenian becomes a black African (Ethiopian); see, further, line 263n.

289   257–58. "No,…/ Seem": The text is probably corrupt. For a survey of attempts to remedy the difficulties, see Furness, 155–56.

290   258. "Seem…loose": pretend to want to break free of Hermia (who is holding him to keep him from fighting; see line 335).

291   258–59. "Take,…not": act as if you really want to follow me, but, once free, you will not show up to fight.

292   259 "tame…, go": meek man, get lost. "Go" is a colloquial imperative expressing hostile dismissal.

260 *Lysander*: Hang off, thou cat, thou burr! Vile thing, let loose,
    Or I will shake thee from me like a serpent.
    Hermia: Why are you grown so rude?[293] What change is this,
    Sweet love?
    Lysander: Thy love? Out, tawny Tartar,[294] out!
    Out, loathed medicine! O, hated potion,[295] hence!
    Hermia: Do you not jest?
265 *Helena*:   Yes, sooth,[296] and so do you.[297]
    Lysander: Demetrius, I will keep my word[298] with thee.
    Demetrius: I would[299] I had your bond. For I perceive
    A weak bond[300] holds you. I'll not trust your word.[301]
    Lysander: What? Should I hurt her, strike her, kill her dead?
270   Although I hate her, I'll not harm her so.
    Hermia: What, can you do me greater harm than hate?
    Hate me? Wherefore? O me, what news,[302] my love?
    Am not I Hermia? Are not you Lysander?
    I am as fair now as I was erewhile.[303]
275   Since night you loved me; yet since night[304] you left me.

---

293 262. "rude": harsh, rough.

294 263. "tawny Tartar": Another insulting reference to Hermia's tan hair and coloring; for Tartar, see line 101n.

295 264. "medicine...potion": Any sort of drug, including poison (referring to her love for him).

296 265. "sooth": truly.

297 265. "Do...you": While the men, affected by the love juice, find nothing strange in their new situation, the women, who try to make sense of it, can understand it only as a cruel hoax, each with herself as the target.

298 266. "word": promise to fight with you.

299 267. "would": wish, would rather.

300 267–68. "bond...bond": The sense shifts from a signed contract to physical restraint (being held by Hermia).

301 267–68. "I...word": Hermia's weak restraint implies Lysander's weak courage and word.

302 272. "what news": what is the matter? what does this mean?

303 274. "erewhile": a short while ago.

304 275. "Since...night": The repeated phrase "since night" shifts from "at the beginning of this night" to "in the course of the night."

Why, then, you left me—O, the gods forbid!—
In earnest, shall I say?
Lysander: Ay, by my life,[305]
And never did desire to see thee more.
Therefore be out of hope, of question, of doubt.
Be certain, nothing truer, 'tis no jest   280
That I do hate thee and love Helena.
Hermia: O me! [*To Helena.*] You juggler![306] You canker-blossom![307]
You thief of love! What, have you come by night
And stolen my love's heart from him?
Helena: Fine, i'faith.
Have you no modesty, no maiden shame,[308]   285
No touch of bashfulness?[309] What, will you tear
Impatient answers from my gentle tongue?
Fie, fie, you counterfeit, you puppet,[310] you!
Hermia: "Puppet"? Why so? Ay, that way goes the game.

---

305   277. "by my life": Lysander swears most often and most strongly
      by his life; see lines 246, 251.
306   282. "juggler": trickster, deceiver.
307   282. "canker-blossom": cankerworm that eats the blossom (of
      love).
308   285. "modesty...shame": Unlike English, Greek has two words for
      shame. One word (*aidôs*), rooted in a sense of awe, is felt before,
      and warns against, an action. The other (*aischutê*), stemming from
      a sense of dishonor or disgrace, is felt after, and results from, an
      action (see, for example, 2.1.74). Helena combines both senses here.
      She explicitly refers to the protective sense of shame, but clearly
      suggests that Hermia should be ashamed for lacking it. The ab-
      sence of "maiden shame" is shameful.
309   284–86. "Fine,...bashfulness": Helena continues to believe that
      Hermia is conspiring with the men to deride her. Now, however,
      she thinks that the plot has reached new phase, with Hermia pre-
      tending to believe that Lysander loves Helena and that Helena has
      stolen his love away from her. With mock praise for her acting per-
      formance, she again accuses Hermia of lacking maidenly modesty
      or shame; see lines 217–19, and line 285n.
310   287. "you...puppet": you pretend to be a friend and a modest
      maiden; see, further, lines 289–90n.

290   Now I perceive[311] that she hath made compare[312]
Between our statures. She hath urged her height,
And with her personage,[313] her tall personage,
Her height, forsooth,[314] she hath prevailed with him.
And are you grown so high in his esteem
295   Because I am so dwarfish and so low?
How low am I, thou painted maypole?[315] Speak!
How low am I?[316] I am not yet so low
But that my nails can reach unto thine eyes.
Helena: I pray you, though you mock me, gentlemen,
300   Let her not hurt me. I was never curst.[317]
I have no gift at all in shrewishness.
I am a right[318] maid for my cowardice.
Let her not strike me. You perhaps may think,
Because she is something[319] lower than myself,

---

311 289–90. "'Puppet,'…perceive": Hermia thinks that Helena's insult suddenly makes everything clear; see, further, lines 289–97n. "Puppet" derives from "poppet," meaning, originally, a small person or figure; see *OED, s.v.* Puppet.

312 290. "compare": comparison. On converting a verb into a noun, see Abbott, §451.

313 292. "personage": personal appearance.

314 293. "forsooth": in truth (contemptuous).

315 296. "painted maypole": A double insult: "painted" means colored over, feigned, phony; "maypole" means overly tall and skinny (see Dent, M778).

316 289–97. "'Puppet,'…I": Hermia, misunderstanding Helena's insult and, taking "puppet" literally to mean a small person or small figure (see lines 289–90n), makes the further mistake of concluding that Helen won Lysander's love by comparing their heights. She then compounds her error by taking her own literal understanding figuratively. If being a puppet means being short, being tall means being held in high esteem. According to Hermia's hermeneutics, littleness is tantamount to lowliness. Hermia's erroneous suspicion may reflect her recognition of Helena's characteristic tendency to compare the two.

317 300. "curst": shrewish, quarrelsome.

318 302. "right": downright, real (see Abbott, §19).

319 304. "something": somewhat.

That I can match[320] her.
Hermia: "Lower"? Hark, again!   305
Helena: Good Hermia, do not be so bitter with me.
    I evermore did love you, Hermia,
    Did ever keep your counsels,[321] never wronged you,
    Save that, in love unto Demetrius,
    I told him of your stealth[322] unto this wood.   310
    He followed you. For love, I followed him.
    But he hath chid me hence[323] and threatened me
    To strike me, spurn me, nay, to kill me too.[324]
    And now, so[325] you will let me quiet go,
    To Athens will I bear my folly back   315
    And follow you no further. Let me go.
    You see how simple and how fond[326] I am.[327]
Hermia: Why, get you gone. Who is't that hinders you?
Helena: A foolish heart that I leave here behind.
Hermia: What, with Lysander?
Helena: With Demetrius.   320
Lysander: Be not afraid. She shall not harm thee, Helena.
Demetrius: No, sir, she shall not, though you take her part.[328]

---

320   305. "can match": am a match for (in a fight).
321   308. "counsels": confidences.
322   310. "stealth": stealing away.
323   312. "chid me hence": tried to drive me away by scolding.
324   309–13. "Save...too": Helena tries to excuse or at least to extenuate her lapse of confidence by claiming that it was an act of love which painfully failed. Both love and painful failure tend to excuse, she suggests. Owing to the one, she could not help doing what she did. Owing to the other, she gained nothing but regret. See, further, 1.1.250–51n.
325   315. "so": provided that.
326   317. "fond": foolish.
327   314–17. "And...am": Helena earlier announced her departure, while admitting some partial (and unspecified) fault, but made no effort to leave (see lines 243–44n). Now, she specifies her fault and asks permission to leave, but again remains (see S.D. line 343).
328   321–22. "Be...part": Both men think that they need to reassure He-

Helena: O, when she is angry, she is keen and shrewd.[329]
She was a vixen[330] when she went to school,
325   And though she be but little, she is fierce.[331]
Hermia: "Little" again? Nothing but "low" and "little"?
Why will you suffer her to flout[332] me thus?
Let me come to her!
Lysander: Get you gone, you dwarf,
You minimus[333] of hindering knotgrass[334] made,
You bead, you acorn.
330 *Demetrius*:   You are too officious[335]
In her behalf that scorns your services.
Let her alone. Speak not of Helena.
Take not her part. For if thou dost intend[336]
Never so little show of love to her,
Thou shalt aby[337] it.
335 *Lysander*:   Now she holds me not.[338]

---

lena of her safety (see lines 299–305). While Lysander tells her that
Hermia will not harm her, Demetrius, in effect challenging
Lysander, says that Hermia will not harm her even if Lysander
takes Helena's part: Demetrius is the only protector she needs.
329 323. "keen and shrewd": bitter and malicious.
330 324. "vixen": ill-tempered quarrelsome woman (the word for a she-fox).
331 323–25. "O,...fierce": Helena's initial complaint emphasized the
two women's former likeness and closeness (see lines 198–219 and
nn). But once Lysander says that he is not jesting and Hermia
blames Helena for stealing his heart (lines 277–84), the two women
stress only their differences in character and temper as well as in
height. In friendship, they see only sameness; in anger, only difference. And they exaggerate both.
332 327. "suffer...flout": allow her to mock.
333 329. "minimus": smallest, most insignificant creature
334 329. "knotgrass": low-growing weed whose juice was supposed to
stunt growth.
335 330. "officious": unduly eager.
336 333. "intend": 1) have in mind, 2) pretend.
337 335. "aby": pay dearly for; see line 175n.
338 335. "she...not": See line 258n.

Now follow, if thou dar'st, to try whose right,
Of thine or mine, is most in Helena.[339]
Demetrius: "Follow"? Nay, I'll go with thee, cheek by jowl.[340]

      Exeunt Demetrius and Lysander.

Hermia: You, mistress, all this coil is long of you.[341]
 Nay, go not back.
Helena: I will not trust you, I,   340
 Nor longer stay in your curst[342] company.
 Your hands than mine are quicker for a fray.[343]
 My legs are longer though, to run away.

        Exit.

Hermia: I am amazed and know not what to say.[344]

        Exit.

Oberon: (*to Puck*) This is thy negligence. Still thou mistak'st, 345
 Or else committ'st thy knaveries willfully.[345]
Puck: Believe me, king of shadows,[346] I mistook.

---

339 336–37. "try…Helena": The men originally argued the rival claims of the right of ancestral law and of love (see 1.1.104–5n). Now Lysander challenges Demetrius to a trial by combat in which manly courage is to decide whose right is stronger.

340 338. "cheek by jowl": cheek by cheek, side by side ("jowl" = jaw); proverbial, see Dent C263. The two schoolgirls sitting side by side has been replaced by the two suitors fighting side by side. War may indeed be part of love; see 1.1.169–71n.

341 339. "all…you": all this turmoil is on account of you. Hermia seems not to notice that her accusation—"long" in the sense of "caused by"—suggests the very sneer that she hates and has threatened to punish.

342 341. "curst": quarrelsome; see line 300n.

343 342. "fray": fight.

344 344. "know…say": The only time Hermia is at a loss for words.

345 345–46. "Still…willfully": you always blunder or else perform your mischievous pranks on purpose; see, further, lines 355–59n.

346 347. "shadows": spirits (fairies).

Did not you tell me I should know the man
By the Athenian garments he had on?[347]

350 And so far[348] blameless proves my enterprise
That I have 'nointed[349] an Athenian's eyes.
And so far am I glad it so did sort,[350]
As[351] this their jangling[352] I esteem a sport.[353]

Oberon: Thou seest these lovers seek a place to fight.

355 Hie,[354] therefore, Robin, overcast the night.
The starry welkin[355] cover thou anon
With drooping fog as black as Acheron,[356]
And lead these testy[357] rivals so astray
As[358] one come not within another's way.[359]

360 Like to Lysander[360] sometime frame thy tongue,
Then stir Demetrius up with bitter wrong.[361]
And sometime rail thou like Demetrius.
And from each other look thou lead them thus,

---

347 345–49. "This...on": The first five lines of Oberon and Puck's exchange are in blank verse.

348 350. "so far": to that extent.

349 351. "'nointed": anointed.

350 352. "sort": turn out.

351 353. "As": because.

352 353. "jangling": wrangling, quarreling.

353 347–53. "Believe...sport": Notwithstanding his claim to innocence, Puck declares that he is delighted with his error.

354 355. "Hie": hurry.

355 356. "welkin": sky.

356 357. "Acheron": Acheron in classical mythology is the black river in the underworld across which Charon ferries the newly dead to reach Hades (see Virgil, *Aeneid*, 6.295–330).

357 358. "testy": irritable, peevish, short-tempered.

358 359. "As": that.

359 355–59. "Hie,...way": Unlike Puck, who cares only for the folly of the lovers' quarrels and not how the duel might end, Oberon wants to avoid a real fight between the men. He cares about people and the effects of his actions on them.

360 360. "Like to Lysander": just like the voice of Lysander.

361 361. "wrong": unfair accusations.

Till o'er their brows death-counterfeiting sleep
With leaden legs and batty[362] wings doth creep.   365
Then crush this herb into Lysander's eye,
Whose liquor[363] hath this virtuous[364] property,
To take from thence all error with his might[365]
And make his eyeballs roll with wonted sight.[366]
When they next wake, all this derision[367]   370
Shall seem a dream and fruitless vision.[368]
And back to Athens shall the lovers wend,
With league whose date[369] till death shall never end.[370]
Whiles I in this affair do thee employ,
I'll to my queen and beg her Indian boy,   375
And then I will her charmed[371] eye release
From monster's view, and all things shall be peace.
Puck: My fairy lord, this must be done with haste,
For night's swift dragons[372] cut the clouds full fast,

---

362 365. "batty": bat-like.
363 367. "liquor": juice.
364 367. "virtuous": powerful, efficacious (inherent quality).
365 368. "with his might": by its power.
366 369. "with wonted sight": Literally an antidote, the drug will end
      Lysander's doting over Helena and return him to his accustomed
      sense of sight.
367 370. "derision": derisible activity.
368 370–71. "When…vision": While a dream mistakes a likeness for
      something real, the lovers will mistake something real for a like-
      ness. Rather than see a dream as unreal when they awake (see
      2.2.144–49n), they will see what was real as a dream.
369 373. "league…date": union whose duration.
370 372–73. "And…end": We must wonder whether Oberon knows of
      Egeus' (and Theseus') ban on Hermia's marrying Lysander, or
      whether he expects it to be waived.
371 376. "charmed": bewitched.
372 379. "night's…dragons": In Greek mythology, Night (Nyx) lives in
      Tartarus, the deepest and darkest part in the Underworld, from
      which she emerges at dusk, then passes swiftly across the sky,
      spreading her dragon wings of darkness over the world, and fi-
      nally returns to Tartarus at dawn (see Hesiod, *Theogony*, 744–58).

380   And yonder shines Aurora's harbinger,[373]
       At whose approach, ghosts wandering here and there
       Troop home to churchyards. Damned spirits all,
       That in crossways and floods have burial,[374]
       Already to their wormy beds are gone.
385   For fear lest day should look their shames upon,[375]
       They willfully themselves exile from light
       And must for aye[376] consort[377] with black-browed night.[378]
Oberon: But we are spirits of another sort.

Puck, "that merry wanderer of the night" (2.1.42), treats the night not as the absence of daylight, but as something existing in its own right. Drawn across the sky in a chariot pulled by dragons, it is a presence, not a privation. For "swift night," see Homer, *Iliad*, 14.261.

373   380. "Aurora's harbinger": dawn's herald (namely, Venus, the morning star). Aurora is the Latin name of Eos, the pre-Olympian goddess of dawn (see Hesiod, *Theogony*, 371–73; Virgil, *Aeneid*, 4.585). A harbinger is a forerunner, who goes ahead and announces the approach of someone or something.

374   383–84. "Damned...burial": all the ghosts of the damned, who are buried at crossroads or underwater (rather than in consecrated grounds). Canon law denies suicides Christian burial. "[A divine service] is not to be used for any that...have laid violent hands upon themselves" (Anonymous, 1559, *Book of Common Prayer*, 451).

375   385. "look...upon": look upon that of which they ought to be ashamed. Elizabethan authors often use the plural when an abstract noun applies to more than one person. On the transposition of prepositions, see Abbott, §203.

376   387. "for aye": forever.

377   387. "consort": keep company.

378   380–87. "And...night": Puck distinguishes two kinds of ghosts or spirits, both Christian: those buried in churchyards and those buried in unsanctified grounds. Both wander at night and flee the sunlight. But while the former troop home as the morning star draws near, the latter are already in bed by then. Driven by shame as well as damned because they are suicides, they "willfully" disappear before the first light of dawn.

I with the Morning's love[379] have oft made sport[380]
And, like a forester,[381] the groves may tread   390
Even till[382] the eastern gate, all fiery red,
Opening on Neptune[383] with fair blessed beams,
Turns into yellow gold his salt-green[384] streams.[385]
But notwithstanding, haste! Make no delay.
We may effect this business yet ere day.   395

Exit.

Puck: Up and down, up and down,
                 I will lead them up and down.
                 I am feared in field and town.
                 Goblin,[386] lead them up and down.[387]
                 Here comes one.   400

---

379   389. "the Morning's love": The mighty hunter Cephalus, after
      whom Aurora, the goddess of morning, lusted, but who remained
      faithful to his wife (see Ovid, *Metamorphoses*, 7.672–862); see, fur-
      ther, 5.1.196–97n.
380   389. "oft made sport": hunted in the early morning.
381   390. "forester": "Forester is an officer of the Forest…sworn to pre-
      serve the Vert and Venison,…and to attend upon the wild beasts"
      (John Manwood, *Laws of the Forest*, 162). He protects the game by
      keeping watch for poachers at night.
382   391. "Even till": until ("even" emphasizes that the time is ex-
      tremely late in comparison with that of other spirits and ghosts);
      see, further, lines 388–93n.
383   392. "Neptune": the sea (a personification).
384   393. "salt-green": sea-green.
385   388–93. "But…streams": Oberon boasts that, unlike the spirits that
      Puck described, he does not have to flee the first light of day. Yet,
      notwithstanding Titania's accusation that he sat "all day" (2.1.66)
      with Phillida, he also seems to say that he too must avoid the full
      light of day; see, further, 4.1.95–96n.
386   399. "Goblin": one of Puck's names; see 2.2.40–41n.
387   396–99. "Up…down": An incantation, presumably to produce the
      blinding fog. The lines are in prose in the Second Quarto and the
      Folio.

Enter Lysander.

Lysander: Where art thou, proud Demetrius? Speak thou now.
Puck: Here, villain, drawn[388] and ready. Where art thou?
Lysander: I will be with thee straight.[389]
Puck: Follow me, then
To plainer[390] ground.

                                        Exit Lysander.

Enter Demetrius.

Demetrius: Lysander, speak again.
405   Thou runaway, thou coward, art thou fled?
       Speak! In some bush? Where dost thou hide thy head?
Puck: Thou coward, art thou bragging to the stars,
       Telling the bushes that thou look'st for wars,
       And wilt not come? Come, recreant![391] Come, thou child![392]
410   I'll whip thee with a rod.[393] He is defiled
       That draws a sword on thee.[394]
Demetrius: Yea, art thou there?
Puck: Follow my voice. We'll try no manhood here.[395]

                                        Exeunt.

Enter Lysander.

Lysander: He goes before me and still dares me on.

---

388   402. "drawn": with drawn sword.
389   403. "straight": straightaway, right away.
390   403. "plainer": smoother, flatter, more open.
391   409. "recreant": quitter, coward.
392   409. "thou child": a child and not a man; see, further line 410n.
393   410. "rod": instrument of punishment, especially for a child.
394   410–11. "He...thee": anyone who treats you like a man by drawing a sword against you disgraces himself.
395   412. "try...here": Puck, who will suggest nothing of the sort to Lysander, describes the fight to Demetrius as a test of manhood; see, further, lines 401–30n.

When I come where he calls, then he is gone.
The villain is much lighter-heeled than I.   415
I followed fast, but faster he did fly,
That[396] fallen am I in[397] dark uneven way,[398]
And here will rest me.

He lies down.

Come, thou gentle day,
For if but once thou show me thy gray light,
I'll find Demetrius and revenge this spite.[399]   420

Sleeps.

Enter Puck and Demetrius.

Puck: Ho, ho, ho! Coward, why com'st thou not?
Demetrius: Abide[400] me, if thou dar'st, for well I wot[401]
        Thou runn'st before me, shifting every place,
        And dar'st not stand[402] nor look me in the face.
        Where art thou now?
Puck: Come hither. I am here.   425
Demetrius: Nay, then, thou mock'st me. Thou shalt buy this dear[403]
        If ever I thy face by daylight see.
        Now go thy way. Faintness constraineth me
        To measure out my length[404] on this cold bed.

[Lies down.]

---

396   417. "That": so that.
397   417. "in": into.
398   417. "uneven way": unlevel ground.
399   420. "spite": bad fortune.
400   422. "abide": wait for, face.
401   422. "wot": know.
402   424. "stand": make a stand.
403   426. "buy this dear": pay dearly for this.
404   429. "measure...length": lie stretched out.

430　By day's approach look to be visited.[405],[406]

[Sleeps.]

Enter Helena.

Helena: O weary night, O long and tedious night,
　　　Abate[407] thy hours! Shine, comforts, from the east,
　　　That I may[408] back to Athens by daylight
　　　From these that my poor company detest.
435　　And sleep, that sometimes shuts up sorrow's eye,
　　　Steal me awhile from mine own company.[409]

[Lies down and sleeps.]

Puck:　　　Yet but three? Come one more.
　　　　　　Two of both kinds makes up four.
　　　　　　Here she comes, curst[410] and sad.
440　　　　　Cupid is a knavish lad
　　　　　　Thus to make poor females mad.[411]

405　430. "look...visited": expect to be attacked.
406　401–30. "Where...visited": Puck's illusive actions, while averting a duel, highlight a characteristic difference between Lysander and Demetrius. When Lysander, who comes ready to fight (lines 401–3), thinks Demetrius has slipped away, he generously praises his rival and blames himself for not being swift enough to keep up with him (lines 415–16). But when Lysander goes off to fight, Demetrius accuses him of being too unmanly to face him (lines 405–6). Puck, accordingly, addresses each man differently. While simply bidding Lysander to follow him to more level or more open ground (lines 403–4), he challenges Demetrius' manhood while accusing him of being a vain braggart (lines 407–9). See, further, 1.1.104–5n.
407　432. "Abate": shorten.
408　433. "may": may go (idiomatic omission of the verb of motion).
409　435–36. "sleep...company": If being awake is to be in one's own company, being asleep may make possible getting away and being secluded from oneself ("steal" has the sense of a furtive action).
410　439. "curst": angry, ill-tempered.
411　437–41. "Yet,...mad": Puck makes no distinction among the lovers,

Enter Hermia.

Hermia: Never so weary, never so in woe,
   Bedabbled with the dew and torn with briers,
   I can no further crawl, no further go.
   My legs can keep no pace with my desires.   445
   Here will I rest me till the break of day.

                                   [*Lies down.*]

Heavens shield Lysander if they mean a fray![412]

                                      [*Sleeps.*]

Puck: On the ground
                  Sleep sound.
                  I'll apply   450
                  To your eye,
            Gentle lover,[413] remedy.

         [*Applies the antidote to Lysander's eyes.*]

               When thou wak'st,
               Thou tak'st

As before (lines 118–21), they are just numbers or ciphers. But having been chastised by Oberon (see lines 345–46n), Puck now seems to care about a proper ending, not a foolish chase. Distancing himself from his former actions, he blames Cupid for doing what he himself said he most enjoys doing (see lines 119n, 121n). And closely repeating the word that Oberon used to blame him (line 346), he describes Cupid pejoratively with the very word ("knavish") which he proudly claimed as his own (see 2.1.33, 42). These are the first signs of change in Puck; see, further, 5.1.357–60n.

412   447. "Heavens…fray": It is unclear whether Hermia is trying to return to Athens (like Helena) or trying to find Lysander. Despite everything, however, she evidently still loves him and prays for his protection.

413   452. "Gentle lover": Cp. what Puck called Lysander when he applied the love juice (see 2.2.76n, 77n). This is Puck's first sweet-sounding chant.

455 True delight
In the sight
Of thy former lady's eye.
And the country proverb known,
That every man should take his own,
460 In your waking shall be shown.
Jack shall have Jill;
Naught shall go ill;
The man shall have his mare[414] again, and all shall be well.[415]

Exit.

---

414   463. "his mare": a bawdy metaphor for the women having sex.
415   459–63. "That…well": Puck's closing charm consists of three proverbs stating that everything will end well, that everyone will be happy (see Dent, M209, A164, and A153). Although seeming now to welcome their happiness, he again speaks of the lovers in an impersonal way, never mentioning them by name: "Jack" and "Jill" mean "every man" and "every woman" (see lines 437–41n). Most importantly, he leaves the love juice on Demetrius' eyes, knowing that the happiness of Demetrius and Helena rests on its never being removed.

Act Four, Scene One

[The wood. The four lovers at a distance lying asleep.]
Enter [Titania,] Queen of Fairies, and [Bottom the] Clown and Fairies
[Peaseblossom, Cobweb, Moth, Mustardseed, and others];
and the King, [Oberon], behind them.

Titania: Come, sit thee down upon this flowery bed,
  While I thy amiable cheeks do coy,[1]
  And stick muskroses[2] in thy sleek smooth head,
  And kiss thy fair large ears, my gentle joy.
Bottom: Where's Peaseblossom?   5
Peaseblossom: Ready.
Bottom: Scratch my head, Peaseblossom. Where's
  Monsieur Cobweb?
Cobweb: Ready.
Bottom: Monsieur Cobweb, good monsieur, get you your   10
  weapons in your hand and kill me a red-hipped
  humble-bee on the top of a thistle, and, good monsieur,
  bring me the honey-bag. Do not fret yourself
  too much in the action, monsieur, and, good monsieur,
  have a care the honey-bag break not; I would   15
  be loath to have you overflown with a honey-bag,
  signior. Where's Monsieur Mustardseed?
Mustardseed: Ready.
Bottom: Give me your neaf,[3] Monsieur Mustardseed. Pray
  you, leave your courtesy,[4] good monsieur.[5]   20

---

1   2. "thy...coy": caress your lovely cheeks.
2   3. "muskroses": roses decorating Titania's bower; see 2.1.252n.
3   19. "neaf": fist, hand; see, further, lines 1–20n.
4   20. "leave...courtesy": stop your bowing and scraping; see, further,
     lines 1–20n.
5   1–20. "Come,... monsieur": Bottom, oblivious to Titania's beauty
     and desire, pays her no attention and, instead, addresses the fairies

Mustardseed: What's your will?

Bottom: Nothing, good monsieur, but to help Cavalery[6]
Cobweb to scratch.[7] I must to the barber's, monsieur,
for methinks I am marvail's[8] hairy about the
25   face. And I am such a tender ass, if my hair do but
tickle me, I must scratch.

Titania: What, wilt thou hear some music, my sweet love?

Bottom: I have a reasonable good ear in music. Let's have
the tongs and the bones.[9]

30   *Titania*: Or say, sweet love, what thou desirest to eat?

Bottom: Truly, a peck of provender.[10] I could munch your
good dry oats. Methinks I have a great desire to a

---

whom she has ordered to be kind and courteous to him (3.1.157–
67). At once consort of the fairy queen and a good democrat, Bottom attempts to be affable to the fairies while giving them orders.
Besides ordering the homey styptic Cobweb (see 3.1.176–77n) to
become a brave hunter (lines 10–17), he addresses Cobweb and
Mustardseed as French, Spanish or Italian men of high rank
("monsieur" [lines 8, 10 (twice), 14 (twice), 17, 19, 20, 22, 23], "Cavalery" [line 22] and "signior" [line17]), and wants them not to
bother too much for him or to hurt themselves in any way. And
contradicting Titania's express order (3.1.157), he tells them to stop
their bowing and scraping and shake his hand instead (lines 19n
and 20n).

6   22. "Cavalery": Bottom's attempt at the Italian or Spanish form of
the title of a Cavalier ("Cavaliere," "Caballero"), designating a gentleman trained to arms.

7   22–23. "help...scratch": Despite paying close attention to the
fairies' names here and when he first met them (see 3.1.172–89nn),
Bottom confuses Peaseblossom's and Cobweb's names; cp. lines
7–13.

8   24. "marvail's": marvelous.

9   29. "the tongs...bones": Crude percussion music. Tongs are struck
by a piece of metal, like the modern triangle. Bones are flat pieces
of bone rattled together between two fingers, producing a sound
like musical spoons.

10   31. "peck of provender": quarter of a bushel of dry food (specifically for beasts).

bottle[11] of hay. Good hay, sweet hay, hath no fellow.[12]
Titania: I have a venturous fairy that shall seek
    The squirrel's hoard and fetch thee new nuts.   35
Bottom: I had rather have a handful or two of dried peas.
    But, I pray you, let none of your people stir[13] me;
    I have an exposition of[14] sleep come upon me.
Titania: Sleep thou, and I will wind thee in my arms.
    Fairies, begone, and be all ways[15] away.   40

                          [Exeunt Fairies.]

    So doth the woodbine the sweet honeysuckle
    Gently entwist; the female ivy so
    Enrings the barky fingers of the elm.[16]
    O, how I love thee! How I dote on thee!

                  [Bottom and Titania sleep.]

            Enter Puck

Oberon: [*coming forward*] Welcome, good Robin. Seest thou this
    sweet sight?   45
    Her dotage now I do begin to pity.
    For, meeting her of late[17] behind the wood,[18]

---

11   33. "bottle": small bundle.
12   33. "fellow": equal. "Asses would prefer hay to gold" (Heraclitus, frag. 9).
13   37. "stir": disturb.
14   38. "exposition of": disposition (inclination) for.
15   40. "all ways": in every direction.
16   41–42. "So...elm": This is the only embrace in the play. The embrace, however, is entirely one-sided. Bottom wishes only to sleep. He sleeps with Titania only in the literal sense. Bottom's insensibility to Titania's beauty and desire spares her the degradation of the women who sleep with asses in some traditional writings (for example, Lucian, *Lucius or the Ass*, 50ff.; Apuleius, *The Golden Ass*, 10.19ff.). For the image of the female ivy leaning on an elm which supports it, see Catullus, *Carmina*, 62.54.
17   47. "of late": recently.
18   47. "of...wood": It is not at all clear when or where this exchange might have taken place.

Seeking sweet favors[19] for this hateful fool,
I did upbraid her and fall out[20] with her.
50   For she his hairy temples then had rounded[21]
With[22] coronet[23] of fresh and fragrant flowers;
And that same dew, which sometime[24] on the buds
Was wont to[25] swell like round and orient[26] pearls,
Stood now within the pretty flouriets'[27] eyes,
55   Like tears that did their own disgrace bewail.[28]
When I had at my pleasure taunted her,
And she in mild terms begged my patience,
I then did ask of her her changeling child,
Which straight she gave me, and her fairy sent
60   To bear him to my bower in fairyland.
And now I have the boy, I will undo
This hateful imperfection of her eyes.[29]

---

19   48. "favors": flowers as love tokens.

20   49. "fall out": quarrel.

21   50. "rounded": surrounded, encircled.

22   51. "With": with the (see Abbott, §89).

23   51. "coronet": garland.

24   52. "sometime": formerly.

25   53. "Was...to": used to.

26   53. "orient": 1) sparkling, lustrous, 2) from the East. Pearls from the seas around India were considered the most beautiful, and their special sheen is called its "orient."

27   54. "flouriets": flowerets (small flowers).

28   55. "disgrace bewail": dishonor lament (for decorating a head so repulsive).

29   46–62. "Her...eyes": Titania said that she keeps the Indian boy for his mother's sake and will not give him up for all of fairyland (2.1.122–37), but now she gives him up without a thought for the boy or his mother. And now that Oberon has the boy, he loses interest in him right away. Neither he nor Titania ever mentions the boy again. What accounts for the change? Oberon and Titania were initially jealous of each other's loves—Oberon of Titania's love for Theseus, and Titania of his loves of Hippolyta and others (see 2.1.64–80nn). The boy—a "changeling" in more than one sense—served as a substitute for the true object of their jealousies. Bottom,

And, gentle Puck, take this transformed scalp
From off the head of this Athenian swain,[30]
That he, awaking when the other[31] do,   65
May all[32] to Athens back again repair[33]
And think no more of this night's accidents[34]
But as the fierce vexation[35] of a dream.[36]
But first I will release the fairy queen.

[*Squeezes the juice on her eyes.*]

Be as thou wast wont to be.   70
See as thou wast wont to see.[37]

---

however, has, by chance, ended the conflict. Consumed by her love for him, Titania is no longer jealous of Oberon's wanderings. Only Bottom now matters to her. At the same time, the contemptible object of Titania's dotage arouses Oberon's pity, which quashes his jealously. Bottom, unlike Theseus, is not a rival, and Oberon could never consider him one. Oberon's plan has worked, but not in the way or for the reason he might have expected. Its success rests on Puck's unauthorized and unforeseen transformation of Bottom's head, which rested in turn on a series of accidents and chance events, including Quince's pointless alteration of the "Pyramus and Thisbe" plot (see 3.1.81–82n). Pure chance permits Oberon's plan to succeed and reconciles the royal couple.

30 64. "swain": 1) lover, 2) lout.
31 65. "other": others (for "other" as a plural, see Abbott, §12).
32 66. "May all": all may.
33 66. "repair": return.
34 67. "accidents": happenings (with the sense of happening by chance and without expectation).
35 68. "fierce vexation": wild agitation.
36 67–68. "think...dream": As we saw before, Oberon intends them to reverse a dream. Instead of taking a resemblance for the reality, they will take the reality for its resemblance. They will, in effect, dream that they had been dreaming; see 3.2.370–71n.
37 70–71. "Be...see": As fits a chant restoring Titania to herself, the first pair of lines of Oberon's chant—each strictly parallel to the other, each opening and closing with the same word, and each echoing both itself and the other—couples as well as rhymes "to

Dian's bud o'er Cupid's flower
Hath such force and blessed power.[38]
Now, my Titania,[39] wake you, my sweet queen.

75 *Titania*: [*waking*] My Oberon, what visions have I seen!
Methought I was enamored of an ass.
Oberon: There lies your love.[40]
Titania: How came these things to pass?
O, how mine eyes do loathe his visage now!
Oberon: Silence awhile.[41] Robin, take off this head.

80 Titania, music call; and strike more dead
Than common sleep[42] of all these five[43] the sense.
Titania: Music, ho, music such as charmeth sleep!
Puck: [*Removing the ass-head from Bottom*]
Now, when thou wak'st, with thine own fool's eyes peep.[44]

---

be" and "to see": to be as one is wont to be means to see as one is
wont to see. To be oneself means to see as oneself.

38   72–73. "Dian's...power": "Dian's bud" is the bud of the Agnus
Castus or Chaste Tree. "That is Diane, the goddess of chastity, /
And for because that she a maiden is, / In her hand the branch she
beareth, this / That *agnus castus* men call properly" (Anonymous,
The Floure and the Leafe, 472–75). Just as the moon's chaste beams
were able to quench Cupid's fiery arrow (2.1.155–64n), Diana's
bud—doting's antidote—has the force and divine power to subdue
the flower that Cupid's arrow wounded.

39   74. "my Titania": Love claims possession of its object: see also "my
sweet queen" [line 74], "My Oberon" [line 75]; and see, further,
2.1.193n. This is the first time Oberon speaks endearingly to Titania.

40   75–77. "My...love": In contrast to his concealing the night's events
from the young lovers by turning them into a dream, Oberon con-
firms the reality of the visions that Titania has seen. Her vision was
not a dream. But see 5.1.77n.

41   79. "Silence awhile": Presumably addressed to the fairies serving
Oberon, so they do not wake the young lovers or Bottom.

42   80–81. "strike...sleep": far deeper than ordinary sleep. "Strike"
refers to "the sense."

43   81. "these five": the lovers and Bottom.

44   83. "Now,...peep": Bottom's eyes, like Titania's, will return to their

142

Oberon: Sound music!

Music.

Come, my queen, take hands with me,

And rock the ground whereon these sleepers be.[45]   85

[*Titania and Oberon dance.*]

Now thou and I are new in amity,
And will tomorrow midnight solemnly[46]
Dance in Duke Theseus' house triumphantly,[47]
And bless it to all fair posterity.[48]
There shall the pairs of faithful lovers be   90
Wedded, with Theseus, all in jollity.[49]

Puck: Fairy king, attend and mark.
     I do hear the morning lark.

---

accustomed way of seeing. It is hard to be sure whether Bottom sees more foolishly with an ass's eyes or his own. In some respects he is never more sensible than when an ass-head (see 3.1.137–41n, 137–44n).

45 85. "rock...be": While the music itself is to charm the mortals' sleep (lines 80–82), the dancers are to rock the ground as a mother rocks a cradle. The dancing is to make sure that the mortals sleep well and awake fully refreshed. No longer taking advantage of people while they are asleep, Oberon now seeks to produce sleep's restorative effects for them.

46 87. "solemnly": with festive celebration; see 1.1.11n.

47 88. "triumphantly": as in a festive triumph; see 1.1.19n.

48 89. "posterity": The First Quarto reads "prosperity": the Second Quarto and Folio, "posterity." The former would point back to 2.1.73; the latter ahead to 5.1.391–400. See Coda, 197–99.

49 88–91. "Dance... jollity": Oberon mentions Theseus by name in only two speeches, which are paired. Where the first marked the initial appearance of his and Titania's jealous quarrel (2.1.76–80), this—the second—marks its resolution. And where the first involved the charge of "break[ing]...faith," the second speaks of "faithful lovers" who are to "be / Wedded." As earlier, Oberon ignores Athens' ancestral law or takes for granted that Theseus will over-rule it; see 3.2.372–73n.

Oberon:		Then, my queen, in silence sad[50]
95		Trip[51] we after night's shade.[52]
		We the globe can compass soon,
		Swifter than the wandering moon.[53]
Titania:		Come, my lord, and in our flight
		Tell me how it came this night
100		That I sleeping here was found
		With these mortals on the ground.[54]

Exeunt Oberon, Titania and Puck.

Wind horns.[55] Enter Theseus and all his train, Hippolyta, Egeus.[56]

Theseus: Go, one of you, find out the forester.[57]
   For now our observation[58] is performed,

---

50   94. "silence sad": sober silence (the opposite of music and dance).
51   95. "Trip": move lightly with quick, short steps.
52   95–96. "Trip...shade": Oberon previously suggested that he does not have to flee the early morning light (see 3.2.388–93n). Now he seems to qualify that boast.
53   96–97. "We...moon": As the initial Fairy had claimed; see 2.1.7n.
54   98–101. "Come...ground": Once more, for Titania, the principal difference between humans and fairies is human mortality (see, further, 3.1.153–54n).
55   S.D. 102. "*Wind horns*": hunting horns. "[M]ighty Theseus, / Who to hunt was so desirous, / And especially for the great hart in May, / That...no day dawned upon him / When he was not...ready to ride / With hunt and horn, and hounds beside him" (Chaucer, *The Knight's Tale*, 1.1673–78).
56   S.D. 102. "*Wind...Egeus*": We have not seen any of these characters since the opening scene. While the fairies are responsible for most of what happens in Acts 2 and 3 and the first 100 lines of Act 4, from now until midnight the Athenians, chiefly Theseus, are responsible for what occurs. As day succeeds night, the Athenian Duke succeeds the fairy king.
57   102. "forester": A sign of the change from the fairy to the human world is that the woods are now, as originally, Theseus' palace woods, with an officer to look after them (see 1.2.94, 103). On foresters, see 3.2.390n.
58   103. "observation": of the rites of Mayday morning; see 1.1.167n.

And, since we have the vaward of the day,[59]
My love shall hear the music of my hounds.   105
Uncouple[60] in the western valley; let them go.
Dispatch,[61] I say, and find the forester.

[*Exit an Attendant.*]

We will, fair queen, up[62] to the mountain's top
And mark the musical confusion
Of hounds and echo in conjunction.   110
Hippolyta: I was with Hercules[63] and Cadmus[64] once,[65]

---

59   104. "we...day": It is still early morning ("vaward means "the
      early part").
60   106. "Uncouple": release. Dogs were chained together in pairs be-
      fore being set free for the hunt.
61   107. "Dispatch": be quick.
62   108. "up": go up.
63   111. "Hercules": The most famous Greek hero, whom Theseus em-
      ulated; see, further, 1.2.25n.
64   111. "Cadmus": The legendary founder of Thebes, whose founding in-
      volved autochthonism is the strictest sense. After killing a dragon sacred
      to Mars, Cadmus sowed its teeth in the ground at Athena's bidding, and
      fully armed warriors at once sprang from the earth and began killing
      each other. At Athena's further instruction, the five survivors made
      peace and helped Cadmus found Thebes (Ovid, *Metamorphoses*, 3.1–
      130). However, the Theban fratricide repeated itself five generations later
      with Oedipus' sons (see 1.1.22–23n for Theseus' role in the aftermath of
      the sons' mutual killings). Fittingly, "A Cadmean victory...turneth to
      the detriment and loss of the winner" (Plutarch, *On Brotherly Love*, 488a;
      Holland, 153). In early Thebes, it seems, there is no end to fratricide be-
      cause there is nothing beyond the realm of one's own. Where Thebes
      stands for the power and danger of the exclusive regard for, or love of,
      one's own, Theseus will moderate that tendency in Athens by overturn-
      ing its patriarchal authority; see, further, 1.1.36–38n, 1.1.95–98n.
65   111. "I...once": Cadmus lived some five generations before Theseus
      (see Sophocles, *Oedipus Tyrannus*, 266–68; Herodotus, *The Histories*,
      5.59). The glaring anachronism, while underscoring the contrast be-
      tween the rival ancient cities' foundings, serves also to emphasize that
      MND as a whole, and the present scene especially, is synchronic. Be-
      ginning with Theseus' reappearance here, the play compresses Athens'

When in a wood of Crete they bayed[66] the bear[67]
With hounds of Sparta.[68] Never did I hear
Such gallant chiding,[69] for, besides the groves,
115   The skies, the fountains,[70] every region near
Seemed all one mutual cry.[71] I never heard
So musical a discord, such sweet thunder.[72,73]
Theseus: My hounds are bred out of the Spartan kind,
So[74] flewed,[75] so sanded;[76] and their heads are hung

---

development from barbaric to civilized into a few key thematic substitutions (for the steps in the transformation, see lines 118–25n, 137n, 138–
39n, 178–80n, 178–84n). Act 4, scene 1—Theseus' central scene—links
the ferocity of ancient heroism on the one hand and the civility of
Athenian democratic politics and intellectual life on the other. The barbaric passes into the civilized. See, further, Introduction, (13–14).

66   112. "bayed": brought to bay (the position of a hunted animal
when, unable to flee farther, it turns, faces the hounds, and defends
itself at close quarters).

67   111–12. "I...bear": On the Amazons' hunting, see Strabo, *Geogra-phy*, 11.5.1.

68   113. "hounds of Sparta": Spartan hounds, which are "a small
breed, with long nostrils and keen scent" (Aristotle, *Generation of Animals*, 781b9), are "swift" (Virgil, *Georgics*, 3.405), "the smartest
creature at chasing down wild prey" (Pindar, frag. 106), and "eager
of prey and of courageous kind" (Seneca, *Hippolytus*,33–35).

69   114. "gallant chiding": noble barking. "Give me the noble Spartan
hound / With whose deep voice Eurotas' banks resound"
(Athenaeus, *Scholars at Dinner*, 1.50 [quoting a lost fragment of Pin-
dar]). The Eurotas River flows past Sparta.

70   115. "fountains": springs.

71   116. "all...cry": one common sound, sounded everywhere.

72   117. "So...thunder": The cry was musical because it was so discordant, sweet because it was so thunderous. To Hippolyta, who still has
the taste of an Amazon queen, war is musical, as thunder is sweet.

73   111–17. "I...thunder": Hippolyta's memory of the Cretan hunt is
her sole expression of deep pleasure.

74   119. "So": like the Spartan hound.

75   119. "flewed": having the large hanging chaps of a deep-mouthed
hound.

76   119. "sanded": sandy-colored.

With ears that sweep away the morning dew;   120
Crook-kneed, and dewlapped[77] like Thessalian bulls;
Slow in pursuit, but matched in mouth like bells,
Each under each.[78] A cry[79] more tunable[80]
Was never holloed to,[81] nor cheered with[82] horn,
In Crete, in Sparta, nor in Thessaly.[83]   125
Judge when you hear. But soft,[84] what nymphs[85] are these?
Egeus: My lord, this is my daughter here asleep,
And this Lysander; this Demetrius is,

---

77   121. "dewlapped": with loose skin around the neck (transferred from use of cattle); see, further, 2.1.50n.

78   122–23. "matched…each": a harmony of individual sounds, like the chime of bells.

79   123. "cry": pack of hounds.

80   123. "tunable": tuneful, harmonious.

81   124. "holloed to": called to for hunting.

82   124. "cheered with": saluted with joy by.

83   118–25. "My…Thessaly": Hippolyta, recounting the time when she, Hercules, and Cadmus hunted bears in Crete, praised the thunderous common cry of the Spartan hounds as unequaled (lines 111–17). Theseus, countering, extols his hounds, although "bred out of the Spartan kind," as superior. Where Hippolyta praised the Spartan hounds for their thunderous common cry, Theseus lauds his for their unparalleled well-tuned harmony of individual sounds. The melodious surpasses the thunderous, harmonious individuals replace a choral unison, as the Athenian exceeds the Spartan (see Plato, *Laws*, 666e). Moreover, owing to an art—the art of breeding—descendants excel their ancestors. In Athens, the new surpasses the old, the excellence of art replaces the authority of age. Crete and Sparta, the oldest and most venerable Greek cities, whose fundamental principle, moreover, is reverence for age, and whose laws are traceable to Zeus and Apollo (Plato, *Laws*, 624aq1–6, 634a1–2, 662c7, d7–e7; *Minos*, 318c1–3), are surpassed by Athens, whose new principle is freedom and art.

84   126. "soft": stop, wait a moment.

85   126. "nymphs": beautiful young women. In Greek, a "nymph" often means a marriageable maiden or a bride; see, further, 2.1.245n.

This Helena, old Nedar's Helena.[86]

130   I wonder of[87] their being here together.

Theseus: No doubt they rose up early to observe

The rite of May, and hearing our intent,

Came here in grace of[88] our solemnity.[89]

But speak, Egeus. Is not this the day

135   That[90] Hermia should give answer of her choice?[91]

Egeus: It is, my lord.

Theseus: Go, bid the huntsmen wake them with their horns.[92]

> *Shout within. Wind horns.*
>
> *The lovers wake and all start up.*

Theseus: Good morrow, friends. Saint Valentine[93] is past.

Begin these wood-birds[94] but to couple now?[95]

---

86   129. "old Nedar's Helena": On the significance of identifying Helena by her patronymic, see 3.2.95n

87   130. "of": at (see Abbott, §174).

88   133. "in grace of": in honor of.

89   133. "solemnity": wedding festival; see, further, 1.1.11n.

90   134. "That": when (see Abbott, §284).

91   131–35. "No…choice": Once again, the marriage dispute between Hermia and her father interrupts Theseus' preparations for his wedding celebration (see 1.1.22–23n).

92   137. "Go,…horns": The music of human art supersedes the musical sound of beasts.

93   137. "Saint Valentine": Chaucer is the first writer to associate this saint's day (Feb. 14) with sexual pairing: "For this was on Saint Valentine's Day / When every bird comes there to choose his mate" (Chaucer, *The Parliament of Fowls*, 309–10). According to a popular belief tracing back at least to him, a person falls in love with the first person of the opposite sex he or she sees on Saint Valentine's Day (Chaucer, *The Legend of Good Women*, Prologue, 145–47). The day, in effect, does the work of love juice. Nothing in this saint's life connects him with such a belief.

94   139. "wood-birds": A triple pun: 1) wooed, 2) senseless, and 3) in a forest; see 2.1.192–93n.

95   138–39. "Saint…now": if birds are to choose their mates on Saint

Lysander: Pardon, my lord.

[*The lovers kneel.*]

Theseus: I pray you all, stand up.   140
    I know you two are rival enemies.
    How comes this gentle concord in the world,
    That hatred is so far from jealousy[96]
    To[97] sleep by hate[98] and fear no enmity?[99]
Lysander: My lord, I shall reply amazedly,[100]   145
    Half sleep, half waking.[101] But as yet, I swear,
    I cannot truly say how I came here.
    But, as I think—for truly would I speak,
    And now I do bethink me,[102] so it is:
    I came with Hermia hither. Our intent   150

Valentine's Day, these lovers are late. Theseus' good-natured tease stands in contrast not only to the tone of his last words to Hermia, warning of the consequence of her continuing to refuse her father's wishes (1.1.117–21). It stands also in contrast to the basis of that warning, by suggesting that the lovers themselves rather than anyone's father are to choose their mates. Wood-birds are free to couple as they wish.

96   143. "jealousy": suspicion, mistrust.
97   144. "To": as to (see Abbott, §281).
98   144. "by hate": by the side of a personal enemy.
99   141–44. "I…enmity": The coupling of lovers agrees with nature, but the sleeping side-by-side of hated foes does not. Since men can fight for love (see 2.2.240–42n, 3.2.255n, 3.2.336–37n), rivalry in love may be tantamount to war. Theseus' perplexed question, containing his only mention of "hatred," "hate, "rival," "jealousy," "enemies," or "enmity," is the heroic warrior's most warlike speech.
100 145. "amazedly": confusedly (as though in a maze).
101 146. "Half…waking": Lysander may mean "sleep" and "waking" either as nouns, the topics of "reply" (his answer will tell of his having been asleep and awake), or as adjectives, characterizing it (his answer will be a mixture of his being half-asleep and half-awake).
102 149. "bethink me": recollect.

Was to be gone from Athens, where we might,
Without[103] the peril of the Athenian law—[104]
Egeus: Enough, enough, my lord You have enough![105]
I beg the law,[106] the law upon his head!
155   They would have stolen away. They would, Demetrius,
Thereby to have defeated[107] you and me:
You of your wife and me of my consent,
Of my consent that she should be your wife.[108]
Demetrius: My lord, fair Helen told me of their stealth,[109]
160   Of this their purpose hither[110] to this wood,
And I in fury hither followed them,

---

103 152. "Without": beyond, outside.

104 148–52. "But…law": Lysander does not give the sort of innocent
excuse that Theseus offered with "[n]o doubt," when he came
upon the lovers (lines 131–35). Instead, he wishes to tell the truth,
and tells it at his and Hermia's "peril of the Athenian law." Egeus
may think that Lysander is artful and cunning (see 1.1.27–38 and
nn), but Lysander answers without the slightest guile or art. As
noted earlier, no one speaks of truth as often as he (see 2.2.35n).

105 153. "Enough…enough": you have enough proof of guilt (from his
confession).

106 154. "beg the law": ask for the application of the law.

107 156. "defeated": defrauded, cheated

108 153–58. "Enough…wife": When Egeus originally invoked the law,
it was Hermia who was to die (1.1.42–45). Now, it is Lysander.
Egeus had claimed that his authority over his daughter rests on
the fact that she is his (1.1.23n, 41–42n). He now seems to assume
that his anger at Lysander gives him authority over him. Anger
extends as it defends one's own. Egeus, echoing his original complaint, speaks in doubles, implicitly or explicitly, in every line: repetition (lines 153–58; cp. 1.1.24–29), including twice mentioning his
"consent" (lines 157, 158; cp. 1.1.25, 40), antithesis (lines 154–58;
cp. 1.1.43–44), anaphora (lines 153–58; cp. 1.1.25, 27, 28, 30, 31, 33,
36), varying words slightly for the same sense (lines 156–58; cp.
1.1.23–26), and charging a double theft (lines 156–57; cp. 1.1.36–
38).

109 159. "stealth": stealthy flight.

110 160. "hither": in coming here (see Abbott, §405).

Fair Helena in fancy[111] following me.
But, my good lord, I wot[112] not by what power—
But by some power it is—my love to Hermia,
Melted as the snow, seems to me now   165
As the remembrance of an idle gaud[113]
Which in my childhood I did dote upon,[114]
And all the faith, the virtue of my heart,
The object and the pleasure of mine eye,
Is only Helena.[115] To her, my lord,   170
Was I betrothed ere I saw Hermia.
But like a sickness[116] did I loathe this food.
But, as in health, come to my natural taste,
Now I do wish it, love it, long for it,
And will forevermore be true to it.[117]   175
Theseus: Fair lovers, you are fortunately met.
Of this discourse we more will hear anon.
Egeus, I will overbear your will,

---

111 162. "fancy": love.
112 164. "wot": know.
113 166. "remembrance…gaud": memory of a worthless trinket.
114 164–67. "my…upon": The love, whose former existence now seems greatly reduced in substance, seems also remote in time (see, further, 3.2.170n).
115 168–70. "And…Helena": With unintended irony, Demetrius describes "faith" as the power ("virtue") of his heart. He likewise pays unwitting tribute to love juice: in seeing Helena, he sees all that he desires to see. She is indeed "[the] apple of his eye" (see 3.2.104n)
116 172. "like a sickness": like one who is sick (the abstract as a metonym for the personal; hence, the antithesis of "as in health" [line 173]).
117 159–75. "My…it": Demetrius has normally been sparing of words. Half of his previous 30 speeches were no more than two lines, and his longest speech was when he woke up with love juice on his eyes and fell in love with Helena—some eight lines (3.2.137–44). The present speech is more than twice that long; see, further, lines 186–98n.

For in the temple by and by,[118] with us,
180 These couples shall eternally be knit.[119]
And, for the morning now is something worn,
Our purposed hunting shall be set aside.
Away with us to Athens. Three and three,
We'll hold a feast in great solemnity.[120],[121]
185 Come, Hippolyta.

---

118   179. "by and by": shortly.
119   178–80. "Egeus,...knit": Theseus summarily deposes the ancient authority of Athenian fathers, allowing the lovers to marry as they choose. Overturning rather than preserving the law (cp. 1.1.20n), he liberates a daughter's romantic desire from her filial duty. The daughter's consent, not the father's, is what now matters. On Theseus' laying the groundwork for the future development of democratic Athens, see Introduction, 11, and n20. On Hermia's father having the name of Theseus' own father, for whose death he bears responsibility, see Introduction, 10–11. From this moment on, Egeus remains completely silent and is alluded to just once in passing (see line 195n). He disappears along with his patriarchal power. The same will be true of Pyramus and Thisbe's parents. Although their parts have been cast, they do not appear in "Pyramus and Thisbe" (see, further, 1.2.56–59n; 5.1.131n) and the father is just briefly alluded to (5.1.173, 338).
120   184. "solemnity": festivity.
121   178–84. "I...solemnity": Theseus' overthrow of the Athenian fathers' authority amounts to the overthrow of the ancestral gods of Athens ("To you your father should be as a god" [1.1.47]). Theseus, however, invokes no god when he takes this action. His only hint of the gods in connection with the marriages is to say that the weddings will take place "in the temple." But even that slim hint seems overstated, for we never see the wedding ceremonies, but only their celebration, which occurs after the newlyweds have "com[e] from the temple" (4.2.15) and which consists of a dramatic performance. In contrast to the Romans, who are always thinking of, turning to, and thanking the gods for everything because they attribute their well-being to their piety (see Introduction, 11, Livy, 44.1.11), the Athenians treat the sacred as largely irrelevant. Once Theseus overturns the patriarchal authority, Athenians mention Olympian or pre-Olympian gods only in the dialogue or description of the artisans' poetry or in

Exeunt Theseus, Hippolyta, Egeus and Train.

Demetrius: These things seem small and undistinguishable,
   Like far-off mountains turned into clouds.
Hermia: Methinks I see these things with parted eye,
   When everything seems double.[122]
Helena: So methinks.
   And I have found Demetrius like a jewel,   190
   Mine own and not mine own.[123]

---

mock oaths (5.1.48, 52, 176, 273–74, 307–8, 323–28) and the word "god" only in profane swearing (4.1.202, 4.2.13–14) or with deliberate irony, calling attention to the absurdity of the artisans' performance (5.1.307, 308). The gods, now existing chiefly in fiction, seem to be largely driven out of Athens by love and replaced by art. Only fairies are now said to follow a god (5.1.369–70).

122   188–89. "Methinks...double": Where things appear to Demetrius to have turned into their opposites and are hard to distinguish (lines 186–87), Hermia sees them as appearing double. She means, most particularly, waking from a dream and recognizing it as a dream—that is, distinguishing a likeness from that of which it is a likeness and at the same time recognizing that she had previously failed to make that distinction. As we saw when she awoke from her dream in the woods, the doubleness involves the recognition of the literalness of a dream (see 2.2.144–49n). More generally, Hermia points to the double vision natural to human thinking. With our body's eye we see what is before us; with our mind's eye we see what it means. Our natural "parted eye" permits us to recognize a likeness as a likeness, an image as an image. Able to see that there is more than meets the eye, we can separate the sight's significance from the sight itself, the meaning or the reality from the appearance. In addition to so much else, we can step back and reflect on our sensing: "Methinks I see...." Ironically, Demetrius has just demonstrated what Hermia indicates. With his mind's eye, he perceived that he perceived, understanding what he saw by likening it to something else, which itself turned into still something else (see, further, Introduction, 4).

123   189–91. "So...own": Helena, while agreeing with Hermia, speaks of desire rather than of knowing. Using both a simile and an antithesis, she describes the doubleness of desire. Like a precious jewel which is found and therefore of uncertain ownership, the ob-

Demetrius: Are you sure
   That we are awake?[124] It seems to me
   That yet we sleep, we dream.[125] Do not you think
   The Duke was here and bid us follow him?
Hermia: Yea,[126] and my father.[127]
195 *Helena*:   And Hippolyta.
Lysander: And he did bid us follow to the temple.
Demetrius: Why, then, we are awake.[128] Let's follow him,
   And by the way let us recount our dreams.[129],[130]

---

ject of desire is at once present and absent. Desired but not yet possessed, it is present in the imagination but absent as a reality (see, further, 1.1.1–4n). The counterpart of an image, which is and is not what it is, the desired object is and is not one's own. Interestingly, unlike the other lovers, no one ever calls Helena "my Helena," nor does she ever call anyone her own.

124 191–92. "Are...awake": This sentence appears only in the Quarto, not in the Folio.

125 191–93. "Are...dream": With the love juice still in his eyes, Demetrius has particular difficulty distinguishing the awake-world from a dream. He fails to recognize that his question answers itself. We distinguish between being awake and dreaming only when awake. It is only after waking that a dream seems to us ("It seems to me...") to be a dream.

126 194. "Yea": An archaic affirmative reply to a question involving a negative.

127 194. "my father": This is Hermia's final word in the play and the only allusion to her father after Theseus eliminates his authority; see, further, lines 178–80n.

128 197. "Why...awake": Demetrius gets things backwards. He concludes from the context and consequences of events that they are awake, when, on the contrary, it is from being awake that he is able to understand the context and the consequences. Dreams make no distinction between true and false.

129 198. "And...dreams": Though now convinced they are awake, Demetrius still thinks that all that happened to them was a dream or collection of dreams. None of the other lovers contradicts him. As Oberon had wished, all the lovers seem to believe that the events in the woods were a dream (see lines 67–68n).

130 186–98. "These...dreams": Demetrius leads the discussion of

Exeunt.

Bottom: (*waking up*) When my cue comes, call me, and I will
    answer. My next[131] is "Most fair Pyramus."[132] Hey-ho![133]   200
    Peter Quince? Flute the bellows-mender? Snout
    the tinker? Starveling? God's my life![134] Stolen hence,
    and left me asleep! I have had a most rare vision.
    I have had a dream past the wit of man to say
    what dream it was. Man is but an ass if he go about[135] to   205
    expound this dream. Methought I was—there
    is no man can tell what. Methought I was—and
    methought I had—but man is but a patched fool[136] if
    he will offer to say what methought I had. The eye of
    man hath not heard, the ear of man hath not seen,   210
    man's hand is not able to taste, his tongue to conceive,
    nor his heart to report what my dream was.[137] I

whether the events were a dream. With as many lines here as the
other three lovers combined, he has the first, last, and virtually the
central speech in the exchange. Demetrius' new garrulousness
may reflect his new love. Originally the most laconic of the four
lovers, he has fallen in love with the most loquacious, and, as he
himself suggested earlier and Titania seemed to demonstrate with
Bottom, a lover should take after his beloved (see 3.1.191–93n). The
love juice has affected more than his love.

131 200. "next": next line.
132 199–200. "When… Pyramus'": Bottom wakes up thinking that he
    is still rehearsing his part in the play. Returning to the moment im-
    mediately before his transformation, he picks up where he left off,
    determined now not to miss his cue (see 3.1.93–96).
133 200. "Hey-ho": yawning.
134 202. "God's my life": A contraction of "God save my life," a com-
    mon oath.
135 205. "go about": tries.
136 208. "patched fool": Professional fools or jesters wore patchwork
    outfits.
137 209–12. "The eye…was": Like Quince, directing his play (see
    3.1.86n), Bottom, elevating his dream, confuses the senses. His
    confusion goes together with his literalness. To Bottom (and

will get Peter Quince to write a ballad[138] of this
dream. It shall be called "Bottom's Dream," because
it hath no bottom;[139] and I will sing it in the latter end
of a play, before the Duke. Peradventure, to make it
the more gracious,[140] I shall sing it at her death.[141]

Exit.

Act Four, Scene Two

[Athens]
Enter Quince, Flute, Snout, and Starveling.

Quince: Have you sent to Bottom's house? Is he come
home yet?
Starveling: He cannot be heard of. Out of doubt he is
transported.[142]

Quince), each sense is isolated from the others, with no power behind them able to discriminate between their natural objects (a
sight, sound, or taste), allow us to perceive that we are sensing,
or interpret what we are sensing. There is nothing beyond the particular sensation itself. The senses, for Bottom, are a plurality
without unity, which, paradoxically, makes them at the same time
a unity without a plurality. In contrast to Hermia's view (see
3.2.177–83n), they are unconnected to and interchangeable with
one another. Any sense can sense anything (cp. Aristotle, *On the
Soul*, 426b12–27a14).

138 213. "ballad": A popular song or poem, usually a narrative, often
celebrating someone or something.
139 215. "no bottom": 1) bottomless profundity, 2) no foundation. On
Bottom's encounter with Titania, see, further, Introduction, 8,
5.1.77n.
140 217. "gracious": graceful, appealing.
141 215–17. "I...death": Bottom, once again relishing the prospect of
his theatrical triumph (see 1.2.66–69n), seems to forget that his
character, Pyramus, is to die before Thisbe.
142 4. "transported": 1) carried off (by spirits), 2) transformed (=
"translated" [3.1.114]).

Flute: If he come not, then the play is marred. It goes not   5
   forward, doth it?
Quince: It is not possible. You have not a man in all Athens
   able to discharge[143] Pyramus but he.[144]
Flute: No, he hath simply the best wit[145] of any handicraft
   man in Athens.[146]   10
Quince: Yea, and the best person[147] too, and he is a very
   paramour for a sweet voice.
Flute: You must say "paragon."[148] A "paramour" is, God bless
   us, a thing of naught.[149]

Enter Snug the joiner.

Snug: Masters, the Duke is coming from the temple, and   15
   there is two or three lords and ladies more married.
   If our sport had gone forward, we had all been
   made men.[150]
Flute: O, sweet bully Bottom![151] Thus hath he lost sixpence   20

---

143 8. "discharge": perform.
144 7–8. "You...he": Bottom's supposed reputation for acting may not
   be altogether unwarranted; see 1.2.35n.
145 9. "wit": intelligence, judgment.
146 7–10. "You...Athens": Quince and Flute, demonstrating a parochial
   perspective, speak as though all Athenians were handicraft men.
147 11. "person": personal appearance, presence; see, further, 1.2.79–82.
148 13. "paragon": person serving as the supreme model.
149 13–14. "A 'paramour'...naught": The young Flute (see 1.2.43–44n)
   corrects the more worldly Quince's malapropism, though his correction only adds to the obscenity. While a "paramour" is someone
   with whom a married person has an adulterous relationship,
   "naught," a much stronger word than today's "naughty," means
   not only something shameful or evil, but, specifically, licentious or
   immoral sex. Flute's invocation "God bless us" shows that he is
   aware of speaking forbidden words.
150 17–18. "made men": men who have made their fortunes; see, further, lines 19–24n.
151 19. "sweet... Bottom": The artisans are concerned for Bottom as
   well as for themselves. He is the only player the others speak of

a day during[152] his life. He could not have 'scaped[153] sixpence
a day. And[154] the Duke had not given him sixpence
a day for playing Pyramus, I'll be hanged.
He would have deserved it. Sixpence a day in
Pyramus, or nothing.[155]

Enter Bottom.

25 *Bottom*: Where are these lads? Where are these hearts?[156]
Quince: Bottom! O most courageous[157] day! O most happy
hour!
Bottom: Masters, I am to discourse[158] wonders. But ask me not
what; for, if I tell you, I am not true Athenian. I will
30 tell you everything right as it fell out.
Quince: Let us hear, sweet Bottom.
Bottom: Not a word of[159] me. All that I will tell you is that the

---

with appreciation or affection. On the term "bully Bottom," see
3.1.7n.
152 20. "during": for the rest of.
153 20. "could…'scaped": must necessarily have earned.
154 21. "And": if.
155 19–24. "O,…nothing": The art of acting has evidently become more
lucrative in Athens than the mechanical arts. Quince and Flute's
deep disappointment, especially combined with their democratic
description of Athens (see lines 7–10n), points to the manner in
which Pericles, an aristocrat who became a great democratic leader,
consolidated democracy in Athens at the expense of the nobles and
the council of the Areopagus, Athens' early aristocratic council. To
win the people's good will and favor, he generously distributed
public money to support the arts, particularly the theater, by paying
for theatrical productions and providing seats for the poor to watch.
Then, with the people's help, he denounced and reduced the Areopagus (Plutarch, *Pericles*, 9.1–3). On his liberality in supplying, and
the frequency of, theatrical performances, see Thucydides, 2.38.1.
156 25. "hearts": a term of friendship.
157 26. "courageous": 1) brave, splendid, 2) (perhaps) a blunder for
"auspicious."
158 28. "to discourse": ready to discourse (see Abbott, §405).
159 32. "of": from.

Duke hath dined. Get your apparel together, good
strings to your beards,[160] new ribbons to your pumps.[161]
Meet presently[162] at the palace. Every man look o'er   35
his part. For the short and the long is, our play is
preferred.[163] In any case,[164] let Thisbe have clean linen,
and let not him that plays the lion pare his nails, for
they shall hang out for the lion's claws.[165] And, most
dear actors, eat no onions nor garlic, for we are to   40
utter sweet breath,[166] and I do not doubt but to hear
them say it is a sweet comedy.[167] No more words.
Away! Go, away!

Exeunt.

160 34. "strings...bears": the strings to tie on your stage beards.
161 34. "ribbons...pumps": cheerful decorations on your light shoes.
162 35. "presently": immediately.
163 36–37. "our...preferred": Certain of success, Bottom suggests that
     their play has already been chosen, when, in fact, it is only on the
     short list and is frowned upon by Philostrate (see 5.1.56–70).
164 37. "In any case": whatever happens.
165 38–39. "Let...claws": Bottom seems to have forgotten his fear of
     bringing in a frightening lion (see 3.1.28–44).
166 41. "breath": Bottom conflates two senses of "breath": 1) the air
     one exhales, 2) the words spoken in a play.
167 41–42. "I...comedy": Unlike Snug and Flute, Bottom says nothing
     about likely monetary rewards (cp. lines 17–18n, 19–24n). Just as
     Athens' handicraft men think they can practice an art of the mind,
     Bottom, always confident of his excellence, is able to overlook
     mere utility and, like Athens itself, show (in his way) a love of
     beauty and fine art.

Act Five, Scene One

Enter Theseus, Hippolyta, and Philostrate, Lords, and Attendants.

Hippolyta: 'Tis strange, my Theseus,[1] that[2] these lovers speak of.
Theseus: More strange than true. I never may[3] believe
    These antique[4] fables nor these fairy toys.[5]
    Lovers and madmen have such seething[6] brains,
    Such shaping fantasies,[7] that apprehend[8]   5

---

1   "my Theseus": Hippolyta never previously referred to Theseus by any term of endearment or even by his name (see 1.1.16–17n). In this and other respects, between her appearance in the woods in the morning (4.1.111–17) and her celebration of her wedding at night, she seems to have passed from Amazon to Athenian. Lawful marriage is a sign, if not the cause, of her becoming civilized.

2   1. "that": that which, what (on the omission of the relative, see Abbott, §244).

3   2. "may": can (see Abbott, §307).

4   3. "antique": 1) ancient, 2) antic, grotesque. Theseus, the legendary founder of Athens, is himself an "antique fable"—a "fabulous antiquity," as Plutarch calls him (Plutarch, *Theseus*, 1.3; North, 1:29); see, further, lines 2–23n.

5   3. "fairy toys": fairy tales. Theseus, who knows nothing of the fairies, describes the lovers' accounts as "fairy toys." His phrase is literally true, though he means it only figuratively, describing unreal or incredible stories, not necessarily ones about fairies. Whether or not Titania led him through the glimmering night, Theseus is entirely unaware of her (see, further, 2.1.77n). To him, fairies are nothing but fairy tales.

6   4. "seething": boiling. According to Galenic humeral physiology, excessive heat caused by violent emotions in the heart are a danger to the brain (see Thomas Vicary, *The Englishman's Treasure*, 16–17). Note the rich quibble on "seething"; and see, further, lines 22–23n

7   5. "shaping fantasies": formative imaginations.

8   5. "apprehend": lay hold of, seizes on.

More than cool reason ever comprehends.[9]
The lunatic, the lover, and the poet
Are of imagination all compact.[10]
One sees more devils than vast hell can hold:
10   That is the madman. The lover, all as frantic,[11]
Sees Helen's[12] beauty in a brow of Egypt.[13]
The poet's eye, in a fine frenzy[14] rolling,
Doth glance from heaven to earth, from earth to heaven,
And as imagination bodies forth[15]
15   The forms of things unknown, the poet's pen
Turns them to shapes and gives to airy nothing
A local habitation and a name.[16]
Such tricks hath strong imagination
That, if it would but apprehend some joy,
20   It comprehends some bringer of that joy.[17]
Or in the night, imagining some fear,[18]

---

9   6. "comprehends": makes sense of, understands.
10   8. "all compact": entirely composed.
11   10. "all as frantic": just as mad.
12   11. "Helen's": Helen of Troy's.
13   11. "a brow of Egypt": a gypsy's face (see, further, 1.1.234n).
14   12. "frenzy": (quasi-divine) poetic madness (see, for example, Plato, *Phaedrus*, 245a).
15   14. "bodies forth": gives bodily form to; see, further, lines 12–17n.
16   12–17. "The poet's…name": The poet, in a disorder akin to madness (see line 12n), looks quickly from heaven to earth and from earth to heaven. But instead of taking in what he sees, he lets his imagination project onto heaven and earth what he has never seen and does not know. Then the poet turns those imaginations into particular figures and gives them a specific place and name. He makes his imaginations seem real by localizing and particularizing them.
17   20–21. "if…joy": imagination does not simply wish for some joy; it imagines that someone or something fulfills its wishes. "Apprehend," here, means imagine or conceive of; "comprehends," means includes.
18   22. "fear": object of fear.

How easy is a bush supposed a bear![19],[20]
Hippolyta: But all the story of the night told over,[21]
And all their minds transfigured so together,[22]
More witnesseth than fancy's images[23]   25

---

19   22–23. "Or...bear": Fear needs a particular object and so will imagine one if its object is unknown. Because we cannot resolve a fear whose object we cannot identify, our fear of the unknown transforms the unknown into a specific, identifiable fear (see 3.2.27–30n). As shown by the lunatic, lover and poet, strong imagination in general "sees" what it only imagines that it sees. What it calls seeing is—in the contemporary antiphrastic slang term—simply "seeing things"; see, further, 3.2.27–30n, and line 4n.

20   2–23. "I...bear": Theseus, the founder of the city renowned for the love of the beautiful and the highest accomplishments in art, disparages both love and art. Their dependence on the imagination lowers them to the level of a lunatic. In a most important way, Athens' founder does not fit into the city he founds. The hero whose actions makes Athens possible, and who is himself the subject of much of the city's great art, has no taste for art. He is antipoetic. A heroic warrior, he appreciates deeds, not poems, action, not imitation. Only what is tactile is real for him. Theseus accordingly fails to recognize the strong connection between imagination, even dreams, and action. As Theseus himself perfectly exemplifies, first we dream of what we will do, then we do it: "[T]he wonderful admiration which Theseus had of Hercules' courage made him in the night that he never dreamed but of his noble acts and doings, and in the daytime pricked forward with emulation and envy of his glory, he determined with himself one day to do the like" (Plutarch, *Theseus*, 6.7; North, 1:35). If poetry imitates men's deeds, men's deeds in turn imitate poetry. Heroic action is not the opposite but rather an imitation of "antique fables."

21   23. "told over": recounted.

22   24. "transfigured so together": changed in the same way, at the same time.

23   25. "More...images": gives evidence of more than the imagination of lovers.

And grows to something of great constancy,[24]
But, howsoever,[25] strange and admirable.[26],[27]

Enter Lysander, Demetrius, Hermia, and Helena.

Theseus: Here come the lovers full of joy and mirth.
Joy, gentle friends! Joy and fresh days of love
Accompany your hearts!
30 *Lysander*: More[28] than to us
Wait in your royal walks, your board, your bed![29]
Theseus: Come now, what masques,[30] what dances shall we have
To wear away this long age of three hours
Between our after-supper[31] and bedtime?
35 Where is our usual manager of mirth?
What revels are in hand? Is there no play

---

24 26. "constancy": consistency (hence reality).
25 27. "howsoever": in any case.
26 27. "strange and admirable": to be wondered at.
27 23–27. "But...admirable": This is the last that anyone refers to the lovers' night in the woods. No one will even hint at the resemblance between the actions of Pyramus and Thisbe those of Lysander and Hermia; see, further, lines 154–63n.
28 30. "More": more joy.
29 30–31. "More...bed": Lysander, unlike before, uses no formal term of address for Theseus and returns a much saltier salutation than he received. Previously, he and Demetrius were always deferential to Theseus. Now, following Theseus' overthrow of patriarchal authority, they speak to him much more as equals. On the other hand, neither Hermia nor Helena says a word in Act 5. Although previously talkative, both remain completely silent even as their husbands (and Hippolyta) banter. The Athenian family becomes democratic in that it comes to be based on the wife's consent, but remains nondemocratic insofar as the husband rules the wife. As Hermia herself put it, the husband is a "lordship" possessing "sovereignty," though a sovereignty based on the wife's wishes or "consent" (see 1.1.79–82n).
30 32. "masques": courtly dramatic entertainment with masked dancers.
31 34. "after-supper": dessert

To ease the anguish of a torturing hour?[32]
Call Philostrate.
Philostrate: [*Coming forward.*] Here, mighty Theseus.
Theseus: Say what abridgment[33] have you for this evening,
    What masque, what music? How shall we beguile   40
    The lazy[34] time if not with some delight?
Philostrate: There is a brief[35] how many sports are ripe.[36]
    Make choice of which your Highness will see first.

                               [*Giving a paper.*]

Theseus: [*Reads*] "The battle with the Centaurs, to be sung
    By an Athenian eunuch to the harp."[37]   45
    We'll none of that. That have I told my love
    In glory of my kinsman[38] Hercules.[39]

---

32   36–37. "Is…hour": As poetry, for Theseus, is mere madness, plays, for him, are nothing more than entertainment, a diversion to help pass the sluggish time.

33   39. "abridgment": entertainment: 1) something to make the time seem shorter, 2) a shortened version of a longer work.

34   41. "lazy": sluggish, slow-moving.

35   42. "brief": short list.

36   42. "sports are ripe": performances are ready.

37   44–45. "'The battle…harp'": The mythical Centaurs are part man, part horse, notoriously savage, brutal, and lascivious creatures. According to the legend, Hercules, on his way to perform one of his Labors, visited Pholoe, one of only two civilized Centaurs. While they were eating, Hercules urged Pholoe to open a cask of wine. Other Centaurs soon smelled the wine and, driven mad by it, rushed into Pholoe's cave and, armed with great rocks, tree trunks, and flaming logs, began plundering the wine. While Pholoe hid himself in terror, Hercules fearlessly fought the attackers, killing most and forcing the rest to flee (Apollodorus, 2.83–87); see, further, lines 46–47n.

38   47. "my kinsmen": Theseus and Hercules were cousins (Plutarch, *Theseus*, 7.1).

39   46–47. "We'll…Hercules": The proposed entertainment epitomizes Theseus' pejorative view of poetry. The heroic deed is to be sung by a eunuch to the music of a harp. Poetry, divorced from reality,

[*Reads*] "The riot of the tipsy Bacchanals,
Tearing the Thracian singer in their rage."[40]
50   That is an old device,[41] and it was played
When I from Thebes came last a conqueror.[42]
[*Reads*] "The thrice-three Muses[43] mourning for the death
Of learning, late deceased in beggary."[44]
That is some satire, keen and critical,
55   Not sorting with a nuptial ceremony.[45]

---

involves an effeminate presentation of manly deeds. In Theseus' view, poetic Athens is an emasculated Athens. Theseus thus rejects the proposal out of hand, saying that he has already told Hippolyta the story "[i]n glory of my kinsman Hercules." He seeks to preserve Hercules as his heroic exemplar; see, further, lines 2–23.

40   48–49. "'The riot...rage'": The Thracian singer is Orpheus, the greatest singer of Greek myth, whose splendid music could tame savage beasts, move rocks and trees, and even gain him entrance into the Underworld. Orpheus descended there to bring back his wife Eurydice, who was allowed to return with him on the condition that he not look back at her until they had reached the light of the sun. But just before reaching the end of the long assent, Orpheus looked back, and Eurydice vanished into the darkness. When Orpheus, wholly despondent, retreated into the woods and spurned the company of women, the Thracian women, chagrined, became drunk and tore him to pieces in a mad fury (Ovid, *Metamorphoses,* 10.1–85, 11.1–43).

41   50. "device": show (with emphasis on its being devised or invented for dramatic presentation).

42   50–51. "That...conqueror": Theseus refers to his ending the Theban internecine war; see, further, 1.1.22–23n.

43   52. "The thrice-three Muses": the nine goddesses presiding over and inspiring learning and the arts, esp. poetry and music (see Hesiod, *Theogony* 1–115).

44   53. "late... beggary": recently died in poverty.

45   54–55. "That...ceremony": This is the only one of the first three proposals that Theseus praises. He rejects it, however, for the same reason that he praises it. As a sharp and censorious ("keen and critical") satire, it is not suitable for a wedding ceremony. Theseus evidently sees an important difference between poetry in general and satire in particular. The latter is essentially political in both its subject and purpose. Although using the language and form of poetry,

[*Reads*] "A tedious brief scene of young Pyramus
And his love Thisbe, very tragical mirth."
"Merry" and "tragical"? "Tedious" and "brief"?
That is hot ice and wondrous strange snow![46]
How shall we find the concord of this discord?[47]   60
Philostrate: A play there is, my lord, some ten words long
    Which is as brief as I have known a play,
    But by ten words, my lord, it is too long,
    Which makes it tedious; for in all the play,
    There is not one word apt, one player fitted.[48]   65
    And tragical, my noble lord, it is.
    For Pyramus therein doth kill himself,
    Which, when I saw rehearsed, I must confess,
    Made mine eyes water; but more merry tears
    The passion[49] of loud laughter never shed.[50]   70
Theseus: What are they that do play it?
Philostrate: Hard-handed men that work in Athens here,
    Which never labored in their minds till now,
    And now have toiled their unbreathed[51] memories
    With this same play, against[52] your nuptial.[53]   75

---

it criticizes and seeks to correct a corruption of the time—in this case, the impoverishment and death of learning. A form of rhetoric in the guise of poetry, its purpose is practical, not theoretical. Its aim is action, not understanding. "[I]ndignation inspires my verse" (Juvenal, *Satire One*, 79).

46 59. "wondrous...snow": wonderfully singular snow.
47 60. "find...discord": reconcile the description's oxymora.
48 65. "There...fitted": neither the script nor the actors are suitable.
49 70. "passion": intensity, strong emotion.
50 66–70. "And...shed": It is a tragedy because it ends in suicide, but a comedy because the players' ludicrous ineptitude transforms it into an unintended farce. The intended tragedy becomes a comic parody of itself.
51 74. "unbreathed": unpracticed, unexercised.
52 75. "against": in preparation for.
53 72–75. "Hard-handed...nuptial": On Greek contempt for artisans, see Herodotus, 2.167.

Theseus: And[54] we will hear it.

Philostrate: No, my noble lord,
It is not for you. I have heard it over,[55]
And it is nothing, nothing in the world,
Unless you can find sport in their intents,[56]

80   Extremely stretched and conned with cruel pain[57]
To do you service.

Theseus: I will hear that play,
For never anything can be amiss
When simpleness[58] and duty tender it.[59]
Go, bring them in, and take your places, ladies.

---

54   76. "And": yes, you are right, and (see Abbott, §97).

55   77. "I...over": Although we saw Puck interrupt the plays after just
10 lines (S.D. 3.1.97), Philostrate thrice claims to have witnessed
the entire play's rehearsal, including its conclusion (see also lines
64–65, 67–68). In a play in which there are many strange twists and
numerous discrepancies between the fairies and the surrounding
play, none seems more curious—and unnecessary to the plot in
any ordinary sense—than Philostrate's repeated instance that he
saw the full play rehearsed. Philostrate's apparently needless
claim, which Shakespeare stresses, seems to suggest that the literal-minded Bottom may have, for once, spoken correctly when
he said his dream "hath no bottom" (4.1.215). It may be as imaginary as Oberon's amorous pursuit of Phillida (see 2.1.65–68n). Theseus draws a sharp line between imagination and reason, poetry
and reality. But the fairies, especially Puck, point up the ambiguous
unity of these pairs. As we see throughout the play, poetry and reality are a "union in partition" (2.1.210). On the level of human
practice, art imitates life while life imitates art (see, further, lines
2–23n). On the level of the nature of imitation itself, an imitation
is, and is not, the imitated.

56   79. "intents": 1) efforts, 2) object of their efforts (learning their
parts).

57   80. "conned...pain": learned with agonizing difficulty (refers to
"intents").

58   83. "simpleness": unpretentiousness, sincerity.

59   81–83. "I...it": Rather than wanting to laugh at the artisans' over-
reaching, Theseus says he will hear the play out of respect for their

[*Exit Philostrate.*]

Hippolyta: I love not to see wretchedness o'ercharged,[60]   85
  And duty in his service perishing.[61]
Theseus: Why, gentle sweet, you shall see no such thing.
Hippolyta: He says they can do nothing in this kind.[62]
Theseus: The kinder we, to give them thanks for nothing.[63]
  Our sport shall be to take what they mistake:[64]   90
  And what poor duty cannot do, noble respect
  Takes it in might, not merit.[65]
  Where I have come,[66] great clerks[67] have purposed
  To greet me with premeditated welcomes,
  Where I have seen them shiver and look pale,   95
  Make periods in the midst of sentences,[68]
  Throttle their practiced accent in their fears,[69]

---

  sincerity and duty in offering it. He will watch their performance
  in the spirit of noble condescension. The harder the players try, the
  less fault he will find; see, further, lines 91–92n.

60 85. "wretchedness o'ercharged": the lowly (both socially and in-
     tellectually) overburdened.
61 86. "duty...perishing": dedicated effort failing completely in its at-
     tempt to do its duty.
62 88. "in this kind": of this kind of activity.
63 89. "The...nothing": Echoing, with a chiasmus and pun, her final
     phrase ("nothing in this kind"), by which Hippolyta meant the sort
     of thing the players can do (see line 88n), Theseus speaks of their
     own kindness in thanking the players for nothing. The more the
     players reach beyond their ability, the greater his kindness in giv-
     ing them thanks.
64 90. "take...mistake": a pun on the antithesis of "take" (accept) and
     "mistake" (get wrong).
65 91–92. "noble...merit": magnanimous regard judges in the light of
     their power ("might"), not their achievement ("merit").
66 93. "Where...come": in places I have visited.
67 93. "great clerks": learned scholars.
68 96. "Make...sentences": See, for example, lines 108–16n.
69 97. "Throttle...fears": have their fears choke their well-trained elo-
     quent speech.

And in conclusion dumbly have broke off,[70]
Not paying me a welcome. Trust me, sweet,
100　Out of this silence yet I picked a welcome,
And in the modesty of fearful duty,[71]
I read as much as from the rattling tongue
Of saucy and audacious eloquence.
Love, therefore, and tongue-tied simplicity
105　In least speak most,[72] to my capacity.[73],[74]

[*Enter Philostrate.*]

Philostrate: So please your Grace, the Prologue is addressed.[75]
Theseus: Let him approach.

Flourish of trumpets.

Enter Quince as Prologue.

Prologue: *If we offend, it is with our goodwill.*[76]
That you should think, we come not to offend,
110　*But*[77] *with good will. To show our simple skill*
That is the true beginning of our end.[78]
Consider, then, we come but in despite.[79]

70　98. "broke off": broken off (before finishing).
71　101. "modesty…duty": deference of timorous duty.
72　104–5. "tongue-tied…most": tongue-tied silence bespeaks deference better than eloquence might have done.
73　105. "to my capacity": in my opinion, as far as I can tell.
74　85–105. "I…capacity": It remains to be seen whether—or in what way—Theseus and Hippolyta live up to their words; see, further, lines 118–25n and 154–63n.
75　106. "Prologue is addressed": Prologue is ready. Prologues, traditionally, greet the audience in a few words, often asking for an indulgent hearing. They also sometimes tell the audience what they need to know to understand the play. Prologue's first speech (lines 108–17) attempts the former; his second speech (lines 126–50), the latter.
76　108. "*our goodwill*": our wish.
77　110. "*But*": "But," as Quince reads it, means "except."
78　111. "*end*": purpose.
79　112. "*in despite*": in contempt.

We do not come, as minding to content you,[80]
Our true intent is. All for your delight,
We are not here. That you should here repent you,[81]   115
The actors are at hand and, by their show,[82]
You shall know all, that you are like to know.
Theseus: This fellow doth not stand upon points.[83]
Lysander: He hath rid[84] his prologue like a rough colt; he knows
     not the stop.[85] A good moral,[86] my lord: it is not enough   120
     to speak, but to speak true.
Hippolyta: Indeed he hath played on this prologue like a child
     on a recorder:[87] a sound, but not in government.[88]

---

80   113. "*minding...you*": intending to please you.
81   108–15. "*If...you*": Quince (Prologue), mispunctuating out of stage-
     fright (see line 96), declares just what he means to deny and denies
     just what he means to declare. The correct reading is: "*If we offend,
     it is with our goodwill* [= our wish] / *That you should think we come,
     not to offend,* / *But* [= on the contrary] *with goodwill to show our simple
     skill.* / *That is the true beginning of our end* [= aim, purpose]. / *Con-
     sider, then,* [that] *we come—but in despite* [in ill will, to vex you]. /
     We do not come—as minding to content you [= to please you]. / *Our
     true intent is all for your delight:* / *We are not here that you should here
     repent you.*" Note that Prologue's meter is neither "eight and six,"
     as Quince himself wanted, nor "eight and eight" as Bottom in-
     sisted (see 3.1.22–25nn), but a more expansive ten and ten.
82   116. "*show*": presentation.
83   118. "stand...points": bother about 1) punctuation, 2) trifles. Until now,
     the nobles have spoken only in verse, and the artisans only in prose,
     except when attempting to act (1.2.27–34, 3.1.78–98). Now that the
     players are performing their play, Shakespeare, to preserve the discon-
     tinuity between the players and their audience, has the nobles switch
     to prose, which they continue until the players' final exit (S.D. line 349).
84   119. "rid": 1) got rid of, 2) ridden.
85   120. "stop": 1) a technical term of horsemanship (see James Hunter,
     Dictionary of Horsemanship, s,v, stop), and 2) a mark of punctuation.
86   120. "moral": moral lesson.
87   123. "recorder": A cylindrical wind instrument, played by blowing
     into a mouthpiece at one end while covering differing combinations
     of holes along the cylinder; frequently a first instrument for children.
88   123. "government": good order, control.

Theseus: His speech was like a tangled chain; nothing
125   impaired,[89] but all disordered.[90] Who is next?

*Enter Pyramus (Bottom), and Thisbe (Flute), and Wall (Snout), and
Moonshine (Starveling), and Lion (Snug), and Prologue (Quince),
a trumpeter before them.*

Prologue: Gentles,[91] perchance you wonder at this show.
    But wonder[92] on, till truth make all things plain.
    This man is Pyramus, if you would know.
    This beauteous lady Thisbe is certain.[93]

---

89   125. "impaired": damaged.
90   118–25. "This…disordered": Contrary to what he seemed to promise when speaking of his "noble respect" for the artisans (see lines
91–92n), Theseus at the first opportunity mocks them, and he and
the others, including Hippolyta, will continue to do so all through
the artisans' performance. Some editors insert a momentary exit
for Quince after he speaks (line 117), but nothing in Shakespeare's
stage directions supports that addition. And Bottom and
Starveling (Moonshine) will soon confirm that they can hear the
audience's critical comments (see lines 180–85, 231–49). See, further, lines 154–63n.
91   126. "Gentles": ladies and gentlemen.
92   126–27. "wonder… wonder": Throughout his speech, Quince (Prologue) frequently echoes words and phrases: "wonder" (lines 126,
127, 133), "this…" (lines 126, 128, 129, 130, 138), "present[eth]" (lines
130, 135), "lovers" (lines 131, 136, 149), "there,…" (line 137), "did…
" (lines 131, 136, 140 [twice], 141, 142), "if you…" (lines 128, 135),
"trusty Thisbe" (lines 139, 144), "with blade" (line145), "bloody…"
(lines 145, 146), and "let…" (lines 133, 149) as well as Lion (138, 142,
149), Moonshine" (lines 135, 136, 149), and "Wall" (lines 131, 132,
149). He also uses redundancies and a correction: "hight by name"
(line 138), "Did…affright" (line 140).
93   129. "certain": Accented on the second syllable (an archaic,
bungling rhyme). Besides lengthening its meter (see lines 108–16n),
Quince uses archaic diction to make his prologue seem more dig-
nified or lofty; see also line 138n. In the manner of archaic poetry,
he also omits articles before some nouns ("blade" [line 145, twice],
"mulberry" [line 147]), treating common nouns as proper names,
denoting individuals rather than classes; see Abbott, §82.

This man with lime and roughcast doth present[94] 130
"Wall," that vile wall which did these lovers sunder;[95]
And through Wall's chink, poor souls, they are content
To whisper, at the which let no man wonder.
This man, with lantern, dog, and bush of thorn,
Presenteth "Moonshine,"[96] for, if you will know, 135
By moonshine did these lovers think no scorn[97]
To meet at Ninus' tomb,[98] there, there to woo.
This grisly beast, which "Lion" hight[99] by name,
The trusty Thisbe coming first by night
Did scare away or rather did affright; 140
And, as she fled, her mantle she did fall,[100],[101]
Which Lion vile with bloody mouth[102] did stain.
Anon comes Pyramus, sweet youth and tall,[103]
And finds his trusty Thisbe's mantle slain.
Whereat, with blade, with bloody blameful blade, 145

---

94   130. "*present*": represent, personate.
95   131. "'*Wall,'...sunder*": Prologue seems to miss the principal part
      of his story. He speaks of Wall separating the lovers, but not of the
      fathers. By personifying the wall and imputing moral qualities to
      it, he eliminates the need for the forbidding fathers, who are men-
      tioned only in passing (lines 173; see lines 172–75n). Underscoring
      the elimination, Snout, who plays Wall, was originally cast as Pyra-
      mus' father (see 1.2.56–59n).
96   134–35. "*This...'Moonshine'*": See lines 247–49n.
97   136. "*think no scorn*": did not disdain.
98   137. "*To...tomb*": To make the prologue seems more learned,
      Quince includes a verbatim translation of Ovid's Latin phrase:
      "*convenient as busta Nini*" (Ovid, *Metamorphoses*, 4.88); see also lines
      141n and 142n.
99   138. "'*hight*'": is called (an anachronism in Shakespeare's day).
100   141. "*fall*": drop (see Abbott, §291).
101   141. "*And,...fall*": Another verbatim translation of Ovid: "*dumque
      fugit, tergo Velamina lapsa reliquit*" (Ovid, *Metamorphoses*, 4.101).
102   142. "*with bloody mouth*": Yet another verbatim translation of Ovid:
      "*cruentato ore*" (Ovid, *Metamorphoses*, 4.104).
103   142. "*tall*": brave.

He bravely broached[104] his boiling bloody breast.[105]
And Thisbe, tarrying in mulberry shade,
His dagger drew, and died. For all the rest,
Let Lion, Moonshine, Wall, and lovers twain
150   At large[106] discourse, while here they do remain.
Theseus: I wonder if the lion be to speak.
Demetrius: No wonder, my lord. One lion may when many
asses do.

           Exeunt Lion, Thisbe, Moonshine, and Prologue.

Wall: In this same interlude[107] it doth befall
155   That I, one Snout by name, present a wall;
And such a wall as I would have you think
That had in it a crannied hole or chink,
Through which the lovers, Pyramus and Thisbe,
Did whisper often, very secretly.
160   This loam, this roughcast, and this stone doth show
That I am that same wall. The truth is so.
And this the cranny is, right and sinister,[108]
Through which the fearful lovers are to whisper.[109]

---

104   146. "bravely broached": gallantly stabbed (with a secondary sense of tapping a cask of wine or ale).

105   145–46. "Whereat,...breast": To make the speech appear more poetic, Quince not only lades it with alliteration throughout, but with special excess in describing Pyramus' suicide—an excess unmatched even by Bottom's impromptu poetry (see 1.2.35n).

106   150. "At large": at full length.

107   154. "interlude": play.

108   162. "sinister": left.

109   154–63. "In...whisper": Wall delivers his own prologue, which was not originally planned (cp. 3.1.63–67). Like Prologue's speech, it contains its own repetitions: "I...wall" (lines 155, 161), "Through... lovers" (lines 158, 163), "That I" (lines 155, 161), "this..." (lines 154, 160, 162), "crannied / cranny (lines 157, 162), "whisper" (lines 159, 163), and redundancies ("a crannied hole or chink" [line 157], "the lovers, Pyramus and Thisbe" [line158]). Moreover, the speech itself is repetitious or redundant (cp. lines 130–33), adding only that the

Theseus: Would you desire lime and hair[110] to speak better?
Demetrius: It is the wittiest[111] partition[112] that ever I heard   165
    discourse, my lord.
Theseus: Pyramus draws near the wall. Silence.

Enter Pyramus.

Pyramus: *O grim-looked[113] night! O night with hue so black!*
    O night, which ever art when day is not!
    O night! O night! Alack, alack, alack!   170

---

actor's name is Snout (line 155) and that the wall includes stone
(cp. lines 150 and 160).

   Wall, however, expands Prologue's remarks on his dramatic
function (lines 155–57). In a drama, the actors' actions take place
in a world discrete from the audience's. The audience must at once
believe and disbelieve that the action is real. It must keep together
and keep apart the twin senses of acting—doing and simulating.
The players, however, afraid of creating too much dramatic illusion (see 1.2.70–73n, 3.1.35–44n), destroy what little they may have
had.

   Theseus and the others in the audience, mimicking the artisans'
misunderstanding of their art, separate the actors from their roles.
They see the players as actors—as men in costume rather than the
characters they are playing—but nevertheless treat them as their
characters. This explains the two major puzzles in Act 5. On the
one hand, seeing the players as actors, those in the audience fail
to see the resemblance of Pyramus and Thisbe to Lysander and
Hermia (see lines 23–27n). But treating them as their characters,
they speak as though the actors were not present and cannot hear
what they say about them (see lines 118–25n). .

110 164. "lime and hair": plasterers' cement (hair was used to help bind
     the plaster).
111 165. "wittiest": most intelligent.
112 165. "partition": 1) a wall, 2) division of a formal speech into parts
     (*partitio*). Here, each meaning is a pun on the other; see Cicero, *Top-
     ics*, 27.
113 168. *"looked"*: A passive participle not used passively; see Abbott,
     §374.

I fear my Thisbe's promise is forgot.[114]
And thou, O wall, O sweet, O lovely wall,
That stand'st between her father's ground and mine,
Thou wall, O wall, O sweet and lovely wall,
175 *Show me thy chink to blink through with mine eyne.*[115]

[*Wall holds up his fingers.*]

Thanks, courteous wall. Jove shield thee well for this.
But what see I? No Thisbe do I see.[116]
O wicked wall, through whom I see no bliss,
Cursed be thy stones for thus deceiving me![117]
180 *Theseus*: The wall, methinks, being sensible,[118] should curse
again.[119]
Pyramus: No, in truth, sir, he should not. "Deceiving me" is
Thisbe's cue. She is to enter now, and I am to spy

---

114 168–71. "*O...forgot*": Bottom, who boasted that he could move
storms by playing Pyramus (1.2.21–23), begins a dozen lines of
nearly nothing but exclamations. In the first of three pairs of alter-
nately rhymed couplets, he addresses the dark night (named five
times in four lines) with fearful cries stressing privation. While
night is described as the absence of day (cp. 3.2.379n), Pyramus'
exclamations of surprise and woe pun on the word "lack." Tragedy
goes together with loss.

115 172–75. "*And...eyne*": Shifting abruptly from fear to hope, Pyramus, continuing his running hyperbole, addresses the second
pair of couplets to the "*sweet and lovely*" wall, with five cries of
"*O.*" This is the sole mention of a father in Quince's play and one
of only two in Act 5; see, further line 131n. The other, also out of
Bottom's mouth, will make a pair with the first; see lines 337–
38n.

116 177. "*But...bliss.*" Pyramus' inverted wording (an antimetabole or
perhaps chiasmus) is meant to stress the contrast.

117 176–79. "*Thanks...me*": The last pair of couplets is addressed to the
wall, at first gratefully, with an invocation to Jove to reward the
"*courteous*" wall, but, then, with another cry of "*O,*" angrily at the
"*wicked*" wall, with a curse upon its stones.

118 180. "*sensible*": capable of feeling,

119 181. "*again*": back, in return.

her through the wall. You shall see it will fall pat[120] as
I told you.[121] Yonder she comes.   185

Enter Thisbe.

Thisbe: O wall, full often hast thou heard my moans
    For parting my fair Pyramus and me.
    My cherry lips have often kissed thy stones,
    Thy stones with lime and hair knit up in thee.[122]
Pyramus: I see a voice! Now will I[123] to the chink   190
    To spy an[124] I can hear my Thisbe's face.[125]
    Thisbe?
Thisbe: My love! Thou art my love, I think!
Pyramus: Think what thou wilt, I am thy lover's grace,[126]
    And, like Limander, am I trusty still.[127]
Thisbe: And I like Helen, till the Fates me kill.   195
Pyramus: Not Shafalus to Procrus was so true.

---

120 184. "pat": exactly.
121 182–85. "No,…you": Bottom, stepping out of character, rejects The-
     seus' jocular suggestion (line 180), which he misunderstands. By
     "should," Theseus meant what the wall ought to do. Bottom, ap-
     parently still intent on making up for his missed cue in rehearsal
     (see 3.1.94–95n; 4.1.199–200n), thinks he meant what comes next
     in the play.
122 186–89. "O…thee": Thisbe, accusing the wall of parting the lovers,
     unwittingly gives her complaint an obscene meaning. Theseus has
     already stated the primary, innocuous meaning of "lime and hair"
     (see line 164n). Thisbe, the most virginal character in the playlet
     (as Flute is in life), gives the phrase the secondary meaning of
     semen and pubic hair, making it, ironically, the bawdiest passage
     in *MND*. See Gordon Williams, *Glossary*, s.v. lime and hair.
123 190. "will I": will I go.
124 191. "an": if.
125 190. "I…face": Pyramus (Bottom) again confuses the senses' func-
     tions; see, further, 3.1.86n, 4.1.209–12n, and line 293n and lines 338–
     40n.
126 193. "thy lover's grace": 1) thy gracious lover, 2) thy beautiful lover.
127 194. "still": always.

Thisbe: As Shafalus to Procrus, I to you.
Pyramus: O kiss me through the hole of this vile wall.
Thisbe: I kiss the wall's hole, not your lips at all.
200 *Pyramus:* Wilt thou at Ninny's tomb[128] meet me straightway?
Thisbe: 'Tide life, 'tide death,[129] I come without delay.[130]

     Exeunt Pyramus (Bottom) and Thisbe (Flute).

Wall: Thus have I, Wall, my part discharged so,
 And, being done, thus Wall away doth go.[131]

          Exit.

Theseus: Now is the wall down[132] between the two neighbors.

---

128 200. *"Ninny's tomb"*: Bottom did not learn from Quince's correction of Flute's error; see 3.1.92–93n. Flute will do no better (see line 252).

129 201. *"'Tide...death"*: come life, come death ("tide" = "betide").

130 194–201. *"And...delay"*: Once they recognize each other, Pyramus and Thisbe begin an exchange—the playlet's only dialogue. Like Hermia and Lysander, whose situation mirrored theirs, Pyramus and Thisbe, speaking in stichomythia, understand their love in the light of literature (see 1.1.135–40n). Pyramus and Thisbe, however, mangle their stories in affirming their fidelity. First, they confuse Limander and Helen for Leander and Hero. Leander, separated from his lover by a stretch of water, swam the Hellespont at night to see Hero, but, when a storm put out the light that she used to guide him, he drowned. When his body washed up on the shore, Hero threw herself from a tower to die on his corpse (see Virgil, *Georgics*, 3.258–63). Then, Pyramus and Thisbe confuse the names of Cephalus and Procris, faithful lovers who falsely and fatally distrusted each other (see Ovid, *Metamorphoses*, 7.672–862; Golding, 7.874–1117). What they mean as a model of trustiness is a cautionary tale of lovers' mistaken distrust.

131 202–3. *"Thus...go"*: As when he first spoke (see lines 154–63n), Wall breaks out of, and comments on, his character, this time without distinguishing himself from his role.

132 204. "wall down": The Quarto reads "moon used"; the Folio, "moral down." Neither seems correct. Various emendations have been proposed, none fully satisfactory. "[W]all down" gains support from Wall's exit and Demetrius' reply (lines 205–6).

Demetrius: No remedy, my lord, when walls are so willful to[133]   205
    hear without warning.[134]
Hippolyta: This is the silliest stuff that ever I heard.
Theseus: The best in this kind[135] are but shadows, and the
    worst are no worse, if imagination amend them.[136]
Hippolyta: It must be your imagination, then, and not theirs.[137]   210
Theseus: If we imagine no worse of them than they of
    themselves, they may pass for excellent men. Here come
    two noble beasts in, a man and a lion.

    Enter Lion (Snug) and Moonshine (Starveling).

Lion: You ladies,[138] you whose gentle hearts do fear
    The smallest monstrous mouse that creeps on floor,   215
    May now perchance both quake and tremble here,
    When lion rough in wildest rage doth roar.
    Then know that I, as Snug the joiner, am
    A lion fell,[139] nor else no lion's dam;[140]

---

133 205. "to": as to.
134 205–6. "walls…warning": if walls are so eager to hear everything
     without warning, this one will resist its removal (alluding to the
     proverb "Walls have ears" [Dent, W19]):
135 208. "in this kind": of this sort (namely, plays or perhaps players).
136 208–9. "The…them": because plays (or players) are nothing but
     shadows of reality, the worst are no worse than the best, if imagi-
     nation makes up for their defects or deficiencies.
137 210. "It…theirs": Hippolyta, agreeing, makes explicit that the spec-
     tator's imagination must correct the reduced reality by reifying the
     play's images and shadows. The spectator must use his own imag-
     ination to translate them back into things that are real. As in The-
     seus' speech on imagination, realism is everything; see lines 2–23n.
138 214. "You ladies": As planned (see 3.1.35–44), Lion (Snug) addresses
     the women in the audience to prevent their mistaking him for a
     real lion. He seems not to realize that his speaking (if nothing else)
     would belie their fear; see 3.1.35–44n.
139 219. "lion fell": 1) fierce lion, 2) lion skin.
140 219. "A lion fell…dam": neither a fierce lion nor the female parent
     of a lion.

220   *For if I should as lion come in strife*
        Into this place, 'twere pity on my life.[141]

Theseus: A very gentle[142] beast, and of a good conscience.

Demetrius: The very best at[143] a beast, my lord, that e'er I saw.

Lysander: This lion is a very fox for his valor.[144]

225 *Theseus*: True, and a goose for his discretion.[145]

Demetrius: Not so, my lord, for his valor cannot carry his
        discretion, and the fox carries the goose.[146]

Theseus: His discretion, I am sure, cannot carry his valor,
        for the goose carries not the fox.[147] It is well. Leave it to

230   his discretion, and let us listen to the moon.

Moonshine: *This lanthorn doth the horned moon present*—[148]

Demetrius: He should have worn the horns on his head.[149]

---

141   221. "*'twere…life*": a sad thing for me.

142   222. "gentle": gentlemanly, well mannered.

143   223. "at": at being.

144   224. "This…valor": As lions "excel in strength and courage," while foxes, "crafty [and] wary" (Topsell, 361, 173), flee dangers, Lion shows that he is unlike the former but like the latter, in fearing to frighten anyone for fear of his own life.

145   225. "a goose…discretion": Just as Lion is a fox, not a lion, for valor, he is a goose, not a fox, for discretion. Geese are said to lack discretion. "[W]here this goose (you see) puts down his head, before there be anything near to touch him" (Philip Sidney, *Arcadia*, 307).

146   226–27. "Not…goose" Demetrius, as though catching Theseus in a self-contradiction, quibbles on the word "carry," using it first to mean support and then to mean carry off or away: Lion's valor (fox) cannot support his discretion (goose), yet the fox carries off the goose.

147   228–29. "His…fox": Theseus, concluding the jibe, reverses the terms, while continuing the confusion between supporting and seizing something.

148   231. "This…present": the lantern (*lanthorn*) symbolizes the crescent (*horned*) moon. Lanterns were commonly made of horn. The modern spelling obscures the pun on "horn."

149   232. "He…head": Demetrius, resorting to a hackneyed joke, takes the timorous Starveling's slenderness as a sign of his unmanliness and accuses him of being a cuckold. Horns are said to adorn a cuckold (see Dent, H625).

Theseus: He is no crescent, and his horns are invisible within
    the circumference.[150]

Moonshine: *This lanthorn doth the horned moon present.*   235
    Myself the man i'th'moon do seem[151] *to be.*

Theseus: This is the greatest error of all the rest;[152] the man
    should be put into the lanthorn. How is it else the man i'th'moon?[153]

Demetrius: He dares not come there for[154] the candle, for you see   240
    it is already in snuff.[155]

Hippolyta: I am aweary of this moon. Would he would change.

Theseus: It appears by his small light of discretion that he is
    in the wane;[156] but yet, in courtesy, in all reason,[157] we
    must stay the time.   245

Lysander: Proceed, Moon.

Moonshine: All that I have to say is to tell you that the
    lanthorn is the moon, I the man i'th'moon, this thornbush
    my thornbush, and this dog my dog.[158]

---

150 233–34. "He...circumference": Theseus, shifting the joke, says that
    Starveling is too thin to be not only a waxing ("crescent") moon,
    but anything other than a new ("invisible") moon.

151 237. "*do seem*": appear.

152 237. "greatest...the rest": A confusion of two constructions of su-
    perlatives; see Abbott, §409.

153 237–39. "This... i'th'moon": the "man i'th'moon" (Moonshine)
    should be in the moon (the lantern), not carrying it.

154 240. "for": for fear of.

155 241. "in snuff": A triple pun: 1) Moonshine is already faint and fee-
    ble ("in snuff"), 2) he needs to have the burnt-out part of himself
    ("snuff") removed, and 3) even before that is tried, he is taking of-
    fence ("in snuff").

156 243–44. "It...wane": Theseus combines ridicule of Starveling's
    slender body and his slender wisdom in the slender moon's small
    light. Showing such light, the moon will quickly vanish.

157 244. "in all reason": as is only reasonable.

158 247–49. "All...dog": The configuration seen in the disc of the full
    moon has been variously interpreted as a man leaning on a fork
    and carrying a bundle of sticks, or as a man with his dog and a
    thorn bush; see line 134; and Ebenezer Cobham Brewer, *Dictionary
    of Phrase and Fable*, s.v. man in the moon, the.

250 *Demetrius*: Why, all these should be in the lanthorn, for all these
are in the moon.[159] But silence. Here comes Thisbe.

Enter Thisbe (Flute).

Thisbe: *This is old Ninny's tomb.*[160] *Where is my love?*
Lion: *O—!*

The Lion roars. Thisbe runs off, [dropping her mantle.]

Demetrius: Well roared, Lion.
255 *Theseus*: Well run, Thisbe.
Hippolyta: Well shone, Moon. Truly, the Moon shines with a
good grace.

[Lion tears Thisbe's mantle, and exit.]

Theseus: Well moused,[161] Lion!
Demetrius: And then came Pyramus.
260 *Lysander*: And so the lion vanished.

Enter Pyramus[162]

Pyramus: *Sweet Moon, I thank thee for thy sunny beams.*[163]
I thank thee, Moon, for shining now so bright,

---

159 250–51. "Why,…moon": Demetrius, mocking the players' literalness, suggests that the word "thorn" is in the word "lanthorn" and
the word "horn" ("the horned moon") is in both words. Hence, the
moon ("horn") should be in the bush ("thorn") and the bush
("thorn") in the moon ("lanthorn"). What is true of the words
should be true of what they name.
160 252. "Ninny's tomb": See line 200n.
161 258. "moused": torn to pieces (as a cat tears a mouse).
162 S.D. 261. "Enter Pyramus": Bottom finally gets to "condole in some
measure" (1.2.23). His grand speech contains two parts of equal
length (lines 261–76, 280–95) and largely similar form, each over-
loaded with nearly continual alliteration, apostrophes, exclamations, repetition, and tortured rhyme. The first part leads up to his
plea to the Fates to let him die. The second depicts his death.
163 261. "sunny beams": A mistranslation of Ovid's "lunae radios"
("lunar rays") (Ovid, *Metamorphoses*, 4.99). Evidently determined

For by thy gracious, golden, glittering gleams,[164]
I trust to take[165] *of truest Thisbe sight.*

      But stay! O spite![166]   265

      But mark, poor knight,

   What dreadful dole[167] *is here?*

     Eyes, do you see?

     How can it be?

   O dainty duck! O dear!   270

     Thy mantle good —

 What! Stained with blood?[168],[169]

Approach, ye Furies fell![170]

   O Fates, come, come!

   Cut thread and thrum,[171]   275

---

    to speak in hyperbole, Pyramus (Bottom) substitutes the direct light of the sun for the reflected light of the moon.

164 263. "*gleams*": Editors often emend the texts' "beams" to "gleams," which fits Quince's frequent excessive alliteration and avoids repeating the rhyming word in line 261.

165 264. "*take*": get, catch (sight of).

166 265. "*spite*": vexation, disaster.

167 267. "*dole*": cause of grief.

168 272. "*Stained...blood*": In Ovid's account, the lion's jaws are dripping with the blood of fresh-slain cattle (Ovid, *Metamorphoses*, 4.96–98). Quince's script does not explain the blood.

169 265–72. "*But...blood*": Pyramus' error, constituting the play's tragic "recognition" and "reversal" (Aristotle, *Poetics*, 1452a22–b9), inverts the players' characteristic literalness. Instead of failing to see an image as an image, Pyramus sees what is not a sign as a sign. He assigns significance where there is none.

170 273. "*Furies fell*": fierce Furies. The Furies (*Erinyes*) are terrifying avenging goddesses, who exact punishment for murder and other serious crimes and are ultimately guardians of civil order. They initially appear on the stage dressed disgustingly in black, with eyes dripping drops of hateful blood and swarming snakes for hair (see Aeschylus, *Libation Bearers*, 1048–50; *Eumenides*, 48–54).

171 274–75. "*O...thrum*": While the three Fates—Clotho, Lachesis, and Atropos—allot, spin, and cut the thread of life (see Hesiod, *Theogony*, 217–20; Plato, *Republic*, 620e), "*thread and thrum*" are a

Quail,[172] *crush, conclude, and quell!*[173]

Theseus: This passion,[174] and the death of a dear friend, would
    go near to make a man look sad.

Hippolyta: Beshrew[175] my heart, but I pity the man.[176]

280 *Pyramus*: O, wherefore, Nature, didst thou lions frame,
        Since lion vile hath here deflowered[177] my dear?
        Which is — no, no — which was the fairest dame
        That lived, that loved, that liked, that looked with cheer?[178],[179]
                Come, tears, confound![180]
285   Out, sword, and wound

---

weaver's terms referring to his warp ("*thread*") and its tufted end
("*thrum*"), which is left attached to the loom when the finished
piece of cloth is cut and removed. Unlike the *thread*, the *thrum* is
unwoven and worth little.

172 276. "*Quail*": overpower.
173 276. "*quell*": slay.
174 277. "*passion*": 1) suffering, 2) passionate speech.
175 279. "*Beshrew*": A very mild curse.
176 279. "*Beshrew...man*": Although tragedy is intended to arouse
     pity (see Aristotle, *Poetics*, 1449b24–28), Hippolyta seems to mean
     that she pities the actor, Bottom, rather than his character, Pyra-
     mus.
177 281. "*lion...deflowered*": Bottom means "devoured." Adding
     salience to his malapropism, "lion" is a heraldic pun on sexual
     rampancy; see Gordon Williams, *Dictionary*, s.v. lion; and note
     3.1.29–30.
178 283. "*cheer*": 1) cheerfulness, 2) (perhaps) face; see 3.2.96n.
179 282–83. "*Which...cheer*": Besides apostrophizing again, as he did
     lavishly in the first part of his speech, Pyramus uses other
     pompous rhetorical tropes to suit the tragic occasion. He asks Na-
     ture a rhetorical question and then attempts to demonstrate both
     his passion and his scrupulousness by interrupting and correcting
     himself: only the living can be spoken of in the present tense; for
     the dead, one must use the past tense. (For *correctio* as an embel-
     lishment, see Quintilian, *Institutes*, 9.1.30). Pyramus also attempts
     to heighten the dramatic effect with a combination of *ploche* and
     alliteration, restating the same word after intervening words that
     repeat the same sound.
180 284. "*confound*": overpower, destroy.

The pap[181] of Pyramus;
   Ay, that left pap,
   Where heart doth hop.

[*Stabs himself.*]

Thus die I, thus, thus, thus!
   Now am I dead;   290
   Now am I fled;
My soul is in the sky.[182]
   Tongue, lose thy light![183]
   Moon, take thy flight!

[*Exit Moonshine.*]

Now die, die, die, die, die.   295

[*Dies.*]

Demetrius: No die, but an ace for him, for he is but one.[184]
Lysander: Less than an ace, man, for he is dead, he is nothing.[185]

---

181   286. *"pap"*: breast, usually referring to a woman's: "Nature hath not given Paps to Men" (John Ray, *Wisdom of God*, 2.236).

182   290–92. *"Now…sky"*: Although he could not speak of dead Thisbe in the present tense (see line 282–83n), Pyramus speaks of himself in the present tense as "dead" and "fled." Unlike Quince's Pyramus, Quince never takes responsibility for Thisbe's imagined death (cp. Ovid, *Metamorphoses*, 4.108–20).

183   293. *"Tongue,…light"*: Pyramus again confuses the senses; on the artisans' sensory confusion, see, further, 3.1.86n, 4.1.209–12n, 5.1.190n, 5.1.338–40n.

184   296. *"No…one"*: A quibble on Pyramus' reechoed dying word and thought (line 295). While a die is one of a pair of dice, an ace is a die marked with one spot. The lowest or worst number with the throw of a die, it is "but one"—just a single point. Pyramus is "but one" because, while a living person is both a body and a soul, a dead person is but a body: "*My soul is in the sky*" (line 292).

185   297. *"Less…nothing"*: To be something means to be alive, as Pyramus suggested (see lines 282–83n). Taking him at his word, Lysander suggests that in order for Pyramus to be one, he must be two. Unless both body and soul, he is nothing.

Theseus: With the help of a surgeon[186] he might yet recover
and yet prove an ass.[187]

300 *Hippolyta*: How chance[188] Moonshine is gone, before Thisbe
comes back and finds her lover?

Theseus: She will find him by starlight.[189]

Enter Thisbe (Flute).

Here she comes, and her passion[190] ends the play.

Hippolyta: Methinks she should not use a long one for such a

305 Pyramus. I hope she will be brief.[191]

Demetrius: A mote[192] will turn the balance, which Pyramus,
which Thisbe, is the better: he for a man, God

---

186 298. "surgeon": medical doctor.

187 299. "prove an ass": show himself to be an ass (a pun on "ace,"
which was similarly pronounced).

188 300. "How chance": how does it happen that.

189 300–2. "How…starlight": This short exchange points to the strik-
ing fact that during the scenes in the woods only the fairies, and
none of the humans, had the benefit of moonlight. Lysander said
that he and Hermia would flee Athens when "Phoebe doth behold / Her silver visage in the wat'ry glass" (1.1.209–10). But
once in the woods, lovers never speak of the moon as shining and
repeatedly complain of darkness (2.2.85, 3.2.60–61, 177–82, 187–
88, 356, 417–19, 431–33). Likewise, the artisans, before entering
the woods, speak of rehearsing there by "moonlight" (1.2.95).
But, once there, they mention a shining moon only when consult-
ing a calendar, and only in regard to performing the play afterwards in Athens. And, even then, they substitute an
impersonation for the moon itself: The shining moon becomes
Moonshine (3.1.46–57).

190 303. "passion": 1) suffering, 2) its expression in words; same as line
277.

191 305. "I…brief": These are Hippolyta's final words. Her change
seems complete. In her opening speech Hippolyta thought that the
four days until her nuptial hour would pass quickly enough (see
1.1.7–11n). In her closing speech she is eager for the remaining minutes to pass quickly.

192 306. "mote": a speck of dust.

warrant us; she for a woman, God bless us!¹⁹³
Lysander: She hath spied him already with those sweet eyes.
Demetrius: And thus she means,¹⁹⁴ *videlicet*—¹⁹⁵   310
Thisbe: *Asleep, my love?*
                    What, dead, my dove?
           O Pyramus, arise!
                    Speak, speak. Quite dumb?
                    Dead, dead? A tomb   315
           Must cover thy sweet eyes.
                    These lily lips,
                    This cherry nose,
           *These yellow cowslip cheeks*¹⁹⁶
                    Are gone, are gone!   320
                    Lovers, make moan;
           His eyes were green as leeks.
                    *O Sisters Three,*¹⁹⁷
                    Come, come to me
           With hands as pale as milk.   325
                    Lay them in gore,
                    Since you have shore

---

193 307–8. "he…bless us": Demetrius, in his last words on Pyramus,
     denigrates his manliness, as he had Starveling's (see line 232n)
     and Lysander's (see 3.2.401–30n). No one disparages the manli-
     ness of other men so much as Demetrius does (see, further,
     1.1.194–201n, 3.2.401–30n). "[W]arrant" means "protect." The
     Folio omits the passage presumably to comply with the 1606
     statute prohibiting using the name of God profanely or jestingly
     on the stage.
194 310. "means": 1) moans or laments, especially for the dead (an old
     sense), 2) lodges a formal complaint (a legal term). For a similar
     combined meaning of the soul's passion and its utterance in
     speech, see lines 277n, 303n.
195 310. "*videlicet*": as you see (a Latin legal term).
196 316–19. "*sweet…cheeks*": Thisbe seems to give each feature of Pyra-
     mus' face an epithet that would seem better suited to a woman
     than to a man; see, further, lines 286n and 307–8n.
197 323. "*Sisters Three*": the three Fates (see lines 274–75n).

With shears his thread of silk.[198]
Tongue, not a word!
330   *Come, trusty sword,*
Come, blade, my breast imbrue![199]

                                   [Stabs herself.]

And farewell, friends.
Thus Thisbe ends.
Adieu, adieu, adieu![200]

                                   [Dies.].

335 *Theseus:* Moonshine and Lion are left[201] to bury the dead.
Demetrius: Ay, and Wall too.
Bottom: [*Starting up.*] No, I assure you, the wall is down that
parted their fathers.[202] [*Flute rises.*] Will it please you to

---

198 328. "*his...silk*": Pyramus' "*thread and thrum*" have become "*his thread of silk*"; see lines 274–75n. Perhaps most especially in death, love idealizes its beloved.

199 331. "*imbrue*": 1) pierce, 2) stain with blood.

200 330–34. "*Come,...adieu*": Thisbe dies in five lines and 17 words, in contrast to Pyramus' 11 lines and 50 words (lines 85–95). Unlike him, she mentions friends, not just herself. Yet, she fails to recognize the tragic crux of her love story. She wants to be killed by Fate, as Pyramus was, and to die by the same sword. But she seems not to realize that Pyramus killed himself for love of her. His silence regarding his responsibility for her imagined death (see lines 290–92n) is matched by her silence regarding her part in his death. In Ovid, Pyramus and Thisbe each takes blame for the other's death. Moreover, Ovid's Thisbe asks their apostrophized parents for a common burial (Ovid, *Metamorphoses*, 4.108–57). Quince's Thisbe, however, never seeks the union in death that their parents denied them in life. Rather than be buried together, Pyramus is to be buried alone (see lines 315–16).

201 335. "*left*": left alive, remain.

202 337–38. "*No,...fathers*": Bottom, rising from the dead and stepping out of character, corrects Demetrius. Bottom is the only character to mention fathers in Act 5, and his two references are paired. As Pyramus, he spoke of the wall that "[*t*]*hat stand'st between her fa-*

see the epilogue or to hear a Bergomask dance[203]
between two of our company?[204]   340
Theseus: No epilogue, I pray you. For your play needs no
excuse.[205] Never excuse. For when the players are all
dead, there need none to be blamed. Marry, if he
that writ it had played Pyramus and hanged
himself in Thisbe's garter,[206] it would have been a fine   345
tragedy; and so it is, truly, and very notably
discharged. But, come, your Bergomask. Let your
epilogue alone.

> [*A dance, and exeunt the players.*]

The iron tongue of midnight[207] hath told[208] twelve.
Lovers, to bed! 'Tis almost fairy time.[209]   350

---

ther's ground and mine" (line 173). As himself, he now insists that
the wall is down. Where the movement of *MND*, a comedy, is from
the authority of fathers to the freedom of their children in marriage, the movement of "Pyramus and Thisbe," a tragedy, is from
the quarreling of fathers to their reconciliation in the deaths of their
children. The authority of fathers in Athens and the wall parting
fathers in the artisans' play are both down.

203   339. "Bergomask dance": a rustic dance, mimicking the people of
Bergamo (an alpine region in today's Italy), often ridiculed as
clownish in their manners and dialect (Robert Nares, *Glossary*, s.v.
Bergomask dance). This is the only dancing by humans in the play
(see, further, 3.1.158n).

204   338-40. "Will...company": While confusing the senses once more,
Bottom seems to have forgotten the ballad that he wanted to sing
at Thisbe's death (see 4.1.212-17).

205   341-42. "No...excuse": needs no apology. Epilogues, like prologues, traditionally address the audience directly and ask for the
audience's indulgence (as Puck's epilogue will [lines 409-24]).

206   344-45. "hanged...garter": A variation of a proverbial expression
of contempt: "He may go hang himself in his own garters" (Dent,
G42).

207   349. "iron...midnight": sound of the midnight bell.

208   349. "told": counted (with a pun on "tolled").

209   350. "fairy time": Fairy time, for Theseus, are the hours between

I fear we shall outsleep the coming morn
As much as we this night have overwatched.[210]
This palpable-gross[211] play hath well beguiled
The heavy gait of night.[212] Sweet friends, to bed.

355 A fortnight hold we this solemnity[213]
In nightly revels and new jollity.

[*Exeunt.*]

Enter Puck [with a broom.]

Puck: Now the hungry lion roars,
And the wolf behowls[214] the moon,
Whilst the heavy[215] plowman snores,

360 All with weary task fordone.[216],[217]

---

midnight and dawn. If there is magic then, it is not that of fairies, but of love.

210 352. "overwatched": stayed up late.

211 353. "palpable-gross": conspicuously 1) rough, coarse, 2) dull, stupid.

212 349–54. "The iron...night": As Theseus had sought, the play has served as a diversion to help pass the slow-moving time (see lines 36–37n). As he initially described his desire and its satisfaction in temporal terms, he does so again in the end. He may still find the night's pace a slow walk ("heavy gait"), but now that it is midnight of his wedding day, "not yet" has become "almost now"; see, further, 1.1.1–4n.

213 355. "fortnight...solemnity": we will have two weeks of festive celebration.

214 358. "behowls": barks, howls at. The Quartos and Folios read "beholds," which editors commonly emend to "behowls," which far better fits the context; see, further, lines 357–60n.

215 359. "heavy": weary, sleepy.

216 360. "fordone": worn out (with a sense of injury; see Abbott, §441).

217 357–60. "Now...fordone": Puck, who, with the other fairies, appears now in Athens for the first time, completes his change from laughing at the harm his pranks cause others to benefitting lovers who know nothing of him, let alone call him Hobgoblin or sweet Puck (see 2.1.34–42 and nn, and 3.2.437–41n). Puck begins his final speech in the play proper by describing three sorts of evils of the

Now the wasted brands[218] do glow,
Whilst the screech-owl, screeching loud,[219]
Puts the wretch that lies in woe
In remembrance of a shroud.[220]
Now it is the time of night   365
That[221] the graves, all gaping wide,
Every one lets forth his sprite
In the church-way paths to glide.[222]
And we fairies, that do run
By the triple Hecate's team[223]   370

---

night. The first concerns predatory beasts (lines 357–60), the second screeching owls (lines 361–64), and the third ghosts (lines 365–68). "[T]riple Hecate" connects them (see line 370n). As for the first sort of evil, the plowman may not labor in vain (cp. 2.1.94), but, as Puck seems to emphasize by rhyming "roars" and "snores," he is nonetheless threatened in his sleep by hungry beasts. He may consequently be "fordone" in another sense as well.

218   361. "wasted brands": nearly burnt-out logs.

219   362. "screech-owl,...loud": "The screech-owl betokens always some heavy news, and is most execrable and accursed...[It] is the very monster of the night, neither crying nor singing out clear, but uttering a certain heavy groan of doleful mourning" (Pliny, 10.34; Holland, 276).

220   361–64. "Now...shroud": The second sort of nocturnal evil concerns imagining one's own imminent death. The owl's shrill screech, which is thought to foretell death (see line 362n), causes the sleepless, dying man to imagine himself as a corpse laid out for burial.

221   366. "That": when (see Abbott, §384).

222   365–68. "Now...glide": The third night-time evil concerns the ghosts or spirits of the dead, which return from the underworld at midnight. "The usual time at which ghosts make their appearance is midnight" (Francis Grose, "Popular Superstitions," 7). Not only some, but all graves, release their dead, as Puck stresses with redundancy: "...the graves, all gaping wide, / Every one lets forth his sprite."

223   370. "triple...team": Hecate, goddess of the moon and all that pertains to darkness and the night, is said to be "threefold." She is called Diana on earth, Phoebe in the sky, and Hecate or Proserpine

From the presence of the sun,
Following darkness like a dream,[224]
Now are frolic.[225] Not a mouse
Shall disturb this hallowed house.
375   I am sent with broom before,
To sweep the dust behind the door.[226]

Enter Oberon and Titania, King and Queen of Fairies,
with all their train.

Oberon: Through the house give glimmering light,
By the dead and drowsy fire.[227]
Every elf and fairy sprite,
380   Hop as light as bird from brier,
And this ditty after me,
Sing and dance it trippingly.[228],[229]

---

in the underworld (Virgil, *Aeneid*, 1.511). Each of her three names or aspects corresponds to one of the night's three sorts of evils, all of which concern death. At the same time, Hecate is honored highly by the Olympian gods, brings victory and glory to warriors and athletes, and is made protector of children by Zeus (Hesiod, *Theogony*, 410–52).

224 369–72. "we...dream": The fairies, like Hecate, are beings of the night. They avoid daylight and follow her chariot or "team," drawn by winged dragons across the nighttime sky.

225 373. "frolic": frolicsome.

226 375–76. "I...door": If Puck initially caused people to lose what they worked for (see 2.1.35–39n), he now does their housecleaning for them. His final transformation is his serviceable domestication. For "Robin good-fellow...sweeping the house at midnight," see Scot, 4.10.

227 377–78. "Through...fire": 1) a royal order addressed to the fairies, or, 2) perhaps more likely, a magical charm addressed to the dim fire itself.

228 380–82. "Hop... trippingly": On the fairies' characteristic movements, see 3.1.158n.

229 377–82. "Through...trippingly": The final appearance of Oberon and Titania pairs up with their first (2.1.60ff.). This time, however, instead of Oberon's disturbing her fairies' dance and refusing to dance with

Titania: First rehearse your song by rote,[230]
    To each word a warbling note.
    Hand in hand, with fairy grace,   385
    Will we sing and bless this place.

Song[231] [*and dance.*]

Oberon: Now, until the break of day,
    Through this house each fairy stray.[232]
    To the best bride-bed will we,[233]
    Which by us shall blessed be,   390
    And the issue[234] there create[235]
    Ever shall be fortunate.
    So shall all the couples three
    Ever true in loving be,
    And the blots of nature's hand[236]   395

---

her on her terms, they happily dance together. And instead of quarreling over a young boy, they have come to bless the newly married couples and their offspring (cp. 3.2.82–142). The "glimmering night" (2.1.77) through which Oberon had jealously accused Titania of leading Theseus to forsake various women has become the "glimmering light" with which Oberon uses his magical powers to increase the glow of the household fire. The taming of the fairies goes together with the moderating or civilizing of Athens' founder and of Athens itself.

230 383. "rehearse…rote": repeat from memory.

231 S.D. 387. "*Song*": The song that Titania wants the fairies to sing seems to have been lost. While the Folio marks Oberon's next (and final) speech as "The Song," and indents and italicizes the lines as a song, the First Quarto prints them in roman as a speech and gives the lines to Oberon. And where Shakespeare typically differentiates his songs metrically from what precedes and follows (for example, 2.2.9–25), these lines, which are chiefly a set of instructions, have the same meter as the previous part of the fairies' dialogue (lines 357ff.).

232 388. "stray": As is their wont, the fairies are to wander until dawn (see 2.1.1n).

233 389. "best…we": we will go to Theseus and Hippolyta's bed.

234 391. "issue": offspring.

235 391. "create": created (see Abbott, §342).

236 395. "blots…hand": ugly natural blemishes.

Shall not in their issue stand.
Never mole, harelip, nor scar,
Nor mark prodigious,[237] such as are
Despised in nativity,[238]
400   Shall upon their children be.[239]
With this field-dew[240] consecrate[241]
Every fairy take his gait,[242]
And each several[243] chamber bless,
Through this palace, with sweet peace.[244]
405   And the owner of it blest,
Ever shall in safety rest.
Trip away. Make no stay.[245]
Meet me all by break of day.[246],[247]

Exeunt [all but Puck].

---

237   398. "mark prodigious": ominous birthmark.

238   399. "nativity": birth.

239   393–400. "So...be": The fairies are to protect, or protect against, two things especially subject to chance: true love and birth defects. The benefits are to be continuous. The couples' true love is to be for "[e]ver," and their children's birth deformities are to be "[n]ever"; see also line 392. We have seen dangers to true love. Oberon lists those of birth defects. He speaks only of visible defects—ones that are ugly as distinguished from unhealthy. They cause a person not to be ill, but to be despised or unloved.

240   401. "field-dew": See 2.1.9n.

241   401. "consecrate": consecrated, blessed (see Abbott, §342).

242   402. "take...gait": make his way, proceed.

243   403, "several": separate.

244   401–6. "With...rest": Oberon adds a third blessing—peace and safety.

245   407. "Trip...stay": move lightly with quick, short steps; do not delay; see lines 380–82n.

246   408. "break of day": As Oberon began the speech with the phrase "break of day," which he rhymed with "stray" (lines 387–88), he ends it with the same phrase, which he rhymes with "stay."

247   387–408. "Now,...day": On the blessings of Theseus and his offspring, see the Coda, 1987–99.

Puck: [*To the audience.*] If we shadows[248] have offended,
       Think but this and all is mended,   410
       That you have but slumbered here
       While these visions did appear.
       And this weak and idle[249] theme,
       No more yielding but[250] a dream,[251]
       Gentles,[252] do not reprehend.[253]   415
       If you pardon, we will mend.[254]
       And, as I am an honest Puck,
       If we have unearned luck
       Now to 'scape the serpent's tongue,[255]
       We will make amends ere[256] long.   420
       Else the Puck a liar call.
       So good night unto you all.
       Give me your hands,[257] if we be friends,
       And Robin shall restore amends.[258]

                                                              [*Exit.*]

---

248 409. "shadows": 1) fairies, 2) actors. Puck called the fairies "shadows" (3.2.347), and Theseus called actors "shadows" (lines 208–9). Puck seems to combine the two senses in addressing the audience.
249 413. "idle": foolish, trifling.
250 414. "No…but": yielding no more than.
251 409–14. "If…dream": Puck's apology is addressed not to all of Shakespeare's audience, but only to those who have been "offended"—those who think the play a "weak and idle theme." Puck's apology is thus no apology at all. Instead of excusing Shakespeare's play, it pointedly if implicitly blames those who think it needs an apology. It tells those who find the play trivial to think that they "have but slumbered here." In an important sense, they have. At least in this respect, Puck is indeed "an honest Puck" (line 417).
252 415. "Gentles": ladies and gentlemen.
253 415. "reprehend": express disapproval.
254 416. "mend": do better next time.
255 419. "serpent's tongue": hisses (from the audience).
256 420. "ere": before.
257 423. "hands": applause.
258 424. "restore amends": make improvements in return.

CODA

MND, we have seen, is an averted tragedy. Theseus' founding of Athens spares Hermia the tragic fate of Pyramus and Thisbe. While the love stories of *Pyramus and Thisbe* and *MND* closely mirror each other—the one as tragedy, the other as comedy—Theseus' revolutionary action permits *MND*'s happy ending with the loving couples marrying and the fairies preparing to bless them and their children. Oberon, in particular, affirms that he and Titania will bless Theseus and Hippolyta's bed, so that "the issue there create / Ever shall be fortunate" (5.1.391–92).

Yet, Shakespeare places at the heart of a comedy an ancient hero whom previous playwrights placed at the heart of tragedies. Moreover, he takes notable—and otherwise unnecessary—steps to call attention to those earlier writings and remind attentive readers that events turn out far from fortunate for Theseus and his issue.

Although ancient writers commonly identify Theseus' Amazon wife not as Hippolyta, but as Antiopa,[1] Shakespeare relegates Antiopa to the ranks of the women Theseus deceived and deserted (see 2.1.80n) and gives the mother of his future son, Hippolytus, the feminine form of the son's name. Shakespeare thus alludes to the tragic story surrounding Phaedra, whom Theseus married after his first wife died, her stepson—Theseus' son—Hippolytus, and Theseus himself.

According to that story, Hippolytus considered Aphrodite vile and was devoted to the goddess Artemis, a virgin huntress whom he revered as the greatest god. He therefore shunned sex and marriage, and devoted himself to hunting. Aphrodite, seeking revenge for his slight, caused his step-mother Phaedra to fall

---

1   For example, Plutarch, *Theseus*, 26. 1–2, 27.4, 28.1; Diodorus Siculus, 4.28.3; Pausanias, 1.2.1; Seneca, *Hippolytus*, 927ff.

passionately in love with him. When he rebuffed her amorous advances, Phaedra, afraid that he would tell Theseus everything, wrote a letter to Theseus falsely accusing Hippolytus of rape and then hanged herself. Theseus, believing the letter, cursed the son, ordered him into exile, and prayed to Poseidon to kill him. When Hippolytus then rode his chariot along the seashore, Poseidon sent a bull from the sea, which terrified the horses and, shattering the chariot, tangled Hippolytus in the reins[2] and dragged him to his death. And so Hippolytus, "through his father's light belief, and stepdame's craft was slain" (Ovid, *Metamorphoses*, 15.471; Golding, 15.556). Only then did Artemis reveal the truth to Theseus.[3]

Just as Oberon's final speech—the last speech in the play itself—points ahead to Hippolytus' murderous step-mother Phaedra, Theseus' first speech—the first speech in the play—points back to his own murderous step-mother, Medea. Where Phaedra, with a credulous Theseus' unwitting help, will bring about the death of his son and her stepson Hippolytus, Medea, a sorceress who murdered her own sons by Jason and married Egeus after Theseus was born, had already tried to murder Theseus before the action of the play, so that her own son by Egeus could succeed him as king.[4] Shakespeare thus frames *MND* with allusions to two deadly step-mothers central to Theseus' tragedy-laden life, as famously depicted by ancient playwrights.

Shakespeare makes the relation of comedy and tragedy a running—often comic—theme of *MND*. As we see most clearly—though not only—in the relation between *Pyramus and Thisbe* and *MND*, tragedy turns into comedy. The tragic outcome is diverted and (except for Egeus) things end happily for everyone. This dramatic transformation is not surprising. A comedy's happy outcome typically springs from unhappy circumstances. Comedy presupposes suffering. "A comedy has in its beginning, at first sight, someone lamenting, and afterwards ends in gladness"

---

2   As echoed his name; see S.D. 1.1.1n.
3   See Euripides, *Hippolytus*; Seneca, *Hippolytus*.
4   See 1.1.4–6n.

(John Lydgate, *Troy Book*, 2.847). What is surprising and highly unusual, however, is that the transformation in *MND* doubles back on itself. As tragedy turns into comedy, comedy turns back into tragedy. Directly contrary to Oberon's blessing, the play's propitious ending proves to be the prelude to a tragic outcome. One might say that *MND*—to borrow the players' inept description of their own play—is "very tragical mirth" (5.1.57).

Something similar could be said of Athens itself. Shakespeare tacitly pairs *MND* with *Timon of Athens*. The former, as I have argued, illustrates, in a comic manner, Pericles' proud description of Athenians as lovers of the beautiful and wisdom (see Introduction, 2–3). In the same oration, however, Pericles cautions that the pursuit of boundless empire and glory could corrupt the citizens and destroy Athenian brilliance. Glory, resting on acquisition, tends to engender greed (Thucydides, 2.65.6–13). Following Pericles' death, the Athenians did just what he had warned against. *Timon* depicts the consequent decline and decay. As we see in that tragedy, the Athenians' love of the beautiful is replaced by a voracious love of gold. Virtually everyone in *Timon* is chasing madly after money. Timon, the most honored man in Athens, is praised, even revered, for his wealth and profligate giving. "Plautus the god of gold / Is but his steward," one admirer says (*TA*, 1.1.275–76). "O he's the very soul of bounty," another exclaims (*TA*,1.2.207), while still another Athenian extols him for possessing "the noblest mind… / That ever goven'd man" (*TA*, 1.1.279–80). In post-Periclean Athens, Athenians esteem prodigality as the highest nobility. Athens still has poets and painters, but they look upon their art as merchandise to be sold at a high price: "Traffic's thy god" (*TA*,1.2.238). And where *MND* concludes with all the women marrying, the only women in *Timon* are two whores who will "do anything for gold" (*TA*, 4.3.152) and a masque of lascivious dancers, led by Cupid (and dressed as Amazons), entertaining a party of carousing men. Indeed, while Cupid promises that the showgirls' entertainment will be sensual, Timon's description of its pleasures is the play's only mention of anything as "beautiful" (1.2.144). As for Theseus, so for Athens: the splendid glory is gone.

BIBLIOGRAPHY

Aeschylus. Choephoroe. In *The Complete Greek Tragedies*, Vol. 1. Translated by Richmond Lattimore. Chicago: The University of Chicago Press, 1959. Cited as *Libation Bearers*.

————. *Eumenides*. In *The Complete Greek Tragedies*, Vol. 1. Translated by Richmond Lattimore. Chicago: The University of Chicago Press, 1959.

Ammianus Marcellinus (4th Century, AD). *Rerum Gestarum*, Vol. 1. Translated by J. C. Rolfe. Loeb Classical Library. Harvard University Press, 1950. Cited as *History*.

Anonymous. *The Floure and the Leafe*, c. 1460–80. Edited by Derek Pearsall. Medieval Institute Publications. Kalamazoo: Western Michigan University, 1990.

Anonymous (7th Century, BC). *Hymn to Hermes*. In *The Homeric Hymns*. Translated by Diana J. Rayor. Berkeley: University of California Press, 2014.

Apollodorus (2nd Century, BC). *Library*. Translated by Keith Aldrich. Lawrence: Coronado Press, 1975.

Appian (2nd Century, AD). *The Civil Wars*. In *Appian's Roman History*, 3 vols. Loeb Classical Library. Harvard University Press, 1972.

Apuleius. *The Golden Ass*, 1566. Translated by Sarah Ruden. New Haven: Yale University Press, 2011.

Aratos de Soles (3rd Century, BC). *Phaenomena*. Translated by Aaron Poochigian. Baltimore: Johns Hopkins University Press, 2010. Cited as *Visible Signs*.

Aristotle. *Generation of Animals*. Translated by A. L. Peck. Loeb Classical Library. Harvard University Press, 1942.

————. *Metaphysics*, 2 vols. Translated by Hugh Tredennick. Loeb Classical Library. Harvard University Press, 1933.

_____. *Nicomachean Ethics*. Focus Philosophical Library. Translated by Joe Sachs. Indianapolis: Hackett Publishing, 2002.

_____. *On Poetics*. Translated by Seth Benardete and Michael Davis. South Bend: St. Augustine Press, 2002.

_____. *On Rhetoric*. Translated by George A. Kennedy. New York: Oxford University Press, 1991.

_____. *On the Soul*. The New Hackett Aristotle. Translated by C. D. C. Reeve. Indianapolis: Hackett Publishing, 2017.

Athenaeus (3rd Century, AD). *The Deipnosophists*, 8 vols. Translated by S. Douglas Olson. Loeb Classical Library. Cambridge: Harvard University Press, 2012. Cited as *Scholars at Dinner*.

Bartholomew the Englishman (13th Century). *On the Properties of Things*. Translated by John Trevisa. London: Thomas East: 1582.

Catullus (1st Century, BC). *Carmina*. In *The Poems of Catullus*. Translated by Peter Green. Berkeley: University of California Press, 2005.

Chapman, George. *The Revenge of Bussy D'Ambois*, 1633. London: Copyright Group, 2017.

Chaucer. *The Knight's Tale*. In *The Riverside Chaucer*. Edited by Larry Dean Benson. Boston: Houghton Mifflin Co., 1987.

_____. "The Legend of Thisbe," in *The Legend of Good Women*. In *The Riverside Chaucer*. Edited by Larry Dean Benson. Boston: Houghton Mifflin Co., 1987.

Cicero. *De inventione*. In *De inventione, De optimo genere oratorum, Topica*. Loeb Classical Library. Translated by H. M. Hubbell. Cambridge: Harvard University Press, 1976. Cited as *On Invention*.

_____. *De natura deorum*. Loeb Classical Library. Translated by H. Rackham. Cambridge: Harvard University Press, 1979. Cited as *On the Nature of the Gods*.

_____. *De officiis*. Loeb Classical Library. Translated by Walter Miller. Cambridge: Harvard University Press, 1975. Cited as *On Duties*.

_____. *Topica*. In *De inventione, De optimo genere oratorum, Topica.* Loeb Classical Library. Translated by H. M. Hubbell. Cambridge: Harvard University Press, 1976. Cited as *Topics*.

Diodorus Siculus (1st Century, BC). *Library of History*. Loeb Classical Library, 12 vols. Translated by C. H. Oldfeather. Cambridge: Harvard University Press, 1957–69. Cited as *Library*.

Dionysius of Halicarnassus (late 1st – early 2nd Century, BC). *Roman Antiquities*. Loeb Classical Library, 12 vols. Translated by Earnest Cary. Cambridge: Harvard University Press, 1961–78.

Euripides. *Hippolytus*. In *The Complete Greek Tragedies*, Vol. 3. Translated by David Grene. Chicago: The University of Chicago Press, 1959.

_____. *The Suppliant Women*. In *The Complete Greek Tragedies*, Vol. 4. Translated by Frank William Jones. Chicago: The University of Chicago Press, 1959.

Grose, Francis. "Popular Superstitions," in *A Provincial Glossary*. London: S. Hooper, 1790.

Henryson, William Dunbar, (15th Century) *The Testament of Cresseid*. London: Faber and Faber, 2009.

Heraclitus, *Fragments: The Collected Wisdom of Heraclitus*. Translated by Brooks Haxton. New York: Penguin Books, 2003.

Herodotus. *The Histories*. Penguin Classics. Translated by Aubrey de Sêincourt. London: Penguin Books, 2003.

Hesiod. *The Shield of Heracles*. In *The Shield. Catalogue of Women. Other Fragments*. Translated by Glenn W. Most. Loeb Classical Library. Cambridge: Harvard University Press, 2018.

_____. *Theogony*. In *Theogony. Works and Days. Testimonia*. Translated by Glenn W. Most. Loeb Classical Library. Cambridge: Harvard University Press, 2018.

Homer. *Iliad*. Hackett Classics. Translated by Stanley Lombardo. Indianapolis: Hackett Publishing, 1997.

Horace (65–8 BC). *Letters*. In *Horace: Satires, Epistles and Ars Poetica.*

Translated by H. Rushton Fairclough. Loeb Classical Library. Cambridge: Harvard University Press, 1970.

Isocrates (436–338 BC). *Panegyricus*. In *The Works of Isocrates*, Vol.1. Loeb Classical Library. Translated by Larue Van Hook. Cambridge: Harvard University Press, 1961.

Juvenal (late 1st – early 2nd Century, AD). *Satire One*. In *Juvenal and Persius*. Loeb Classical Library. Translated by Susanna Morton Braund. Cambridge: Harvard University Press, 2004.

Livy (58 BC – 17 AD). *Ab urbe condita libri*. Loeb Classical Library, 14 vols. Translated by B. O. Foster, F. G. Moore, Alfred C. Schlesinger, and Evan T. Sage. Cambridge: Harvard University Press, 1965–79. Cited as *History*.

Lucian (2nd Century, AD). *Lucius or the Ass*. In *Lucian*, Loeb Classical Library, 8 vols. Translated by M. D. Macleod. Cambridge: Harvard University Press, 1961.

Lydgate, John. *Lydgate's Troy Book*, 1412–20. The Early English Text Society. London: K. Paul, Trench, Trübner & Co., 1906–35.

Manwood, John. *A Brief Collection of the Laws of the Forest*, 1592. In *Manwood's Treatise of the Forest Laws*. London: B. Lintott, 1717. Cited as *Laws of the Forest*.

More, Thomas. "Six Lines on the Island of Utopia," 1516, in *Utopia*. Edited by George M. Logan. Cambridge: Cambridge University Press, 1995.

Ovid (43 BC – 17 AD). *The Art of Love*. In *The Loves; The Art of Beauty; The Remedies for Love; and The Art of Love*. Translated by Rolfe Humphries. Bloomington: Indiana University Press, 1957.

____. In *Thomas Heywood's "Art of Love,"* c.1609. Edited by M. L. Stapleton. Ann Arbor: University of Michigan Press, 2000. Cited as Heywood.

____. *Metamorphoses*. Loeb Classical Library, 2 vols. Translated by Frank Justin Miller. Cambridge: Harvard University Press, 1976.

____. *Shakespeare's Ovid: being Arthur Golding's translation of the Metamorphoses*, 1567. Edited by W.H.D. Rouse. New York: W.W. Norton and Co., 1966.

Pollux, Julius (2ⁿᵈ Century, AD). *Onomasticon*. Translated by Leland A. Hall. Eugene: University of Oregon Press, 1960.

Pausanias (2ⁿᵈ Century, AD). *Description of Greece*. Loeb Classical Library, 6 vols. Translated by W. H. S. Jones. Cambridge: Harvard University Press, 1918.

Pindar (5ᵗʰ Century, BC), *Fragments*. In *Nemean Odes, Isthmian Odes, Fragments*. Loeb Classical Library. Translated by William H. Race. Cambridge: Harvard University Press. 1997.

Plato. *Laws*. Translated by Thomas L. Pangle. New York: Basic Books, 1980.

____. *Minos*. In *Charmides, Alcibiades, Hipparchus, The Lovers, Theages, Minos and Epinomis*. Loeb Classical Library. Translated by W. R. M. Lamb. Cambridge: Harvard University Press. 1927.

____. *Phaedrus*. In *Euthyphro, Apology, Crito, Phaedo, Phaedrus*. Loeb Classical Library. Translated by Harold North Fowler. Cambridge: Harvard University Press. 1966.

____. *Republic*. Translated by Allan Bloom. New York: Basic Books, 1968.

Pliny. *Natural History*, Loeb Classical Library. Translated by H. Rackham, 10 vols. Cambridge: Harvard University Press, 1938–63.

____. Translated by Philemon Holland. London: Adam Islip, 1601. Cited as Holland.

Plutarch. *Lives of Noble Greeks and Romans*. Loeb Classical Library, 11 vols. Translated by Bernadotte Perrin. Cambridge: Harvard University Press. 1967–75.

____. *Moralia*. Loeb Classical Library, 14 vols. Translated by F. C. Babbitt, et. al. Cambridge: Harvard University Press, 1957–70.

_____. *North's Plutarch*, 1579. Translated by Sir Thomas North, 8 vols. London: David Nutt, 1895. Cited as North.

_____. *The Philosophy, Commonly Called, the Morals*. Translated by Philemon Holland. London: Arnold Hatfield, 1603. Cited as Holland.

Propertius (50–15, BC). *Elegies*. Loeb Classical Library. Translated by H.E. Butler. Cambridge: Harvard University Press, 1962.

Ptolemy, (2nd century AD), *Almagest*. Santa Fe: Green Lion Press, 2014.

Quintilian (1st Century, AD). *Institutio Oratoria*. Loeb Classical Library, 4 vols. Translated by W. R. Paton. Cambridge: Harvard University Press, 1966–80. Cited as *Institutes*.

Ray, John. *Wisdom of God Manifested in the Works of Creation*, 3rd ed. London: Samuel Smith and Benjamin Walford, 1701. Cited as *Wisdom of God*.

Scot, Reginald. *The Discovery of Witchcraft*, 1584. London: John Rodker, 1930.

Seneca (1st Century, AD). *Hippolytus*. In *Seneca: His Tenne Tragedies*. Translated by John Studley. Edited by Thomas Newton, 1581. Bloomington: Indiana University Press, 1964.

Sidney, Philip, Sir. *The Countess of Pembroke's Arcadia*, 1593. London: George Routledge and Sons, 1907. Cited as *Arcadia*.

Sophocles. *Antigone*. In *The Complete Greek Tragedies*, Vol. 2. Translated by Elizabeth Wyckoff. Chicago: The University of Chicago Press, 1959.

_____. *Oedipus the King*. In *The Complete Greek Tragedies*, Vol. 2. Translated by David Grene. Chicago: The University of Chicago Press, 1959. Cited as *Oedipus Tyrannus*.

Strabo (64 or 63 BC – c. 24 AD). *Geography*. Translated by Duane W. Roller. Cambridge: Cambridge University Press, 2014.

Theocritus (3rd Century, BC), *Idylls*. Translated by Anthony Verity. New York: Oxford University Press, 2002.

Thucydides. *The Peloponnesian War*. Translated by Steven Lattimore. Indianapolis: Hackett Publishing, 1998.

Vicary, Thomas (c.1490 – 1561). *The Englishman's Treasure*. London: Thomas Creede, 1596.

Virgil. *Aeneid*. Lombardo Edition. Translated by Stanley Lombardo. Indianapolis: Hackett Publishing, 2005.

_____. *Eclogues*. Translated by Len Krisak. Philadelphia: University of Pennsylvania Press, 2010.

_____. *Georgics*. Translated by Kristina Chew. Indianapolis: Hackett Publishing, 2002.

Wilson, Thomas. *The Arte of Rhetorique*. London: John Kingston, 1560.

Xenophon, *Constitution of the Athenians*. In *Xenophon on Government*. Edited by Vivienne Gray. New York: Cambridge University Press, 2007.

Other Works of Shakespeare

Coriolanus. Focus. Edited by Jan H. Blits. Indianapolis: Hackett Publishing, 2020.

Timon of Athens, Arden Edition. Edited by H.J. Oliver. London: Methuen and Co., 1965. Cited as *TA*.

References

Anonymous, *Book of Common Prayer: The Texts of 1549, 1559, and 1662*. Edited by Brian Cummings. Oxford: Oxford University Press, 2011.

Black, Henry Campbell. *A Law Dictionary*, 2nd ed. St. Paul: West Publishing Co., 1910.

Brewer, Ebenezer Cobham. *Dictionary of Phrase and Fable*, 1870. Compiled by Adrian Room. 16th edition. New York: Harper Resource, 1999.

Dent, R. W. *Shakespeare's Proverbial Language*. Berkeley: University of California Press, 1981.

Furness, Horace Howard. *A Midsummer Night's Dream*. The New Variorum Shakespeare, 1895, New York: Dover Publications, 1963.

Gerard, John, 1597. *The Herbal or the History of Plants*, London: Adam Islip, 1633. Cited as *Herbal*.

Hunter, James. *A Complete Dictionary of Farriery & Horsemanship*. Dublin: P. Wogan, P. Byrne, J. Rice, and J. Moore, 1796. Cited as *Dictionary of Horsemanship*.

Nares, Robert. *A Glossary of Words, Phrases, Names and Allusions in the Works of English Authors*. London: Geroge Routledge and Sons, 1905. Cited as *Glossary*.

Osgood, Frances S. *The Poetry of Flowers and the Flowers of Poetry*. New York: J.C. Riker, 1848.

Rushton, William L. *Shakespeare a Lawyer*. London: Longman, Brown, et. al., 1858.

Sharp, Cecil J. and Macilwaine, Herbert C. *The Morris Book*. London: Novello and Co., 1907.

Tilley, Morris Palmer. *A Dictionary of Proverbs*. Ann Arbor: University of Michigan Press, 1950.

Tomlins, Thomas Edlyne. *The Law-Dictionary*, 2 vols. London: Payne and Foss, 1820.

Topsell, Edward. *The History of Four-Footed Beasts and Serpents and Insects*. 3 vols. 1607. New York: De Capo Press, 1967. Cited as *The History of Four-Footed Beasts*.

Williams, Gordon. *Dictionary of Sexual Language and Imagery in Shakespearean and Stuart Literature*, 3 vols. London: Athlone Press, 1994. Cited as *Dictionary*.

_____. *Glossary of Shakespeare's Sexual Language*. London: Athlone Press, 1997. Cited as *Glossary*.

INDEX

References are to line numbers of notes and to page numbers of the Preface, the Introduction, and the Coda.

as real, seen as, 2.1.82–117
vs. realism, 5.1.2–23n,
  5.1.210
and senses, 1.1.234
and wishes, 5.1.20–21
See also image, imitation, love
imitation, 2.1.123–34
  as mockery, 2.2.122
  twin meanings of, Introduc-
    tion, 4
See also art, image, imagination,
  "Pyramus and Thisbe,"
  Shakespeare, and individual
  characters
Isocrates, *Panegyricus*, 1.1.7–11

Juvenal, *Satire One*, 5.1.54–55

Leander and Hero, *See* "Pyramus
  and Thisbe"
literalness. *See* artisans, dreams,
  imagination, love, thinking
  and individual characters
Livy, *History*, 2.1.158, 4.1.178–84
love,
  and art, common ground of,
    Introduction, 4
  artifice of, 1.1.28–35, 1.1.192–93
  beautiful, of the, Introduction,
    2–3, 10
  brevity of, 1.1.135–40, 1.1.141–49
  as challenge or conquest,
    1.1.194–201, 1.1.244–45,
    2.2.97–98
  and disgust, 2.1.212
  and doting, 1.1.108–9, 1.1.225
  essence of, 2.1.182
  and fawning, 2.1.203–4,
    2.1.202–10
  and happiness, 1.1.76–78,
    1.1.206–7, 1.1.226, 3.2.144,
    3.2.459–63

and hatred, 2.2.140–41,
  3.2.189–90
and idealization, Introduction,
  5, 1.1.234, 3.2.137,
  5.1.328
and jealousy, 1.1.244–45,
  4.1.46–62, 5.1.377–82
and knowledge, 1.1.229–31
and literalness, Introduction, 5
as literature and art, Introduction, 3–4, 1.1.132–34, 1.1.156,
  1.1.235–39, 2.1.65–68,
  2.1.230–34, 2.1.235, 2.2.105–6,
  2.2.120–21, 5.1.194–201
and love juice, Introduction, 8,
  3.2.31–34, 3.2.265
madness of, Introduction, 9,
  2.1.182, 5.1.2–23
memory of a former love,
  2.2.111, 3.2.170, 4.1.164–67
and the mind, 1.1.234
moderated, Introduction, 10,
  5.1.377–82, 5.1.393–400
of one's own, 1.2.11–12, 4.1.111
and poetry, Introduction, 3–4,
  2.1.65–68, 5.1.2–23
and possession, claimed by,
  2.1.193, 4.1.74, 4.1.189–91
and reciprocity of, 1.1.206–7,
  1.1.226, 2.2.28, 2.2.79–80,
  3.1.91
and rejection, 1.1.229–31,
  2.1.199–201
and sight, Introduction, 9,
  n15, 1.1.56, 1.1.234,
  1.1.250–51
  vs. touch, Introduction, 8
and speech, 2.1.193, 2.1.199–
  201, 2.2.102, 2.2.129, 3.1.191–
  93, 4.1.186–98
true/false, Introduction, 6,
  3.2.91, 5.1.393–400